W9-DAS-914

WITHDRAWN

NEW THINKING ABOUT
EVOLUTION

NEW THINKING ABOUT
EVOLUTION

EDITED BY JOHN P. RAFFERTY, ASSOCIATE EDITOR, EARTH SCIENCES

Britannica®
Educational Publishing

IN ASSOCIATION WITH

ROSEN
EDUCATIONAL SERVICES

Published in 2011 by Britannica Educational Publishing
(a trademark of Encyclopædia Britannica, Inc.)
in association with Rosen Educational Services, LLC
29 East 21st Street, New York, NY 10010.

Distributed exclusively by Rosen Educational Services.
For a listing of additional Britannica Educational Publishing titles, call toll free (800) 237-9932.

First Edition

Britannica Educational Publishing
Michael I. Levy: Executive Editor
J.E. Luebering: Senior Manager
Marilyn L. Barton: Senior Coordinator, Production Control
Steven Bosco: Director, Editorial Technologies
Lisa S. Braucher: Senior Producer and Data Editor
Yvette Charboneau: Senior Copy Editor
Kathy Nakamura: Manager, Media Acquisition
John P. Rafferty: Associate Editor, Earth Sciences

Rosen Educational Services
Nicholas Croce: Editor
Nelson Sá: Art Director
Cindy Reiman: Photography Manager
Matthew Cauli: Designer, Cover Design
Introduction by Daniel R. Faust

Library of Congress Cataloging-in-Publication Data

New thinking about evolution / edited by John P. Rafferty. — 1st ed.
    p. cm. — (21st century science)
"In association with Britannica Educational Publishing, Rosen Educational Services."
Includes bibliographical references and index.
ISBN 978-1-61530-129-4 (library binding)
1. Evolution (Biology) I. Rafferty, John P.
QH366.2.N483 2011
576.8 — dc22

2010000848

CONTENTS

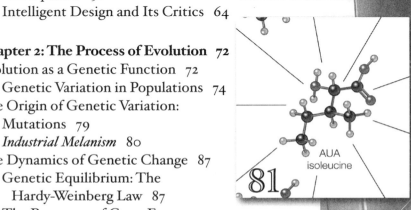

AUA
isoleucine

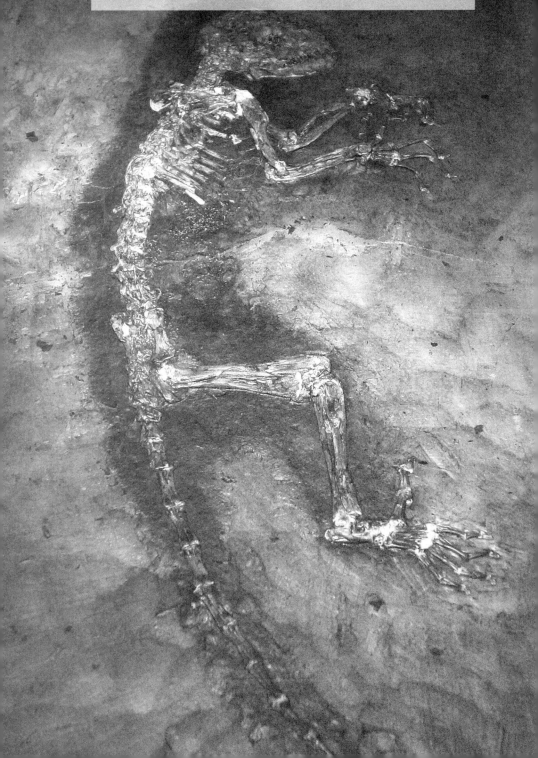

In 2009, while the world celebrated the 200th anniversary of Charles Darwin's birth, scientists announced the discovery of the oldest fossilized skeleton of an ancestral human. The significance of the timing should be clear. Darwin, the 19th-century English naturalist and author of *On the Origin of the Species*, argued for the theory of evolution, going so far as to provide an accurate but incomplete scientific explanation for the process. And, it was the work of Darwin and those who came after him that formed the foundation for the modern theories of evolution. Earlier scientists, such as Swedish naturalist Carolus Linnaeus, had theorized that humans and great apes were related, basing this assumption on similarities in morphology and anatomy; however, after Darwin published his theories, the scientific community began searching for a direct "missing link" between apes and humans.

Throughout history, human cultures have tried to develop explanations for the creation of the world and the diversity of plants and animals, including humans, that populate it. The ancient Greeks, for example, proposed that animals could be transformed from one species into another, or created as an amalgamation of parts from different animals, while traditional Judaic and Christian teachings attributed the origins of the various species of plants and animals to a single, omnipotent God. By the Middle Ages, some intellectuals theorized that organisms could change over time through natural processes; however, this school of thought was not widely accepted until much later.

It was during the Enlightenment of the 18th century that ideas of change and progress began to take hold. While philosophers theorized about the progress of the human mind and spirit, naturalists turned their attention to the progress of the human body. Several years before Charles Darwin was even born, intellectuals had started to advance the notion that organisms could become adapted to their environments through the modification or eradication of organs or biological structures. The French naturalist Jean-Baptiste Lamarck championed this theory of the inheritance of acquired characteristics (also known as Lamarckism). And, while this concept was disproved by the 20th century, Lamarck's ideas did lead to the gradual acceptance of the theories of biological evolution, as well as spurring on future investigation.

By Darwin's time, it was understood that the world operated according to a set of natural laws. The work of individuals like Copernicus, Galileo, and Newton established that the universe was governed by the laws of science. Darwin would apply similar laws to the natural world as well. During his five-year voyage aboard the HMS *Beagle*, Darwin would accumulate evidence to prove that evolution had occurred, that different organisms share a common ancestor, and that organisms change over time. To account for this third assertion—that organisms change over time—Darwin proposed the concept of natural selection. Natural selection, according to Darwin, is the process that aids in adaptation, preserving "favourable variations" and rejecting "injurious variations."

The ramifications of Darwin's ideas became clear. In fact, it was Darwin himself who stated that his theories of natural selection would be a light "thrown on the origin of man and his history." The traditional belief that humans were the creation of a divine intelligence had to be reevaluated. If, as Darwin's theory of natural selection suggests, the organisms we see every day have changed—or evolved—over time, is the same true of humans? Did modern humans emerge from a lesser-developed species? What did our earliest ancestors look like? Since the similarities between humans and apes had already been recognized, could these two groups share a common ancestor? The hunt was on for the "missing link."

Three years before Darwin published *On the Origin of the Species*, "Neanderthal man" was discovered in Germany and sparked the development of paleoanthropology and the study of human evolution. The idea that humans could have evolved from "lesser species" was not only radical, but it was controversial, as well. Even men who had supported Darwin's theory of natural selection—like British naturalist Alfred Russel Wallace and Scottish geologist Charles Lyell—scoffed at the idea that the human brain could have developed through the process of natural selection. However, as more and more scientists joined the search for a human ancestor, the debate soon turned from whether humans were the product of natural selection to which modern human traits emerged first.

The prevailing theory at the end of the 19th and the beginning of the 20th century was that the trait that makes us most human is the modern human brain. Therefore, efforts to unearth our earliest ancestors focused on discovering a specimen with a large brain. However, as new fossilized evidence was uncovered, it became clear that our ancestors developed a modern bipedal stance before they developed an enlarged modern brain. The scientific community was outraged. They were willing to accept that modern humans were the result of Darwinian natural selection, but they couldn't accept that our ancestors developed modern bodies before modern brains. In fact, this widely held bias led to one of the most famous hoaxes in the field of human evolution: Piltdown Man.

"Discovered" in 1912, the Piltdown Man fossils consisted of fragments of a skull and jawbone that were found by workers in a gravel pit in Piltdown, England. The fragments were brought to English amateur archaeologist Charles Dawson, who heralded the find as evidence of a human ancestor with a modern human brain. Although looked upon with some skepticism from the start, *Eoanthropus dawsoni* (or "Dawson's dawn man") wasn't officially exposed as a fraud until 1953, when it was revealed to consist of parts of a modern human skull and the jawbones of an orangutan. Despite being a forgery, Piltdown Man has a place in the history of human evolutionary theory as indicative of one of the largest hurdles the field had to face. Hubris made it difficult for most people—whether the public or the scientific community—to accept that we had evolved from ancestors who did not possess a fully developed modern brain.

The second half of the 20th century provided a bounty of fossil evidence—among it "Lucy" in 1974 and "Ardi" in 1994—that our ancestors developed upright bipedalism long before an increased brain. "Lucy" was the name given to a roughly 40 percent complete skeleton of an *Australopithecus afarensis* discovered in Ethiopia in 1974. Providing further evidence that bipedalism preceded brain growth, Lucy had a skull size similar to that of apes but a skeleton that had developed to allow for bipedal locomotion. Lucy would reign as one of the earliest known human ancestors for more than twenty years, when an older specimen, *Ardipithecus ramidus*, was discovered.

Ardipithecus ramidus—or "Ardi"—was discovered, like Lucy, in the Afar desert of Ethiopia. Not only was Ardi the oldest fossil skeleton of a human ancestor, living around 4.4 million years ago, but scientists also claim that this discovery should finally put to rest the popular belief that a missing link existed that possessed traits of both humans and modern apes. In fact, Ardi possessed modifications in her pelvis, legs, and feet that allowed her to move through the trees in a fashion similar to species that were far more primitive than chimpanzees and gorillas.

What the previous episodes prove is that the study of evolutionary theory is, itself, a constantly evolving science. When Darwin's concept of natural selection was first introduced, even its proponents lacked a suitable explanation of exactly how the "favourable variations" could be passed from one generation to the next. Around the time that Darwin's *On the Origin of the Species* was published, an Augustinian monk in Austria-Hungary was experimenting with peas in the monastery garden. The monk, Gregor Mendel, used the results of his experiments to formulate the basic principles of the theory of heredity. According to Mendel's theories, biological inheritance occurs through "particulate factors" that are inherited from both parents; Mendel's "particulate factors" would eventually become known as genes.

Not to discount the contributions of individuals like Mendel, perhaps the greatest contribution to the field of evolution since Darwin's initial theories would not come until 1953. That year, American geneticist and biophysicist James Watson and British biophysicist Francis Crick published an article that described the double helix structure of DNA (or deoxyribonucleic acid), the material responsible for genetic heredity. Watson and Crick's discovery opened whole new avenues of thought regarding evolutionary biology. Now, biologists knew not only how traits were inherited—through genes—but also the mechanism through which these genes were passed from one generation to the next—DNA.

At the end of the 20th century, new techniques were developed to fully exploit science's new understanding of DNA and evolution. Biologists could now, for example, explore genetic variation on a molecular level. This new molecular understanding of evolution led to the concept of the "molecular clock." According to this theory, the amount of divergence between the DNA of two different species should create a reliable estimate of when those two species diverged from a common ancestor, allowing scientists to reconstruct the evolutionary history of a species. And, while scientists have since proven that the molecular clock theory is not exact, it continues to provide fairly reliable evidence into the 21st century.

Perhaps the greatest boon to the study of evolution in the 21st century is the success of the Human Genome Project. The Human Genome Project was an international project with the primary goal to determine the sequence of chemical pairs that make up DNA and to identify and map the 20,000 to 25,000 genes that make up the human genome. The project began in 1990 and, after releasing a working draft in 2000, was completed in 2003. While the stated objective of the Human Genome Project was to understand the genetic makeup of human DNA, the project has also successfully mapped the genome of more than 20 other organisms, including the rat, the mosquito, the fruit fly, and the bacterium *Escherichia coli*.

In the decades since Darwin's work was published, scientists have all but confirmed each of Darwin's theories. Most experts agree that it is no longer accurate to call Darwin's findings "theory"; they have become an accepted part of the study of biology.

While Darwin may have accurately theorized the basics of evolution, modern research has shown that evolution may, in fact, work in ways that Darwin and his contemporaries could never have imagined. Although earlier naturalists stated that natural selection occurred slowly over time, modern scientists have found that evolution may actually occur quite rapidly. The current school of thought best explains gaps in the fossil record, which 19th-century scientists took to indicate the existence of "missing links" between species. Modern science, however, claims that these gaps simply indicate places where evolution took a radical leap forward. Whether it occurs quickly or slowly, scientists know one thing for certain: evolution modifies existing structures by trial and error. This is why the skeletal structures of a chimpanzee's hand, a dolphin's fin, and a bat's wing are not radically different, since they all arose from a similar structure. Similarly, despite what proponents of creation science and intelligent design may argue, the human brain, though remarkable, could not have appeared on its own and must have developed from earlier, less-developed structures.

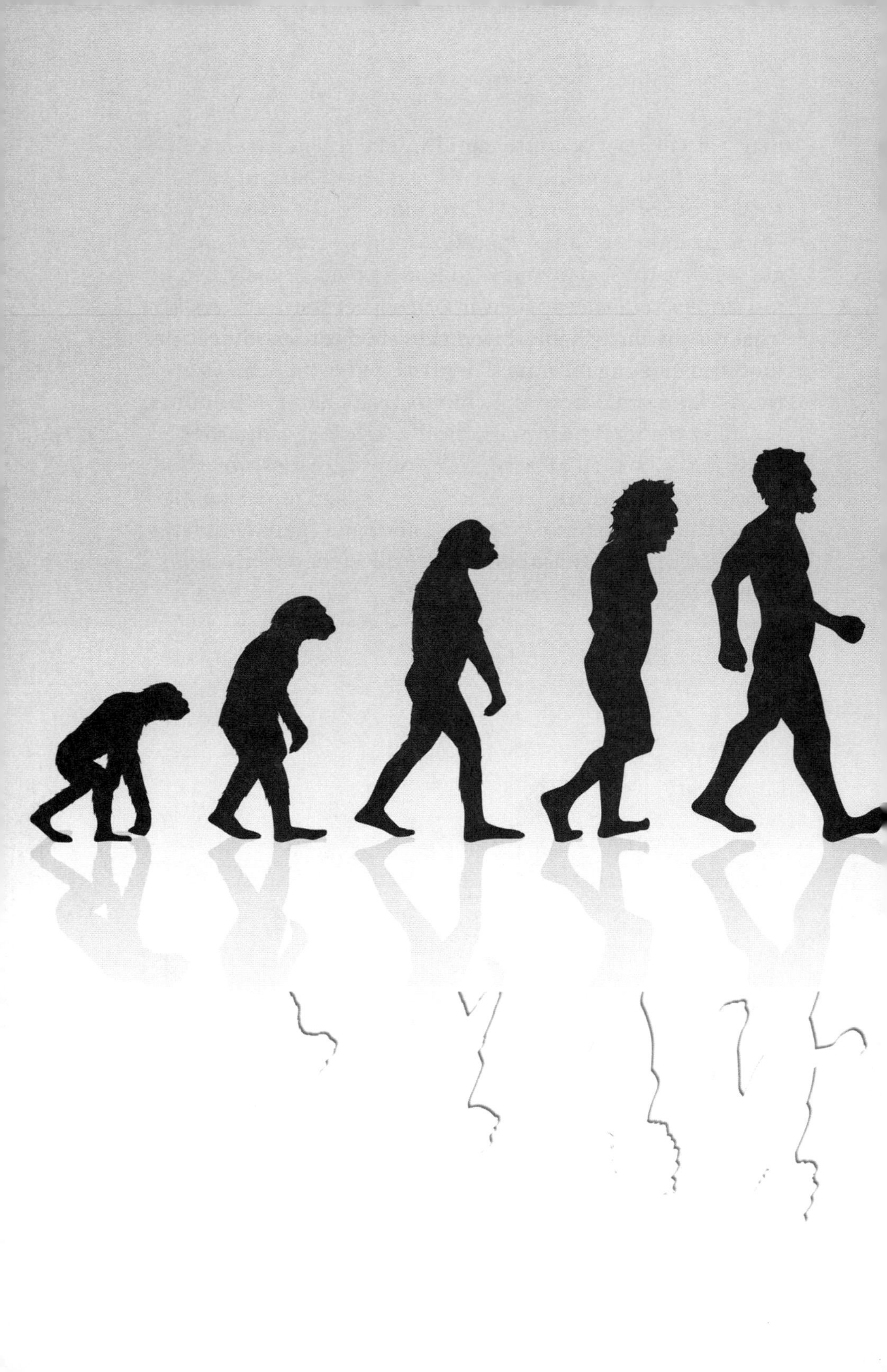

CHAPTER 1
UNDERSTANDING EVOLUTION

In biology the theory of evolution postulates that the various types of plants, animals, and other living things on Earth have their origin in other preexisting types and that the distinguishable differences are due to modifications in successive generations. The theory of evolution is one of the fundamental keystones of modern biological theory.

The diversity of the living world is staggering. More than 2 million existing species of organisms have been named and described; many more remain to be discovered—from 10 million to 30 million, according to some estimates. What is impressive is not just the numbers but also the incredible heterogeneity in size, shape, and way of life—from lowly bacteria, measuring less than a thousandth of a millimetre in diameter, to stately sequoias, rising 100 metres (300 feet) above the ground and weighing several thousand tons; from bacteria living in hot springs at temperatures near the boiling point of water to fungi and algae thriving on the ice masses of Antarctica and in saline pools at -23 °C (-9 °F); and from giant tube worms discovered living near hydrothermal vents on the dark ocean floor to spiders and larkspur plants existing on the slopes of Mount Everest more than 6,000 metres (19,700 feet) above sea level.

The virtually infinite variations on life are the fruit of the evolutionary process. All living creatures are related by descent from common ancestors. Humans and other mammals descend from shrewlike creatures that lived more than 150 million years ago; mammals, birds, reptiles, amphibians, and fishes share as ancestors aquatic worms that lived 600 million years ago; and all plants and animals derive from bacteria-like microorganisms that originated more than 3 billion years ago. Biological evolution

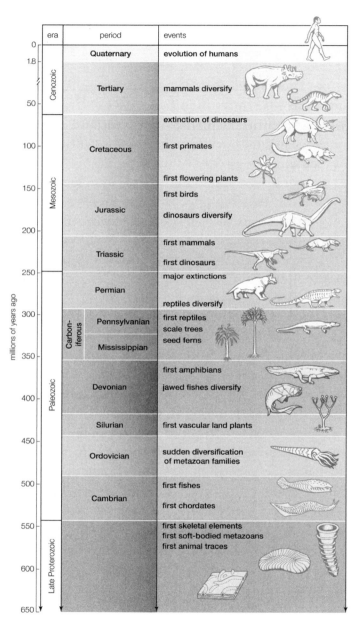

The geologic time scale from 650 million years ago to the present, showing major evolutionary events. Encyclopædia Britannica, Inc.

is a process of descent with modification. Lineages of organisms change through generations; diversity arises because the lineages that descend from common ancestors diverge through time.

The 19th-century English naturalist Charles Darwin argued that organisms come about by evolution, and he provided a scientific explanation, essentially correct but incomplete, of how evolution occurs and why it is that organisms have features — such as wings, eyes, and kidneys — clearly structured to serve specific functions. Natural selection was the fundamental concept in his explanation. Natural selection occurs because individuals having more-useful traits, such as more-acute vision or swifter legs, survive better and produce more progeny than individuals with less-favourable traits. Genetics, a science born in the 20th century, reveals in detail how natural selection works and led to the development of the modern theory of evolution. Beginning in the 1960s, a related scientific discipline, molecular biology, enormously advanced knowledge of biological evolution and made it possible to investigate detailed problems that had seemed completely out of reach only a short time previously — for example, how similar the genes of humans and chimpanzees might be (they differ in about 1–2 percent of the units that make up the genes).

THE EVIDENCE FOR EVOLUTION

Darwin and other 19th-century biologists found compelling evidence for biological evolution in the comparative study of living organisms, in their geographic distribution, and in the fossil remains of extinct organisms. Since Darwin's time, the evidence from these sources has become considerably stronger and more comprehensive, while biological disciplines that emerged more recently—genetics, biochemistry, physiology, ecology, animal behaviour (ethology), and especially molecular biology—have supplied powerful additional evidence and detailed confirmation. The amount of information about evolutionary history stored in the DNA and proteins of living things is virtually unlimited; scientists can reconstruct any detail of the evolutionary history of life by investing sufficient time and laboratory resources.

Evolutionists no longer are concerned with obtaining evidence to support the fact of evolution but rather are concerned with what sorts of knowledge can be obtained from different sources of evidence. The following sections identify the most productive of these sources and illustrate the types of information they have provided.

The Fossil Record

Paleontologists have recovered and studied the fossil remains of many thousands of organisms that lived in the past. This fossil record shows that many kinds of extinct organisms were very different in form from any now living. It also shows successions of organisms through time, manifesting their transition from one form to another.

When an organism dies, it is usually destroyed by other forms of life and by weathering processes. On rare occasions some body parts—particularly hard ones such as shells, teeth, or bones—are preserved by being buried in mud or protected in some other way from predators and weather. Eventually, they may become petrified and preserved indefinitely with the rocks in which they are embedded. Methods such as radiometric dating—measuring the amounts of natural radioactive atoms that remain in certain minerals to determine the

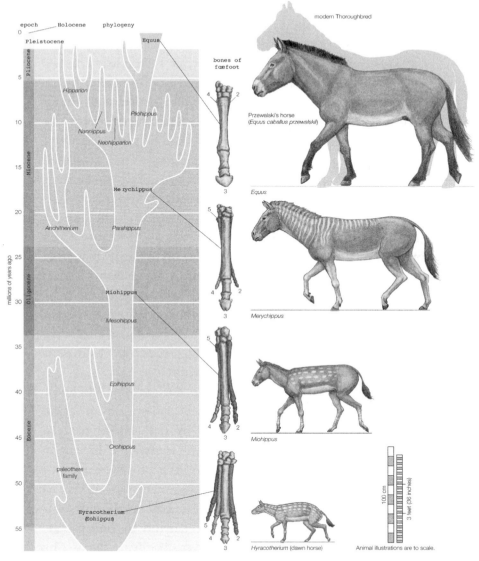

Evolution of the horse over the past 55 million years. The present-day Przewalski's horse is believed to be the only remaining example of a wild horse—i.e., the last remaining modern horse to have evolved by natural selection. Numbered bones in the forefoot illustrations trace the gradual transition from a four-toed to a one-toed animal.

Encyclopædia Britannica, Inc.

23

elapsed time since they were constituted—make it possible to estimate the time period when the rocks, and the fossils associated with them, were formed.

Radiometric dating indicates that Earth was formed about 4.5 billion years ago. The earliest fossils resemble microorganisms such as bacteria and cyanobacteria (blue-green algae); the oldest of these fossils appear in rocks 3.5 billion years old. The oldest known animal fossils, about 700 million years old, come from the so-called Ediacara fauna, small wormlike creatures with soft bodies. Numerous fossils belonging to many living phyla and exhibiting mineralized skeletons appear in rocks about 540 million years old. These organisms are different from organisms living now and from those living at intervening times. Some are so radically different that paleontologists have created new phyla in order to classify them. The first vertebrates, animals with backbones, appeared about 400 million years ago; the first mammals, less than 200 million years ago. The history of life recorded by fossils presents compelling evidence of evolution.

The fossil record is incomplete. Of the small proportion of organisms preserved as fossils, only a tiny fraction have been recovered and studied by paleontologists. In some cases the succession of forms over time has been reconstructed in detail. One example is the evolution of the horse. The horse can be traced to an animal the size of a dog having several toes on each foot and teeth appropriate for browsing; this animal, called the dawn horse (genus *Hyracotherium*), lived more than 50 million years ago. The most recent form, the modern horse (*Equus*), is much larger in size, is one-toed, and has teeth appropriate for grazing. The transitional forms are well preserved as fossils, as are many other kinds of extinct horses that evolved in different directions and left no living descendants.

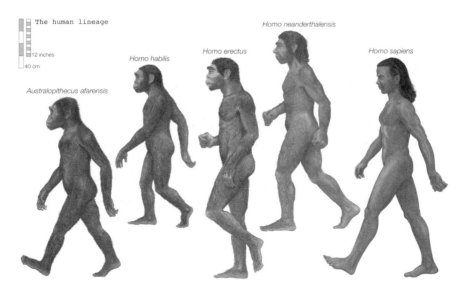

The human lineage

12 inches
40 cm

Australopithecus afarensis

Homo habilis

Homo erectus

Homo neanderthalensis

Homo sapiens

Five hominins—members of the human lineage after it separated at least seven million to six million years ago from lineages going to the apes—are depicted in an artist's interpretations. All but Homo sapiens, *the species that comprises modern humans, are extinct and have been reconstructed from fossil evidence.* Encyclopædia Britannica, Inc.

Using recovered fossils, paleontologists have reconstructed examples of radical evolutionary transitions in form and function. For example, the lower jaw of reptiles contains several bones, but that of mammals only one. The other bones in the reptile jaw unmistakably evolved into bones now found in the mammalian ear. At first, such a transition would seem unlikely—it is hard to imagine what function such bones could have had during their intermediate stages. Yet paleontologists discovered two transitional forms of mammal-like reptiles, called therapsids, that had a double jaw joint (i.e., two hinge points side by side)—one joint consisting of the bones that persist in the mammalian jaw and the other composed of the quadrate and articular bones, which eventually became the hammer and anvil of the mammalian ear.

For skeptical contemporaries of Darwin, the "missing link"—the absence of any known transitional form between apes and humans—was a battle cry, as it remained for uninformed people afterward. Not one but many creatures intermediate between living apes and humans have since been found as fossils. The oldest known fossil hominins—i.e., primates belonging to the human lineage after it separated from lineages going to the apes—are 6 million to 7 million years old, come from Africa, and are known as *Sahelanthropus* and *Orrorin* (or *Praeanthropus*), which were predominantly bipedal when on the ground but which had very small brains. *Ardipithecus* lived about 4.4 million years ago, also in Africa. Numerous fossil remains from diverse African origins are known of *Australopithecus*, a hominin that appeared between 3 million and 4 million years ago. *Australopithecus* had an upright human stance but a cranial capacity of less than 500 cc (equivalent to a brain weight of about 500 grams), comparable to that of a gorilla or a chimpanzee and about one-third that of humans. Its head displayed a mixture of ape and human characteristics—a low forehead and a long, apelike face but with teeth proportioned like those of humans. Other early hominins partly contemporaneous with *Australopithecus* include *Kenyanthropus* and *Paranthropus*; both had comparatively small brains, although some species of *Paranthropus* had larger bodies. *Paranthropus* represents a side branch in the hominin lineage that became extinct. Along with increased cranial capacity, other human characteristics have been found in *Homo habilis*, which lived about 1.5 million to 2 million years ago in Africa and had a cranial capacity of more than 600 cc (brain weight of 600 grams), and in *H. erectus*, which lived between 0.5 million and more than 1.5 million years ago, apparently ranged widely over Africa, Asia, and Europe, and had a cranial capacity of 800 to 1,100 cc (brain weight of 800 to 1,100 grams). The brain sizes of *H. ergaster*, *H. antecessor*, and *H. heidelbergensis* were roughly that of the brain of *H. erectus*, some of which species were partly contemporaneous, though they lived in different regions of the Eastern Hemisphere.

STRUCTURAL SIMILARITIES

The skeletons of turtles, horses, humans, birds, and bats are strikingly similar, in spite of the different ways of life of these animals and the diversity of their environments. The correspondence, bone by bone, can easily be seen not only in the limbs but also in every other part of the body. From a purely practical point of view, it is incomprehensible that a turtle should swim, a horse run, a person write, and a bird or a bat fly with forelimb structures built of the same bones. An engineer could design better limbs in each case. But if it is accepted that all of these skeletons inherited their structures from a common ancestor and became modified only as they adapted to different ways of life, the similarity of their structures makes sense.

Comparative anatomy investigates the homologies, or inherited similarities, among organisms in bone structure and in other parts of the body. The correspondence of structures is typically very close among some organisms — the different varieties of songbirds, for instance—but becomes less so as the organisms being compared are less closely related in their evolutionary history. The similarities are less between mammals and birds than they are among mammals, and they are still less between mammals and fishes. Similarities in structure, therefore, not only manifest evolution but also help to reconstruct the phylogeny, or evolutionary history, of organisms.

Comparative anatomy also reveals why most organismic structures are not perfect. Like the forelimbs of turtles, horses, humans, birds, and bats, an organism's body parts are less than perfectly adapted because they are modified from an inherited structure rather than designed from completely "raw" materials for a specific purpose. The imperfection of structures is evidence for evolution and against antievolutionist arguments that invoke intelligent design.

EMBRYONIC DEVELOPMENT AND VESTIGES

Darwin and his followers found support for evolution in the study of embryology, the science that investigates the development of organisms from fertilized egg to time of birth or hatching. Vertebrates, from fishes through lizards to humans, develop in ways that are remarkably similar during early stages, but they become more and more differentiated as the embryos approach maturity. The similarities persist longer between organisms that are more closely related (e.g., humans and monkeys) than between those less closely related (humans and sharks). Common developmental patterns reflect evolutionary kinship. Lizards and humans share a developmental pattern inherited from their remote common ancestor; the inherited pattern of each was modified only as the separate descendant lineages evolved in different directions. The common embryonic stages of the two creatures reflect the constraints imposed by this common inheritance, which prevents changes that have not been necessitated by their diverging environments and ways of life.

The embryos of humans and other nonaquatic vertebrates exhibit gill slits even though they never breathe through gills. These slits are found in the embryos of all vertebrates because they share as common ancestors the fish in which these structures first evolved. Human embryos also exhibit by the fourth week of development a well-defined tail, which reaches maximum length at six weeks. Similar embryonic tails are found in other mammals, such as dogs, horses, and monkeys; in humans, however, the tail eventually shortens, persisting only as a rudiment in the adult coccyx.

A close evolutionary relationship between organisms that appear drastically different as adults can sometimes be recognized by their embryonic homologies. Barnacles, for example, are sedentary crustaceans with little apparent likeness to such free-swimming crustaceans as lobsters, shrimps, or copepods. Yet barnacles pass through a free-swimming larval stage, the nauplius, which is unmistakably similar to that of other crustacean larvae.

Embryonic rudiments that never fully develop, such as the gill slits in humans, are common in all sorts of animals. Some, however, like the tail rudiment in humans, persist as adult vestiges, reflecting evolutionary ancestry. The most familiar rudimentary organ in humans is the vermiform appendix. This wormlike structure attaches to a short section of intestine called the cecum, which is located at the point where the large and small intestines join. The human vermiform appendix is a functionless vestige of a fully developed organ present in other mammals, such as the rabbit and other herbivores, where a large cecum and appendix store vegetable cellulose to enable its digestion with the help of bacteria. Vestiges are instances of imperfections—like the imperfections seen in anatomical structures—that argue against creation by design but are fully understandable as a result of evolution.

BIOGEOGRAPHY

Darwin also saw a confirmation of evolution in the geographic distribution of plants and animals, and later knowledge has reinforced his observations. For example, there are about 1,500 known species of *Drosophila* vinegar flies in the world; nearly one-third of them live in Hawaii and nowhere else, although the total area of the archipelago is less than one-twentieth the area of California or Germany. Also in Hawaii are more than 1,000 species of snails and other land mollusks that exist nowhere else. This unusual diversity is easily explained by evolution. The islands of Hawaii are extremely isolated and have had few colonizers—i.e, animals and plants that arrived there from elsewhere and established populations. Those species that did colonize the islands found many unoccupied ecological niches, local environments suited to sustaining them and lacking predators that would prevent them from multiplying. In response, these species rapidly diversified; this process of diversifying in order to fill ecological niches is called adaptive radiation.

Each of the world's continents has its own distinctive collection of animals and plants. In Africa are rhinoceroses, hippopotamuses, lions, hyenas, giraffes, zebras, lemurs, monkeys with narrow noses and nonprehensile tails, chimpanzees, and gorillas. South America, which extends over much the same latitudes as Africa, has none of these animals; it instead has pumas, jaguars, tapir, llamas, raccoons, opossums, armadillos, and monkeys with broad noses and large prehensile tails.

These vagaries of biogeography are not due solely to the suitability of the different environments. There is no reason to believe that South American animals are not well suited to living in Africa or those of Africa to living in South America. The islands of Hawaii are no better suited than other Pacific islands for vinegar flies, nor are they less hospitable than other parts of the world for many absent organisms. In fact, although no large mammals are native to the Hawaiian islands, pigs and goats have multiplied there as wild animals since being introduced by humans. This absence of many species from a hospitable environment in which an extraordinary variety of other species flourish can be explained by the theory of evolution, which holds that species can exist and evolve only in geographic areas that were colonized by their ancestors.

MOLECULAR BIOLOGY

The field of molecular biology provides the most detailed and convincing evidence available for biological evolution. In its unveiling of the nature of DNA and the workings of organisms at the level of enzymes and other protein molecules, it has shown that these molecules hold information about an organism's ancestry. This has made it possible to reconstruct evolutionary events that were previously unknown and to confirm and adjust the view of events already known. The precision with which these events can be reconstructed is one reason the evidence from molecular biology is so compelling. Another reason is that molecular evolution has shown all living organisms, from bacteria to humans, to be related by descent from common ancestors.

A remarkable uniformity exists in the molecular components of organisms—in the nature of the components as well as in the ways in which they are assembled and used. In all bacteria, plants, animals, and humans, the DNA comprises a different sequence of the same four component nucleotides, and all the various proteins are synthesized from different combinations and sequences of the same 20 amino acids, although several hundred other amino acids do exist. The genetic code by which the information contained in the DNA of the cell nucleus is passed on to proteins is virtually everywhere the same. Similar metabolic pathways—sequences of biochemical reactions—are used by the most diverse organisms to produce energy and to make up the cell components.

This unity reveals the genetic continuity and common ancestry of all organisms. There is no other rational way to account for their molecular uniformity when numerous alternative structures are equally likely. The genetic code serves as an example. Each particular sequence of three nucleotides in the nuclear DNA acts as a pattern for the production of exactly the same amino acid in all organisms. This is no more necessary than it is for a language to use a particular combination of letters to represent a particular object. If it is found that certain sequences of letters— *planet, tree, woman*—are used with identical meanings in a number of different books, one can be sure that the languages used in those books are of common origin.

Genes and proteins are long molecules that contain information in the sequence of their components in much the same way as sentences of the English language contain information in the sequence of their letters and words. The sequences that make up the genes are passed on from parents to offspring and are identical except for occasional changes introduced by mutations. As an illustration, one may assume that two books are being compared. Both books are 200 pages long and contain the same number of chapters. Closer examination reveals that the two books are identical page for page and word for word, except that an occasional word—say, one in 100—is different. The two books cannot have been written independently; either one has been copied from the other, or both have been copied, directly or indirectly, from the same original book. Similarly, if each component nucleotide of DNA is represented by one letter, the complete sequence of nucleotides in the DNA of a higher organism would require several hundred books of hundreds of pages, with several thousand letters on each page. When the "pages" (or sequences of nucleotides) in these "books" (organisms) are examined one by one, the correspondence in the "letters" (nucleotides) gives unmistakable evidence of common origin.

The two arguments presented above are based on different grounds, although both attest to evolution. Using the alphabet analogy, the first argument says that languages that use the same dictionary—the same genetic code and the same 20 amino acids—cannot be of independent origin. The second argument, concerning similarity in the sequence of nucleotides in the DNA (and thus the sequence of amino acids in the proteins), says that books with very similar texts cannot be of independent origin.

The evidence of evolution revealed by molecular biology goes even further. The degree of similarity in the sequence of nucleotides or of amino acids can be precisely quantified. For example, in humans and chimpanzees, the protein molecule called cytochrome c, which serves a vital function in respiration within cells, consists of the same 104 amino acids in exactly the same order. It differs, however, from the cytochrome c of rhesus monkeys by 1 amino acid, from that of horses by 11 additional amino acids, and from that of tuna by 21 additional amino acids. The degree of similarity reflects the recency of common ancestry. Thus, the inferences from comparative anatomy and other disciplines concerning evolutionary history can be tested in molecular studies of DNA and proteins by examining their sequences of nucleotides and amino acids.

The authority of this kind of test is overwhelming; each of the thousands of genes and thousands of proteins contained in an organism provides an independent test of that organism's evolutionary history. Not all possible tests have been performed, but many hundreds have been done, and not one has given evidence contrary to evolution. There is probably no other notion in any field of science that has been as extensively tested and as thoroughly corroborated as the evolutionary origin of living organisms.

HISTORY OF EVOLUTIONARY THEORY

The work of naturalist Charles Darwin was a critical turning point in the history of evolutionary theory. Before Darwin, a number of thinkers attempted to explain the diversity of life on Earth. The first such attempts were essentially outgrowths of various religious and philosophical traditions. Subsequent attempts to describe how new species emerged entertained such notions as spontaneous generation, the fixity of species, and the passing on of characters acquired during life from parent to offspring. After Darwin developed his theory of natural selection, a number of other thinkers fine-tuned and solidified Darwin's arguments. His work was merged with that of Austrian geneticist Gregor Mendel, and evolutionary theory was linked to new developments in other scientific fields. Later, the knowledge gained from exploring the characteristics and behaviour of DNA was applied to questions of natural selection.

EARLY IDEAS

All human cultures have developed their own explanations for the origin of the world and of human beings and other creatures. Traditional Judaism and Christianity explain the origin of living beings and their adaptations to their environments—wings, gills, hands, flowers—as the handiwork of an omniscient God. The philosophers of ancient Greece had their own creation myths. Anaximander proposed that animals could be transformed from one kind into another, and Empedocles speculated that they were made up of various combinations of preexisting parts. Closer to modern evolutionary ideas were the proposals of early church fathers such as Gregory of Nazianzus and Augustine, both of whom maintained that not all species of plants and animals were created by God; rather, some had developed in historical times from God's creations. Their motivation was not biological but religious—it would have been impossible to hold representatives of all species in a single vessel such as Noah's Ark; hence, some species must have come into existence only after the Flood.

The notion that organisms may change by natural processes was not investigated as a biological subject by Christian theologians of the Middle Ages, but it was, usually incidentally, considered as a possibility by many, including Albertus Magnus and his student Thomas Aquinas. Aquinas concluded, after detailed discussion, that the development of living creatures such as maggots and flies from nonliving matter such as decaying meat was not incompatible with Christian faith or philosophy. But he left it to others to determine whether this actually happened.

The idea of progress, particularly the belief in unbounded human progress, was central to the Enlightenment of the 18th century, particularly in France among such philosophers as the marquis de Condorcet and Denis Diderot and such scientists as Georges-Louis Leclerc, comte de Buffon. But belief in progress did not necessarily lead to the development of a theory of evolution. Pierre-Louis Moreau de Maupertuis proposed the spontaneous generation and extinction of organisms as part of his theory of origins, but he advanced no theory of evolution—i.e., the transformation of one species into another through knowable, natural causes. Buffon, one of the greatest naturalists of the time, explicitly considered—and rejected—the possible descent of several species from a common ancestor. He postulated that organisms arise from organic molecules by spontaneous generation, so that there could be as many kinds of animals and plants as there are viable combinations of organic molecules.

The English physician Erasmus Darwin, grandfather of Charles Darwin, offered in his *Zoonomia; or, The Laws of Organic Life* (1794–96) some evolutionary speculations, but they were not further developed and had no real influence on subsequent theories. The Swedish botanist Carolus Linnaeus devised the hierarchical system of plant and animal classification that is still in use in a modernized form. Although he insisted on the fixity of species, his classification system eventually contributed much to the acceptance of the concept of common descent.

The great French naturalist Jean-Baptiste de Monet, chevalier de Lamarck, held the enlightened view of his age that living organisms represent a progression, with humans as the highest form. From this idea he proposed, in the early years of the 19th century, the first broad theory of evolution. Organisms evolve through eons of time from lower to higher forms, a process still going on, always culminating in human beings. As organisms become adapted to their environments through their habits, modifications occur. Use of an organ or structure reinforces it; disuse leads to obliteration. The characteristics acquired by use and disuse, according to this theory, would be inherited. This assumption, later called the inheritance of acquired characteristics (or Lamarckism), was thoroughly disproved in the 20th century. Although his theory did not stand up in the light of later knowledge, Lamarck made important contributions to the gradual acceptance of biological evolution and stimulated countless later studies.

CHARLES DARWIN

The founder of the modern theory of evolution was Charles Darwin. The son and grandson of physicians, he enrolled as a medical student at the University of Edinburgh. After two years, however, he left to study at the University of Cambridge and prepare to become a clergyman. He was not an exceptional student, but he was deeply interested in natural history. On Dec. 27, 1831, a few months after his graduation from Cambridge, he sailed as a naturalist aboard the HMS *Beagle* on a round-the-world trip that lasted until October 1836. Darwin was often able to disembark for extended trips ashore to collect natural specimens.

The discovery of fossil bones from large extinct mammals in Argentina and the observation of numerous species of finches in the Galapagos Islands were among the events credited with stimulating Darwin's interest in how species originate. In 1859 he published *On the Origin of Species by Means of Natural Selection*, a treatise establishing the theory of evolution and, most important, the role of natural selection in determining its course. He published many other books as well, notably *The Descent of Man and Selection in Relation to Sex* (1871), which extends the theory of natural selection to human evolution.

Darwin must be seen as a great intellectual revolutionary who inaugurated a new era in the cultural history of humankind, an era that was the second and final stage of the Copernican revolution that had begun in the 16th and 17th

LAMARCKISM

Lamarckism is a theory of organic evolution based on the principle that physical changes in organisms during their lifetime—such as greater development of an organ or a part through increased use—could be transmitted to their offspring. The doctrine, proposed by the French naturalist J. B. Lamarck in 1809, influenced evolutionary thought through most of the 19th century. Lamarck believed that in animals, a new environment calls forth new needs that the animal seeks to satisfy by some effort. Thus, new needs engender new habits, which modify the parts cumulatively and permanently: for example, the giraffe, seeking to browse higher and higher on the leaves of trees on which it feeds, stretches its neck, and continuation of the habit for a long time results in a gradual lengthening of the limbs and neck. In the early 20th century, neo-Lamarckism incorporated the Darwinian theory of natural selection in its basic postulate that organic evolution is caused by the action of natural selection on the acquired characters.

Lamarckism was discredited by most geneticists after the 1930s, but certain of its ideas continued to be held in the Soviet Union. Incorporated in state-approved—but professionally disavowed—schools of Michurinism and Lysenkoism, they dominated and severely handicapped Soviet research in genetics through mid-20th century.

centuries under the leadership of men such as Nicolaus Copernicus, Galileo, and Isaac Newton. The Copernican revolution marked the beginnings of modern science. Discoveries in astronomy and physics overturned traditional conceptions of the universe. Earth no longer was seen as the centre of the universe but was seen as a small planet revolving around one of myriad stars; the seasons and the rains that make crops grow, as well as destructive storms and other vagaries of weather, became understood as aspects of natural processes; the revolutions of the planets were now explained by simple laws that also accounted for the motion of projectiles on Earth.

The significance of these and other discoveries was that they led to a conception of the universe as a system of matter in motion governed by laws of nature. The workings of the universe no longer needed to be attributed to the ineffable will of a divine Creator; rather, they were brought into the realm of science — an explanation of phenomena through natural laws. Physical phenomena such as tides, eclipses, and positions of the planets could now be predicted whenever the causes were adequately known. Darwin accumulated evidence showing that evolution had occurred, that diverse organisms share common ancestors, and that living beings have changed drastically over the course of Earth's history. More important, however, he extended to the living world the idea of nature as a system of matter in motion governed by natural laws.

Before Darwin, the origin of Earth's living things, with their marvelous contrivances for adaptation, had been attributed to the design of an omniscient God. He had created the fish in the waters, the birds in the air, and all sorts of animals and plants on the land. God had endowed these creatures with gills for breathing, wings for flying, and eyes for seeing, and he had coloured birds and flowers so that human beings could enjoy them and recognize God's wisdom. Christian theologians, from Aquinas on, had argued that the presence of design, so evident in living beings, demonstrates the existence of a supreme Creator; the argument from design was Aquinas's "fifth way" for proving the existence of God. In 19th-century England the eight Bridgewater Treatises were commissioned so that eminent scientists and philosophers would expand on the marvels of the natural world and thereby set forth "the Power, wisdom, and goodness of God as manifested in the Creation."

The British theologian William Paley in his *Natural Theology* (1802) used natural history, physiology, and other contemporary knowledge to elaborate the argument from design. If a person should find a watch, even in an uninhabited desert, Paley contended, the harmony of its many parts would force him to conclude that it had been created by a skilled watchmaker; and, Paley went on, how much more intricate and perfect in design is the human eye, with its transparent lens, its retina placed at the precise distance for forming a distinct image, and its large nerve transmitting signals to the brain.

The argument from design seems to be forceful. A ladder is made for climbing, a knife for cutting, and a watch for telling time; their functional design leads to the conclusion that they have been fashioned by a carpenter, a smith, or a watchmaker. Similarly, the obvious functional design of animals and plants seems to denote the work of a Creator. It was Darwin's genius that he provided a natural explanation for the organization and functional design of living beings.

Darwin accepted the facts of adaptation—hands are for grasping, eyes for seeing, lungs for breathing. But he showed that the multiplicity of plants and animals, with their exquisite and varied adaptations, could be explained by a process of natural selection, without recourse to a Creator or any designer agent. This achievement would prove to have intellectual and cultural implications more profound and lasting than his multipronged evidence that convinced contemporaries of the fact of evolution.

Darwin's theory of natural selection is summarized in the *Origin of Species* as follows:

> *As many more individuals are produced than can possibly survive, there must in every case be a struggle for existence, either*

one individual with another of the same species, or with the individuals of distinct species, or with the physical conditions of life . . . Can it, then, be thought improbable, seeing that variations useful to man have undoubtedly occurred, that other variations useful in some way to each being in the great and complex battle of life, should sometimes occur in the course of thousands of generations? If such do occur, can we doubt (remembering that many more individuals are born than can possibly survive) that individuals having any advantage, however slight, over others, would have the best chance of surviving and of procreating their kind? On the other hand, we may feel sure that any variation in the least degree injurious would be rigidly destroyed. This preservation of favourable variations and the rejection of injurious variations, I call Natural Selection.

Natural selection was proposed by Darwin primarily to account for the adaptive organization of living beings; it is a process that promotes or maintains adaptation. Evolutionary change through time and evolutionary diversification (multiplication of species) are not directly promoted by natural selection, but they often ensue as by-products of natural selection as it fosters adaptation to different environments.

Modern Conceptions

The modern conception of evolution is the product of three distinct phases of thought and research that followed Darwin's publication of the *Origin of Species*. The first phase included the period immediately following the release of *Origin of Species*, whereas the second was characterized by the synthesis of Darwinian natural selection with Mendelian genetics in 1940. The most recent phase of evolutionary theory began with the discovery of the chemical structure of DNA in 1953 and is grounded in the application of the tools of genetics research, including DNA sequencing, electrophoresis, and the polymerase chain reaction.

SIR JOSEPH DALTON HOOKER
(b. June 30, 1817, Halesworth, Suffolk, Eng.—d. Dec. 10, 1911, Sunningdale, Berkshire)

Sir Joseph Dalton Hooker was an English botanist noted for his botanical travels and studies and for his encouragement of Charles Darwin and of Darwin's theories. The younger son of Sir William Jackson Hooker, he was assistant director of the Royal Botanic Gardens at Kew from 1855 to 1865 and, succeeding his father, was then director from 1865 to 1885.

Hooker, unlike his father, had the benefit of a formal education and was graduated from the University of Glasgow with an M.D., in 1839.

Through his familiarity with his father's herbarium, he was well prepared for the first of his many travels—as surgeon-botanist aboard HMS *Erebus* on the Antarctic expedition of 1839–43. Thereafter, a steady stream of publications followed, punctuated by his own travels: *The Botany of the Antarctic Voyage of H.M. Discovery-Ships Erebus and Terror in 1839–1843* (1844–60); *Rhododendrons of Sikkim Himalya* (1849); The *Flora of British India*

Sir Joseph Dalton Hooker.
© Photos.com/Jupiterimages

(1872–97); *Handbook of the New Zealand Flora* (1864); and *Journal of a Tour in Marocco and the Great Atlas* (1878). His last major botanical expedition, to the Rocky Mountains and California (1877), led to the publication of several important papers concerning the relationship of American and Asian floras. His travels resulted in the discovery of species new to science, many of which were soon introduced to horticultural circles. Even more important, however, were the data, which gained him an international reputation as a plant geographer.

In 1851 Joseph Hooker married Frances Henslow, the daughter of a botanist. Six children survived her death in 1874. By his second wife, Hyacinth Symonds Jardine, whom he married in 1876, he had two sons. He became assistant director of Kew in 1855, a position he retained until 1865, when he succeeded his father as director, serving in that capacity until his own retirement in 1885. Many honours came to Hooker, including the presidency of the Royal Society (1872–77) and a knighthood (1877). He remained active until shortly before his death.

One of the most significant results of his travels was an attempt to explain the geographical distribution of plants and their seemingly anomalous variations. As a close friend of Charles Darwin and one well acquainted with the latter's early work, Hooker, along with the geologist Sir Charles Lyell, presided at the historic meeting of the Linnean Society (London) in July 1858. It was their function to adjudicate the priority claims concerning natural selection as the mechanism for evolution, which had been advanced simultaneously by Darwin and Alfred Russel Wallace. By lending his support to a scientific claim that was soon to be attacked on extrascientific grounds, Hooker was among the first to demonstrate the importance and applicability of the evolutionary theory to botany in general and to plant geography in particular. The capstone to Hooker's career came in 1883 with the publication of the final volume of the *Genera Plantarum*, written in conjunction with George Bentham. This world flora, describing 7,569 genera and approximately 97,000 species of seed-bearing plants, was based on a personal examination of the specimens cited, the vast majority of which were deposited at Kew.

The Darwinian Aftermath

The publication of the *Origin of Species* produced considerable public excitement. Scientists, politicians, clergymen, and notables of all kinds read and discussed the book, defending or deriding Darwin's ideas. The most visible actor in the controversies immediately following publication was the English biologist T.H. Huxley, known as "Darwin's bulldog," who defended the theory of evolution with articulate and sometimes mordant words on public occasions as well as in numerous writings. Evolution by natural selection was indeed a favourite topic in society salons during the 1860s and beyond. But serious scientific controversies also arose, first in Britain and then on the Continent and in the United States.

One occasional participant in the discussion was the British naturalist Alfred Russel Wallace, who had hit upon the idea of natural selection independently and had sent a short manuscript about it to Darwin from the Malay Archipelago, where he was collecting specimens and writing. On July 1, 1858, one year before the publication of the *Origin*, a paper jointly authored by Wallace and Darwin was presented, in the absence of both, to the Linnean Society in London—with apparently little notice. Greater credit is duly given to Darwin than to Wallace for the idea of evolution by natural selection; Darwin developed the theory in considerably more detail, provided far more evidence for it, and was primarily responsible for its acceptance. Wallace's views differed from Darwin's in several ways, most importantly in that Wallace did not think natural selection sufficient to account for the origin of human beings, which in his view required direct divine intervention.

A younger English contemporary of Darwin, with considerable influence during the latter part of the 19th and in the early 20th century, was Herbert Spencer. A philosopher rather than a biologist, he became an energetic proponent of evolutionary ideas, popularized a number of slogans, such as "survival of the fittest" (which was taken up by Darwin in later editions of the *Origin*), and engaged in social and metaphysical speculations. His ideas considerably damaged proper understanding and acceptance of the theory of evolution by natural selection. Darwin wrote of Spencer's speculations:

> *His deductive manner of treating any subject is wholly opposed to my frame of mind . . . His fundamental generalizations (which have been compared in importance by some persons with Newton's laws!) which I dare say may be very valuable under a philosophical point of view, are of such a nature that they do not seem to me to be of any strictly scientific use.*

Most pernicious was the crude extension by Spencer and others of the notion of the "struggle for existence" to human economic and social life that became known as social Darwinism.

The most serious difficulty facing Darwin's evolutionary theory was the lack of an adequate theory of inheritance that would account for the preservation through the generations of the variations on which natural selection was supposed to act. Contemporary theories of "blending inheritance" proposed that offspring merely struck an average between the characteristics of their parents. But as Darwin became aware, blending inheritance (including his own theory of "pangenesis," in which each organ and tissue of an organism throws off tiny contributions of itself that are collected in the sex organs and determine the configuration of the offspring) could not account for the conservation of variations, because differences between variant offspring would be halved each generation, rapidly reducing the original variation to the average of the preexisting characteristics.

The missing link in Darwin's argument was provided by Mendelian genetics. About the time the *Origin of Species* was published, the Augustinian monk Gregor Mendel was starting a long series of experiments with peas in the garden of his monastery in Brünn, Austria-Hungary (now Brno, Czech Republic). These experiments and the analysis of their results are by any standard an example of masterly scientific method. Mendel's paper, published in 1866 in the *Proceedings of the Natural Science Society of Brünn*, formulated the fundamental principles of the theory of heredity that is still current. His theory accounts for biological inheritance through particulate factors (now known as genes) inherited one from each parent, which do not mix or blend but segregate in the formation of the sex cells, or gametes.

Mendel's discoveries remained unknown to Darwin, however, and, indeed, they did not become generally known until 1900, when they were simultaneously rediscovered by a number of scientists on the Continent. In the meantime, Darwinism in the latter part of the 19th century faced an alternative evolutionary theory known as neo-Lamarckism. This hypothesis shared with Lamarck's the importance of use and disuse in the development and obliteration of organs, and it added the notion that the environment acts directly on organic structures, which explained their adaptation to the way of life and environment of the organism. Adherents of this theory discarded natural selection as an explanation for adaptation to the environment.

Prominent among the defenders of natural selection was the German biologist August Weismann, who in the 1880s published his germ plasm theory. He distinguished two substances that make up an organism: the soma, which comprises most body parts and organs, and the germ plasm, which contains the cells that give rise to the gametes and hence to progeny. Early in the development of an egg, the germ plasm becomes segregated from the somatic cells that give rise to the rest of the body. This notion of a radical separation between germ plasm and soma—that is, between the reproductive tissues and all other body tissues—prompted Weismann to assert that inheritance of acquired characteristics was impossible, and it opened the way for his championship of natural selection as the only major process that would account for biological evolution. Weismann's ideas became known after 1896 as neo-Darwinism.

THE SYNTHETIC THEORY

The rediscovery in 1900 of Mendel's theory of heredity, by the Dutch botanist and geneticist Hugo de Vries and others, led to an emphasis on the role of heredity in evolution. De Vries proposed a new theory of evolution known as mutationism, which essentially did away with natural selection as a major evolutionary process. According to de Vries (who was joined by other geneticists such as William Bateson in England), two kinds of variation take place in organisms. One is the "ordinary" variability observed among individuals of a species, which is of no lasting consequence in evolution because, according to de Vries, it could not "lead to a transgression of the species border [i.e., to establishment of new species] even under conditions of the most stringent and continued selection." The other consists of the changes brought about by mutations, spontaneous alterations of genes that result in large modifications of the organism and give rise to new species: "The new species thus originates suddenly, it is produced by the existing one without any visible preparation and without transition."

Mutationism was opposed by many naturalists and in particular by the so-called biometricians, led by the English statistician Karl Pearson, who defended Darwinian natural selection as the major cause of evolution through the cumulative effects of small, continuous, individual variations (which the biometricians assumed passed from one generation to the next without being limited by Mendel's laws of inheritance).

The controversy between mutationists (also referred to at the time as Mendelians) and biometricians approached a resolution in the 1920s and '30s through the theoretical work of geneticists. These scientists used mathematical arguments to show, first, that continuous variation (in such characteristics as body size, number of eggs laid, and the like) could be explained by Mendel's laws and, second, that natural selection acting cumulatively on small variations could yield major evolutionary changes in form and function. Distinguished members of this group of theoretical geneticists were R.A. Fisher and J.B.S. Haldane in Britain and Sewall Wright in the United States. Their work contributed to the downfall of mutationism and, most important, provided a theoretical framework for the integration of genetics into Darwin's theory of natural selection. Yet their work had a limited impact on contemporary biologists for several reasons—it was formulated in a mathematical language that most biologists could not understand; it was almost exclusively theoretical, with little empirical corroboration; and it was limited in scope, largely omitting many issues, such as speciation (the process by which new species are formed), that were of great importance to evolutionists.

A major breakthrough came in 1937 with the publication of *Genetics and the Origin of Species* by Theodosius Dobzhansky, a Russian-born American naturalist and experimental geneticist. Dobzhansky's book advanced a reasonably comprehensive account of the evolutionary process in genetic terms, laced with experimental evidence supporting the theoretical argument. *Genetics and the Origin of Species* may be considered the most important landmark in the formulation of what came to be known as the synthetic theory of evolution, effectively combining Darwinian natural selection and Mendelian genetics. It had an enormous impact on naturalists and experimental biologists, who rapidly embraced the new understanding of the evolutionary process as one of genetic change in populations. Interest in evolutionary studies was greatly stimulated, and contributions to the theory soon began to follow, extending the synthesis of genetics and natural selection to a variety of biological fields.

The main writers who, together with Dobzhansky, may be considered the architects of the synthetic theory were the German-born American zoologist Ernst Mayr, the English zoologist Julian Huxley, the American paleontologist George Gaylord Simpson, and the American botanist George Ledyard Stebbins. These researchers contributed to a burst of evolutionary studies in the traditional biological disciplines and in some emerging ones—notably population genetics and, later, evolutionary ecology. By 1950 acceptance of Darwin's theory of evolution by natural selection was universal among biologists, and the synthetic theory had become widely adopted.

Molecular Biology and Earth Sciences

The most important line of investigation after 1950 was the application of molecular biology to evolutionary studies. In 1953 the American geneticist James Watson and the British biophysicist Francis Crick deduced the molecular structure of DNA (deoxyribonucleic acid), the hereditary material contained in the chromosomes of every cell's nucleus. The genetic information is encoded within the sequence of nucleotides that make up the chainlike DNA molecules. This information determines the sequence of amino acid building blocks of protein molecules, which include, among others, structural proteins such as collagen, respiratory proteins such as hemoglobin, and numerous enzymes responsible for the organism's fundamental life processes. Genetic information contained in the DNA can thus be investigated by examining the sequences of amino acids in the proteins.

In the mid-1960s laboratory techniques such as electrophoresis and selective assay of enzymes became available for the rapid and inexpensive study of differences among enzymes and other proteins. The application of these techniques to evolutionary problems made possible the pursuit of issues that earlier could not be investigated — for example, exploring the extent of genetic variation in natural populations (which sets bounds on their evolutionary potential) and determining the amount of genetic change that occurs during the formation of new species.

Comparisons of the amino acid sequences of corresponding proteins in different species provided quantitatively precise measures of the divergence among species evolved from common ancestors, a considerable improvement over the typically qualitative evaluations obtained by comparative anatomy and other evolutionary subdisciplines. In 1968 the Japanese geneticist Motoo Kimura proposed the neutrality theory of molecular evolution, which assumes that, at the level of the sequences of nucleotides in DNA and of amino acids in proteins, many changes are adaptively neutral; they have little or no effect on the molecule's function and thus on an organism's fitness within its environment. If the neutrality theory is correct, there should be a "molecular clock" of evolution; that is, the degree to which amino acid or nucleotide sequences diverge between species should provide a reliable estimate of the time since the species diverged. This would make it possible to reconstruct an evolutionary history that would reveal the order of branching of different lineages, such as those leading to humans, chimpanzees, and orangutans, as well as the time in the past when the lineages split from one another. During the 1970s and '80s it gradually became clear that the molecular clock is not exact; nevertheless, into the early 21st century it continued to provide the most reliable evidence for reconstructing evolutionary history.

The laboratory techniques of DNA cloning and sequencing have provided a new and powerful means of investigating evolution at the molecular level. The fruits of this technology began to accumulate during the 1980s following the development of automated DNA-sequencing machines and the invention of the polymerase chain reaction (PCR), a simple and inexpensive technique that obtains, in a few hours, billions or trillions of copies of a specific DNA sequence or gene. Major research efforts such as the Human Genome Project further improved the technology for obtaining long DNA sequences rapidly and inexpensively. By the first few years of the 21st century, the full DNA sequence—i.e., the full genetic complement, or genome—had been obtained for more than 20 higher organisms, including human beings, the house mouse (*Mus musculus*), the rat *Rattus norvegicus*, the vinegar fly *Drosophila melanogaster*, the mosquito *Anopheles gambiae*, the nematode worm *Caenorhabditis elegans*, the malaria parasite *Plasmodium falciparum*, the mustard weed *Arabidopsis thaliana*, and the yeast *Saccharomyces cerevisiae*, as well as for numerous microorganisms.

The Earth sciences also experienced, in the second half of the 20th century, a conceptual revolution with considerable consequence to the study of evolution. The theory of plate tectonics, which was formulated in the late 1960s, revealed that the configuration and position of the continents and oceans are dynamic, rather than static, features of Earth. Oceans grow and shrink, while continents break into fragments or coalesce into larger masses. The continents move across Earth's surface at rates of a few centimetres a year, and over millions of years of geologic history this movement profoundly alters the face of the planet, causing major climatic changes along the way. These previously unsuspected massive modifications of Earth's past environments are, of necessity, reflected in the evolutionary history of life. Biogeography, the evolutionary study of plant and animal distribution, has been revolutionized by the knowledge, for example, that Africa and South America were part of a single landmass some 200 million years ago and that the Indian subcontinent was not connected with Asia until geologically recent times.

Ecology, the study of the interactions of organisms with their environments, has evolved from descriptive studies — "natural history" — into a vigorous biological discipline with a strong mathematical component, both in the development of theoretical models and in the collection and analysis of quantitative data. Evolutionary ecology is an active field of evolutionary biology; another is evolutionary ethology, the study of the evolution of animal behaviour. Sociobiology, the evolutionary study of social behaviour, is perhaps the most active subfield of ethology. It is also the most controversial, because of its extension to human societies.

THE CULTURAL IMPACT OF EVOLUTIONARY THEORY

Few scientific ideas have ignited more controversy in religious circles than evolutionary theory. Although it has been widely adopted by the scientific community, extending into several subdisciplines of biology, religious opposition to evolutionary theory has appeared periodically since Darwin's time. Many mainstream Christian denominations have grown to accept evolutionary theory; however, some fundamentalist groups continue to perceive it as a threat to their belief systems.

SCIENTIFIC ACCEPTANCE AND EXTENSION TO OTHER DISCIPLINES

The theory of evolution makes statements about three different, though related, issues: (1) the fact of evolution—that is, that organisms are related by common descent; (2) evolutionary history—the details of when lineages split from one another and of the changes that occurred in each lineage; and (3) the mechanisms or processes by which evolutionary change occurs.

The first issue is the most fundamental and the one established with utmost certainty. Darwin gathered much evidence in its support, but evidence has accumulated continuously ever since, derived from all biological disciplines. The evolutionary origin of organisms is today a scientific conclusion established with the kind of certainty attributable to such scientific concepts as the roundness of Earth, the motions of the planets, and the molecular composition of matter. This degree of certainty beyond reasonable doubt is what is implied when biologists say that evolution is a "fact"; the evolutionary origin of organisms is accepted by virtually every biologist.

But the theory of evolution goes far beyond the general affirmation that organisms evolve. The second and third issues—seeking to ascertain evolutionary relationships between particular organisms and the events of evolutionary history, as well as to explain how and why evolution takes place—are matters of active scientific investigation. Some conclusions are well established. One, for example, is that the chimpanzee and the gorilla are more closely related to humans than is any of those three species to the baboon or other monkeys. Another conclusion is that natural selection, the process postulated by Darwin, explains the configuration of such adaptive features as the human eye and the wings of birds. Many matters are less certain, others are conjectural, and still others—such as the characteristics of the first living things and when they came about—remain completely unknown.

Since Darwin, the theory of evolution has gradually extended its influence to other biological disciplines, from physiology to ecology and from biochemistry to systematics. All biological knowledge now includes the phenomenon of evolution. In the words of Theodosius Dobzhansky, "Nothing in biology makes sense except in the light of evolution."

The term *evolution* and the general concept of change through time also have penetrated into scientific language well beyond biology and even into common language.

Astrophysicists speak of the evolution of the solar system or of the universe; geologists, of the evolution of Earth's interior; psychologists, of the evolution of the mind; anthropologists, of the evolution of cultures; art historians, of the evolution of architectural styles; and couturiers, of the evolution of fashion. These and other disciplines use the word with only the slightest commonality of meaning—the notion of gradual, and perhaps directional, change over the course of time.

Toward the end of the 20th century, specific concepts and processes borrowed from biological evolution and living systems were incorporated into computational research, beginning with the work of the American mathematician John Holland and others. One outcome of this endeavour was the development of methods for automatically generating computer-based systems that are proficient at given tasks. These systems have a wide variety of potential uses, such as solving practical computational problems, providing machines with the ability to learn from experience, and modeling processes in fields as diverse as ecology, immunology, economics, and even biological evolution itself.

To generate computer programs that represent proficient solutions to a problem under study, the computer scientist creates a set of step-by-step procedures, called a genetic algorithm or, more broadly, an evolutionary algorithm, that incorporates analogies of genetic processes—for instance, heredity, mutation, and recombination—as well as of evolutionary processes such as natural selection in the presence of specified environments. The algorithm is designed typically to simulate the biological evolution of a population of individual computer programs through successive generations to improve their "fitness" for carrying out a designated task. Each program in an initial population receives a fitness score that measures how well it performs in a specific "environment"—for example, how efficiently it sorts a list of numbers or allocates the floor space in a new factory design. Only those with the highest scores are selected to "reproduce," to contribute "hereditary" material—i.e., computer code—to the following generation of programs. The rules of reproduction may involve such elements as recombination (strings of code from the best programs are shuffled and combined into the programs of the next generation) and mutation (bits of code in a few of the new programs are changed at random). The evolutionary algorithm then evaluates each program in the new generation for fitness, winnows out the poorer performers, and allows reproduction to take place once again, with the cycle repeating itself as often as desired. Evolutionary algorithms are simplistic compared with biological evolution, but they have provided robust and powerful mechanisms for finding solutions to all sorts of problems in economics, industrial production, and the distribution of goods and services.

Darwin's notion of natural selection also has been extended to areas of human discourse outside the scientific setting, particularly in the fields of sociopolitical theory and economics. The extension can be only metaphoric, because in Darwin's intended meaning natural selection applies only to hereditary variations in entities endowed with biological reproduction—that is, to living organisms. That natural selection is a natural process in the living world has been taken by some as a justification for ruthless competition and for "survival of the fittest" in the struggle for economic advantage or for political hegemony. Social Darwinism was an influential social philosophy in some circles through the late 19th and early 20th centuries, when it was used as a rationalization for racism, colonialism, and social strati-fication. At the other end of the political spectrum, Marxist theorists have resorted to evolution by natural selection as an explanation for humankind's political history.

Darwinism understood as a process that favours the strong and successful and eliminates the weak and failing has been used to justify alternative and, in some respects, quite diametric economic theories. These theories share in common the premise that the valuation of all market products depends on a Darwinian process. Specific market commodities are evaluated in terms of the degree to which they conform to specific valuations emanating from the consumers. On the one hand, some of these economic theories are consistent with theories of evolutionary psychology that see preferences as determined largely genetically; as such, they hold that the reactions of markets can be predicted in terms of largely fixed human attri-butes. The dominant neo-Keynesian and monetarist schools of economics make predictions of the macroscopic behaviour of economies based the interrelationship of a few variables; money supply, rate of inflation, and rate of unemployment jointly determine the rate of economic growth. On the other hand, some minority economists, such as the 20th-century Austrian-born British theorist F.A. Hayek and his followers, predicate the Darwinian process on individual preferences that are mostly under-determined and change in erratic or unpredictable ways. According to them, old ways of producing goods and ser-vices are continuously replaced by new inventions and behaviours. These theorists affirm that what drives the economy is the ingenuity of individuals and corpora-tions and their ability to bring new and better products to the market.

RELIGIOUS CRITICISM AND ACCEPTANCE

The theory of evolution has been seen by some people as incompatible with religious beliefs, particularly those of Christianity. The first chapters of the biblical book of Genesis describe God's creation of the world, the plants, the animals, and human beings. A literal interpretation of Genesis seems incompatible with the gradual evolution of humans and other organisms by natural processes. Independently of the biblical narrative, the Christian beliefs in the immortality of the soul and in humans as "created in the image of God" have appeared to many as contrary to the evolutionary origin of humans from nonhuman animals.

Religiously motivated attacks started during Darwin's lifetime. In 1874 Charles Hodge, an American Protestant theologian, published *What Is Darwinism?*, one of the most articulate assaults on evolutionary theory. Hodge perceived Darwin's theory as "the most thoroughly naturalistic that can be imagined and far more atheistic than that of his predecessor Lamarck." He argued that the design of the human eye evinces that "it has been planned by the Creator, like the design of a watch evinces a watchmaker." He concluded that "the denial of design in nature is actually the denial of God."

Other Protestant theologians saw a solution to the difficulty through the argument that God operates through intermediate causes. The origin and motion of the planets could be explained by the law of gravity and other natural processes without denying God's creation and providence. Similarly, evolution could be seen as the natural process through which God brought living beings into existence and developed them according to his plan. Thus, A.H. Strong, the president of Rochester Theological Seminary in New York state, wrote in his *Systematic Theology* (1885):

"We grant the principle of evolution, but we regard it as only the method of divine intelligence." The brutish ancestry of human beings was not incompatible with their excelling status as creatures in the image of God. Strong drew an analogy with Christ's miraculous conversion of water into wine: "The wine in the miracle was not water because water had been used in the making of it, nor is man a brute because the brute has made some contributions to its creation." Arguments for and against Darwin's theory came from Roman Catholic theologians as well.

Gradually, well into the 20th century, evolution by natural selection came to be accepted by the majority of Christian writers. Pope Pius XII in his encyclical *Humani generis* (1950; "Of the Human Race") acknowledged that biological evolution was compatible with the Christian faith, although he argued that God's intervention was necessary for the creation of the human soul. Pope John Paul II, in an address to the Pontifical Academy of Sciences on Oct. 22, 1996, deplored interpreting the Bible's texts as scientific statements rather than religious teachings, adding:

> *New scientific knowledge has led us to realize that the theory of evolution is no longer a mere hypothesis. It is indeed remarkable that this theory has been progressively accepted by researchers, following a series of discoveries in various fields of knowledge. The convergence, neither sought nor fabricated, of the results of work that was conducted independently is in itself a significant argument in favor of this theory.*

Similar views were expressed by other mainstream Christian denominations. The General Assembly of the United Presbyterian Church in 1982 adopted a resolution stating that "Biblical scholars and theological schools . . .

find that the scientific theory of evolution does not conflict with their interpretation of the origins of life found in Biblical literature." The Lutheran World Federation in 1965 affirmed that "evolution's assumptions are as much around us as the air we breathe and no more escapable. At the same time theology's affirmations are being made as responsibly as ever. In this sense both science and religion are here to stay, and . . . need to remain in a healthful tension of respect toward one another." Similar statements have been advanced by Jewish authorities and those of other major religions. In 1984 the 95th Annual Convention of the Central Conference of American Rabbis adopted a resolution stating: "Whereas the principles and concepts of biological evolution are basic to understanding science . . . we call upon science teachers and local school authorities in all states to demand quality textbooks that are based on modern, scientific knowledge and that exclude 'scientific' creationism."

Opposing these views were Christian denominations that continued to hold a literal interpretation of the Bible. A succinct expression of this interpretation is found in the Statement of Belief of the Creation Research Society, founded in 1963 as a "professional organization of trained scientists and interested laypersons who are firmly committed to scientific special creation":

The Bible is the Written Word of God, and because it is inspired throughout, all of its assertions are historically and scientifically true in the original autographs. To the student of nature this means that the account of origins in Genesis is a factual presentation of simple historical truths.

Many Bible scholars and theologians have long rejected a literal interpretation as untenable, however, because the

Bible contains incompatible statements. The very beginning of the book of Genesis presents two different creation narratives. Extending through chapter 1 and the first verses of chapter 2 is the familiar six-day narrative, in which God creates human beings—both "male and female"—in his own image on the sixth day, after creating light, Earth, firmament, fish, fowl, and cattle. But in verse 4 of chapter 2 a different narrative starts, in which God creates a male human, then plants a garden and creates the animals, and only then proceeds to take a rib from the man to make a woman.

Biblical scholars point out that the Bible is inerrant with respect to religious truth, not in matters that are of no significance to salvation. Augustine, considered by many the greatest Christian theologian, wrote in the early 5th century in his *De Genesi ad litteram* (*Literal Commentary on Genesis*):

> *It is also frequently asked what our belief must be about the form and shape of heaven, according to Sacred Scripture. Many scholars engage in lengthy discussions on these matters, but the sacred writers with their deeper wisdom have omitted them. Such subjects are of no profit for those who seek beatitude. And what is worse, they take up very precious time that ought to be given to what is spiritually beneficial. What concern is it of mine whether heaven is like a sphere and Earth is enclosed by it and suspended in the middle of the universe, or whether heaven is like a disk and the Earth is above it and hovering to one side.*

Augustine adds later in the same chapter: "In the matter of the shape of heaven, the sacred writers did not wish to teach men facts that could be of no avail for their salvation." Augustine is saying that the book of Genesis is not an elementary book of astronomy. It is a book about religion, and it is not the purpose of its religious authors to settle questions about the shape of the universe that are of no relevance whatsoever to how to seek salvation. In the same vein, John Paul II said in 1981:

> *The Bible itself speaks to us of the origin of the universe and its make-up, not in order to provide us with a scientific treatise but in order to state the correct relationships of man with God and with the universe. Sacred scripture wishes simply to declare that the world was created by God, and in order to teach this truth it expresses itself in the terms of the cosmology in use at the time of the writer. Any other teaching about the origin and make-up of the universe is alien to the intentions of the Bible, which does not wish to teach how the heavens were made but how one goes to heaven.*

John Paul's argument was clearly a response to Christian fundamentalists who see in Genesis a literal description of how the world was created by God. In modern times biblical fundamentalists have made up a minority of Christians, but they have periodically gained considerable public and political influence, particularly in the United States. Opposition to the teaching of evolution in the United States can largely be traced to two movements with 19th-century roots, Seventh-day Adventism and Pentecostalism. Consistent with their emphasis on the seventh-day Sabbath as a memorial of the biblical Creation, Seventh-day Adventists have insisted on the recent creation of life and the universality of the Flood, which they believe deposited the fossil-bearing rocks. This distinctively Adventist interpretation of Genesis became the hard core of "creation science" in the late 20th century and was incorporated into the "balanced-treatment" laws of Arkansas and Louisiana (discussed below). Many

William Jennings Bryan (lower left, with fan) and Clarence Darrow (centre right, arms folded) in a Dayton, Tennessee, courtroom during the Scopes trial, July 1925. Library of Congress, Washington, D.C.

Pentecostals, who generally endorse a literal interpretation of the Bible, also have adopted and endorsed the tenets of creation science, including the recent origin of Earth and a geology interpreted in terms of the Flood. They have differed from Seventh-day Adventists and other adherents of creation science, however, in their tolerance of diverse views and the limited import they attribute to the evolution-creation controversy.

During the 1920s, biblical fundamentalists helped influence more than 20 state legislatures to debate antievolution laws, and four states—Arkansas, Mississippi, Oklahoma, and Tennessee—prohibited the teaching of evolution in their public schools. A spokesman for the antievolutionists was William Jennings Bryan, three times the unsuccessful

Democratic candidate for the U.S. presidency, who said in 1922, "We will drive Darwinism from our schools." In 1925 Bryan took part in the prosecution of John T. Scopes, a high school teacher in Dayton, Tennessee, who had admittedly violated the state's law forbidding the teaching of evolution.

In 1968 the Supreme Court of the United States declared unconstitutional any law banning the teaching of evolution in public schools. After that time Christian fundamentalists introduced bills in a number of state legislatures ordering that the teaching of "evolution science" be balanced by allocating equal time to creation science. Creation science maintains that all kinds of organisms abruptly came into existence when God created the universe, that the world is only a few thousand years old, and that the biblical Flood was an actual event that only one pair of each animal species survived. In the 1980s Arkansas and Louisiana passed acts requiring the balanced treatment of evolution science and creation science in their schools, but opponents successfully challenged the acts as violations of the constitutionally mandated separation of church and state. The Arkansas statute was declared unconstitutional in federal court after a public trial in Little Rock. The Louisiana law was appealed all the way to the Supreme Court of the United States, which ruled Louisiana's "Creationism Act" unconstitutional because, by advancing the religious belief that a supernatural being created humankind, which is embraced by the phrase *creation science*, the act impermissibly endorses religion.

INTELLIGENT DESIGN AND ITS CRITICS

William Paley's *Natural Theology*, the book by which he has become best known to posterity, is a sustained argument explaining the obvious design of humans and their parts, as well as the design of all sorts of organisms, in themselves and in their relations to one another and to their environment. Paley's keystone claim is that "there cannot be design without a designer; contrivance, without a contriver; order, without choice; . . . means suitable to an end, and executing their office in accomplishing that end, without the end ever having been contemplated." His book has chapters dedicated to the complex design of the human eye; to the human frame, which, he argues, displays a precise mechanical arrangement of bones, cartilage, and joints; to the circulation of the blood and the disposition of blood vessels; to the comparative anatomy of humans and animals; to the digestive system, kidneys, urethra, and bladder; to the wings of birds and the fins of fish; and much more. For more than 300 pages, Paley conveys extensive and accurate biological knowledge in such detail and precision as was available in 1802, the year of the book's publication. After his meticulous description of each biological object or process, Paley draws again and again the same conclusion—only an omniscient and omnipotent deity could account for these marvels and for the enormous diversity of inventions that they entail.

On the example of the human eye he wrote:

> I know no better method of introducing so large a subject, than that of comparing . . . an eye, for example, with a telescope. As far as the examination of the instrument goes, there is precisely the same proof that the eye was made for vision, as there is that the telescope was made for assisting it. They are made upon the same principles; both being adjusted to the laws by which the transmission and refraction of rays of light are regulated . . . For instance, these laws require, in order to produce the same effect, that the rays of light, in passing from water into the eye, should be refracted by a more convex surface than

when it passes out of air into the eye. Accordingly we find that the eye of a fish, in that part of it called the crystalline lens, is much rounder than the eye of terrestrial animals. What plainer manifestation of design can there be than this difference? What could a mathematical instrument maker have done more to show his knowledge of [t]his principle, his application of that knowledge, his suiting of his means to his end . . . to testify counsel, choice, consideration, purpose?

It would be absurd to suppose, he argued, that by mere chance the eye:

should have consisted, first, of a series of transparent lenses— very different, by the by, even in their substance, from the opaque materials of which the rest of the body is, in general at least, composed, and with which the whole of its surface, this single portion of it excepted, is covered: secondly, of a black cloth or canvas—the only membrane in the body which is black—spread out behind these lenses, so as to receive the image formed by pencils of light transmitted through them; and placed at the precise geometrical distance at which, and at which alone, a distinct image could be formed, namely, at the concourse of the refracted rays: thirdly, of a large nerve communicating between this membrane and the brain; without which, the action of light upon the membrane, however modified by the organ, would be lost to the purposes of sensation.

The strength of the argument against chance derived, according to Paley, from a notion that he named *relation* and that later authors would term *irreducible complexity*. Paley wrote:

When several different parts contribute to one effect, or, which is the same thing, when an effect is produced by the joint action

*of different instruments, the fitness of such parts or instru-
ments to one another for the purpose of producing, by their
united action, the effect, is what I call relation; and wherever
this is observed in the works of nature or of man, it appears to
me to carry along with it decisive evidence of understanding,
intention, art . . . all depending upon the motions within, all
upon the system of intermediate actions.*

Natural Theology was part of the canon at Cambridge
for half a century after Paley's death. It thus was read by
Darwin, who was an undergraduate student there between
1827 and 1831, with profit and "much delight." Darwin was
mindful of Paley's relation argument when in the *Origin of
Species* he stated: "If it could be demonstrated that any
complex organ existed, which could not possibly have
been formed by numerous, successive, slight modifications, my theory would absolutely break down. But I can
find out no such case . . . We should be extremely cautious
in concluding that an organ could not have been formed
by transitional gradations of some kind."

In the 1990s several authors revived the argument
from design. The proposition, once again, was that living
beings manifest "intelligent design"—they are so diverse
and complicated that they can be explained not as the outcome of natural processes but only as products of an
"intelligent designer." Some authors clearly equated this
entity with the omnipotent God of Christianity and other
monotheistic religions. Others, because they wished to
see the theory of intelligent design taught in schools as an
alternate to the theory of evolution, avoided all explicit
reference to God in order to maintain the separation
between religion and state.

The call for an intelligent designer is predicated on the
existence of irreducible complexity in organisms. In

Michael Behe's book *Darwin's Black Box: The Biochemical Challenge to Evolution* (1996), an irreducibly complex system is defined as being "composed of several well-matched, interacting parts that contribute to the basic function, wherein the removal of any one of the parts causes the system to effectively cease functioning." Contemporary intelligent-design proponents have argued that irreducibly complex systems cannot be the outcome of evolution. According to Behe, "Since natural selection can only choose systems that are already working, then if a biological system cannot be produced gradually it would have to arise as an integrated unit, in one fell swoop, for natural selection to have anything to act on." In other words, unless all parts of the eye come simultaneously into existence, the eye cannot function; it does not benefit a precursor organism to have just a retina, or a lens, if the other parts are lacking. The human eye, they conclude, could not have evolved one small step at a time, in the piecemeal manner by which natural selection works.

The theory of intelligent design has encountered many critics, not only among evolutionary scientists but also among theologians and religious authors. Evolutionists point out that organs and other components of living beings are not irreducibly complex—they do not come about suddenly, or in one fell swoop. The human eye did not appear suddenly in all its present complexity. Its formation required the integration of many genetic units, each improving the performance of preexisting, functionally less-perfect eyes. About 700 million years ago, the ancestors of today's vertebrates already had organs sensitive to light. Mere perception of light—and, later, various levels of vision ability—were beneficial to these organisms living in environments pervaded by sunlight. As is discussed more fully below in the section Diversity and Extinction, different kinds of eyes have independently evolved at least 40 times in animals, which exhibit a full range, from very uncomplicated modifications that allow individual cells or simple animals to perceive the direction of light to the sophisticated vertebrate eye, passing through all sorts of organs intermediate in complexity. Evolutionists have shown that the examples of irreducibly complex systems cited by intelligent-design theorists—such as the bio-chemical mechanism of blood clotting or the molecular rotary motor, called the flagellum, by which bacterial cells move—are not irreducible at all; rather, less-complex versions of the same systems can be found in today's organisms.

Evolutionists have pointed out as well that imperfections and defects pervade the living world. In the human eye, for example, the visual nerve fibres in the eye converge on an area of the retina to form the optic nerve and thus create a blind spot; squids and octopuses do not have this defect. Defective design seems incompatible with an omnipotent intelligent designer. Anticipating this criticism, Paley responded that "apparent blemishes . . . ought to be referred to some cause, though we be ignorant of it." Modern intelligent-design theorists have made similar assertions; according to Behe, "The argument from imperfection overlooks the possibility that the designer might have multiple motives, with engineering excellence often-times relegated to a secondary role." This statement, evolutionists have responded, may have theological validity, but it destroys intelligent design as a scientific hypothesis, because it provides it with an empirically impenetrable shield against predictions of how "intelligent" or "perfect" a design will be. Science tests its hypotheses by observing whether predictions derived from them are the case in the observable world. A hypothesis that cannot be tested empirically—that is, by observation or experiment—is not scientific. The implication of this line of reasoning for U.S. public schools has been recognized not only by scientists but also by nonscientists, including politicians and policy makers. The liberal U.S. senator Edward Kennedy wrote in 2002 that "intelligent design is not a genuine scientific theory and, therefore, has no place in the curriculum of our nation's public school science classes."

Scientists, moreover, have pointed out that not only do imperfections exist but so do dysfunctions, blunders, oddities, and cruelties prevail in the world of life. For this reason theologians and religious authors have criticized the theory of intelligent design, because it leads to conclusions about the nature of the designer at odds with the omniscience, omnipotence, and omnibenevolence that they, like Paley, identify as the attributes of the Creator. One example of a "blunder" is the human jaw, which for its size has too many teeth; the third molars, or wisdom teeth, often become impacted and need to be removed. Whereas many people would find it awkward, to say the least, to attribute to God a design that a capable human engineer would not even wish to claim, evolution gives a good account of this imperfection. As brain size increased over time in human ancestors, the concurrent remodeling of the skull entailed a reduction of the jaw so that the head of the fetus would continue to fit through the birth canal of the adult female. Evolution responds to an organism's needs not by optimal design but by tinkering, as it were—by slowly modifying existing structures through natural selection. Despite the modifications to the human jaw, the woman's birth canal remains much too narrow for easy passage of the fetal head, and many thousands of babies die during delivery as a result. Science makes this understandable as a consequence of the evolutionary enlargement of the human brain; females of other animals do not experience this difficulty.

The world of life abounds in "cruel" behaviours. Numerous predators eat their prey alive; parasites destroy their living hosts from within; in many species of spiders and insects, the females devour their mates. Religious scholars in the past had struggled with such dysfunction and cruelty because they were difficult to explain by God's design. Evolution, in one respect, came to their rescue. A contemporary Protestant theologian called Darwin the "disguised friend," and a Roman Catholic theologian wrote of "Darwin's gift to theology." Both were acknowledging the irony that the theory of evolution, which at first had seemed to remove the need for God in the world, now was convincingly removing the need to explain the world's imperfections as outcomes of God's design.

CHAPTER 2
THE PROCESS OF EVOLUTION

The process of evolution is largely a genetic process. Populations of organisms are made up of a pool of various genes. Mutations in an individual's genetic code may produce traits that increase an organism's survival and reproductive success. Beneficial mutations may be passed along from parent to offspring, whereas those that substantially decrease the ability of the organism to survive often perish with the individual before the individual can reproduce. The more advantageous the trait, the more frequent it will become in a population. Over several generations, the population will become better adapted to its environment.

EVOLUTION AS A GENETIC FUNCTION

The central argument of Darwin's theory of evolution starts with the existence of hereditary variation. Experience with animal and plant breeding had demonstrated to Darwin that variations can be developed that are "useful to man." So, he reasoned, variations must occur in nature that are favourable or useful in some way to the organism itself in the struggle for existence. Favourable variations are ones that increase chances for survival and procreation. Those advantageous variations are preserved and multiplied from generation to generation at the expense of less-advantageous ones. This is the process known as natural selection. The outcome of the process is an organism that is well adapted to its environment, and evolution often occurs as a consequence.

Natural selection, then, can be defined as the differential reproduction of alternative hereditary variants, determined by the fact that some variants increase the likelihood that the organisms having them will survive and reproduce more successfully than will organisms carrying alternative variants. Selection may occur as a result of differences in survival, in fertility, in rate of development, in mating success, or in any other aspect of the life cycle. All of these differences can be incorporated under the term *differential reproduction* because all result in natural selection to the extent that they affect the number of progeny an organism leaves.

Darwin maintained that competition for limited resources results in the survival of the most-effective competitors. Nevertheless, natural selection may occur not only as a result of competition but also as a result of some aspect of the physical environment, such as inclement weather. Moreover, natural selection would occur even if all the members of a population died at the same age, simply because some of them would have produced more offspring than others. Natural selection is quantified by a measure called Darwinian fitness or relative fitness. Fitness in this sense is the relative probability that a hereditary characteristic will be reproduced; that is, the degree of fitness is a measure of the reproductive efficiency of the characteristic.

Biological evolution is the process of change and diversification of living things over time, and it affects all aspects of their lives—morphology (form and structure), physiology, behaviour, and ecology. Underlying these changes are changes in the hereditary materials. Hence, in genetic terms evolution consists of changes in the organism's hereditary makeup.

Evolution can be seen as a two-step process. First, hereditary variation takes place; second, selection is made of those genetic variants that will be passed on most effectively to the following generations. Hereditary variation also entails two mechanisms—the spontaneous mutation of one variant into another and the sexual process that recombines those variants to form a multitude of variations. The variants that arise by mutation or recombination are not transmitted equally from one generation to another. Some may appear more frequently because they are favourable to the organism; the frequency of others may be determined by accidents of chance, called genetic drift.

Genetic Variation in Populations

The amount of genetic variation in a given population influences the rate at which that population evolves. Genetic variation itself is governed by the pool of alleles in the population. Although environmental pressures and randomness bring about evolution in populations over time, the traits of many animals and plants may be artificially selected by humans. Molecular techniques developed during the middle of the 20th century may also be used to alter an organism's existing genetic structure.

The Gene Pool

The gene pool is the sum total of all the genes and combinations of genes that occur in a population of organisms of the same species. It can be described by citing the frequencies of the alternative genetic constitutions. Consider, for example, a particular gene (which geneticists call a locus), such as the one determining the MN blood groups in humans. One form of the gene codes for the M blood group, while the other form codes for the N blood group; different forms of the same gene are called alleles. The MN gene pool of a particular population is specified by giving the frequencies of the alleles M and N. Thus, in the United States the M allele occurs in people of European descent with a frequency of 0.539 and the N allele with a frequency of 0.461—that is, 53.9 percent of the alleles in the population are M and 46.1 percent are N. In other populations these frequencies are different; for instance, the frequency of the M allele is 0.917 in Navajo Indians and 0.178 in Australian Aboriginals.

The necessity of hereditary variation for evolutionary change to occur can be understood in terms of the gene pool. Assume, for instance, a population in which there is no variation at the gene locus that codes for the MN blood groups; only the M allele exists in all individuals. Evolution of the MN blood groups cannot take place in such a population, since the allelic frequencies have no opportunity to change from generation to generation. On the other hand, in populations in which both alleles M and N are present, evolutionary change is possible.

GENETIC VARIATION AND RATE OF EVOLUTION

The more genetic variation that exists in a population, the greater the opportunity for evolution to occur. As the number of gene loci that are variable increases and as the number of alleles at each locus becomes greater, the likelihood grows that some alleles will change in frequency at the expense of their alternates. The British geneticist R.A. Fisher mathematically demonstrated a direct correlation between the amount of genetic variation in a population and the rate of evolutionary change by natural selection. This demonstration is embodied in his fundamental theorem of natural selection (1930): "The rate of increase in fitness of any organism at any time is equal to its genetic variance in fitness at that time."

This theorem has been confirmed experimentally. One study employed different strains of *Drosophila serrata*, a species of vinegar fly from eastern Australia and New Guinea. Evolution in vinegar flies can be investigated by breeding them in separate "population cages" and finding out how populations change over many generations.

Experimental populations were set up, with the flies living and reproducing in their isolated microcosms. Single-strain populations were established from flies collected either in New Guinea or in Australia; in addition, a mixed population was constituted by crossing these two strains of flies. The mixed population had the greater initial genetic variation, since it began with two different single-strain populations. To encourage rapid evolutionary change, the populations were manipulated such that the flies experienced intense competition for food and space. Adaptation to the experimental environment was measured by periodically counting the number of individuals in the populations.

Two results deserve notice. First, the mixed population had, at the end of the experiment, more flies than the single-strain populations. Second, and more relevant, the number of flies increased at a faster rate in the mixed population than in the single-strain populations. Evolutionary adaptation to the environment occurred in both types of population; both were able to maintain higher numbers as the generations progressed. But the rate of evolution was more rapid in the mixed group than in the single-strain groups. The greater initial amount of genetic variation made possible a faster rate of evolution.

MEASURING GENE VARIABILITY

Because a population's potential for evolving is determined by its genetic variation, evolutionists are interested in discovering the extent of such variation in natural populations. It is readily apparent that plant and animal species are heterogeneous in all sorts of ways—in the flower colours and growth habits of plants, for instance, or the shell shapes and banding patterns of snails. Differences are more readily noticed among humans—in facial features, hair and skin colour, height, and weight—but such morphological differences are present in all groups of organisms. One problem with morphological variation is that it is not known how much is due to genetic factors and how much may result from environmental influences.

Animal and plant breeders select for their experiments individuals or seeds that excel in desired attributes—in the protein content of corn (maize), for example, or the milk yield of cows. The selection is repeated generation after generation. If the population changes in the direction favoured by the breeder, it becomes clear that the original stock possessed genetic variation with respect to the selected trait.

The results of artificial selection are impressive. Selection for high oil content in corn increased the oil content from less than 5 percent to more than 19 percent in 76 generations, while selection for low oil content reduced it to below 1 percent. Thirty years of selection for increased egg production in a flock of White Leghorn chickens increased the average yearly output of a hen from 125.6 to 249.6 eggs. Artificial selection has produced endless varieties of dog, cat, and horse breeds. The plants grown for food and fibre and the animals bred for food and transportation are all products of age-old or modern-day artificial selection. Since the late 20th century, scientists have used the techniques of molecular biology to modify or introduce genes for desired traits in a variety of organisms, including domestic plants and animals; this field has become known as genetic engineering or recombinant DNA technology. Improvements that in the past were achieved after tens of generations by artificial selection can now be accomplished much more effectively and rapidly (within a single generation) by molecular genetic technology.

The success of artificial selection for virtually every trait and every organism in which it has been tried suggests that genetic variation is pervasive throughout natural populations. But evolutionists like to go one step further and obtain quantitative estimates. Only since the 1960s, with the advances of molecular biology, have geneticists developed methods for measuring the extent of genetic variation in populations or among species of organisms. These methods consist essentially of taking a sample of genes and finding out how many are variable and how variable each one is. One simple way of measuring the variability of a gene locus is to ascertain what proportion of the individuals in a population are heterozygotes at that locus. In a heterozygous individual the two genes for a trait, one received from the mother and the other from the father, are different. The proportion of heterozygotes in the population is, therefore, the same as the probability that two genes taken at random from the gene pool are different.

Techniques for determining heterozygosity have been used to investigate numerous species of plants and animals. Typically, insects and other invertebrates are more varied genetically than mammals and other vertebrates, and plants bred by outcrossing (crossing with relatively unrelated strains) exhibit more variation than those bred by self-pollination. But the amount of genetic variation is in any case astounding. Consider as an example humans, whose level of variation is about the same as that of other mammals. The human heterozygosity value at the level of proteins is stated as $H = 0.067$, which means that an individual is heterozygous at 6.7 percent of his genes, because the two genes at each locus encode slightly different proteins. The Human Genome Project demonstrated that there are at least 30,000 genes in humans. This means that a person is heterozygous at no fewer than $30,000 \times 0.067 =$

2,010 gene loci. An individual heterozygous at one locus (*Aa*) can produce two different kinds of sex cells, or gametes, one with each allele (*A* and *a*); an individual heterozygous at two loci (*AaBb*) can produce four kinds of gametes (*AB*, *Ab*, *aB*, and *ab*); an individual heterozygous at *n* loci can potentially produce 2*n* different gametes. Therefore, a typical human individual has the potential to produce $2^{2,010}$, or approximately 10^{605} (1 with 605 zeros following), different kinds of gametes. That number is much larger than the estimated number of atoms in the universe, about 10^{80}.

It is clear, then, that every sex cell produced by a human being is genetically different from every other sex cell and, therefore, that no two persons who ever existed or will ever exist are likely to be genetically identical — with the exception of identical twins, which develop from a single fertilized ovum. The same conclusion applies to all organisms that reproduce sexually; every individual represents a unique genetic configuration that will likely never be repeated again. This enormous reservoir of genetic variation in natural populations provides virtually unlimited opportunities for evolutionary change in response to the environmental constraints and the needs of the organisms.

The Origin of Genetic Variation: Mutations

Life originated about 3.5 billion years ago in the form of primordial organisms that were relatively simple and very small. All living things have evolved from these lowly beginnings. At present there are more than two million known species, which are widely diverse in size, shape, and way of life, as well as in the DNA sequences that contain their genetic information. What has produced the pervasive genetic variation within natural populations and the

INDUSTRIAL MELANISM

Industrial melanism is the darkness—of the skin, feathers, or fur—acquired by a population of animals living in an industrial region where the environment is soot-darkened. The melanization of a population increases the probability that its members will survive and reproduce; it takes place over the course of many generations as the result of natural selection of the lighter, more conspicuous animals by predators.

genetic differences among species? There must be some evolutionary means by which existing DNA sequences are changed and new sequences are incorporated into the gene pools of species.

The information encoded in the nucleotide sequence of DNA is, as a rule, faithfully reproduced during replication, so that each replication results in two DNA molecules that are identical to each other and to the parent molecule. But heredity is not a perfectly conservative process; otherwise, evolution could not have taken place. Occasionally "mistakes," or mutations, occur in the DNA molecule during replication, so that daughter cells differ from the parent cells in the sequence or in the amount of DNA. A mutation first appears in a single cell of an organism, but it is passed on to all cells descended from the first. Mutations can be classified into two categories—gene, or point, mutations, which affect only a few nucleotides within a gene, and chromosomal mutations, which either change the number of chromosomes or change the number or arrangement of genes on a chromosome.

Gene Mutations

A gene mutation occurs when the nucleotide sequence of the DNA is altered and a new sequence is passed on to the offspring. The change may be either a substitution of one

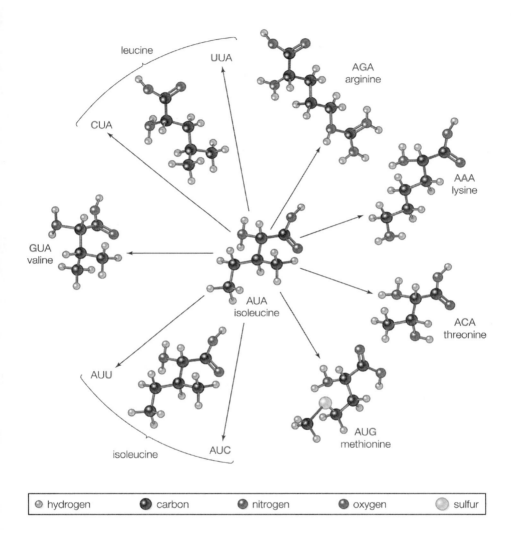

The effect of base substitutions, or point mutations, on the messenger-RNA codon AUA, which codes for the amino acid isoleucine. Substitutions at the first, second, or third position in the codon can result in nine new codons corresponding to six different amino acids in addition to isoleucine itself. The chemical properties of some of these amino acids are quite different from those of isoleucine. Replacement of one amino acid in a protein by another can seriously affect the protein's biological function.
Encyclopædia Britannica, Inc.

or a few nucleotides for others or an insertion or deletion of one or a few pairs of nucleotides.

The four nucleotide bases of DNA, named adenine, cytosine, guanine, and thymine, are represented by the letters A, C, G, and T, respectively. A gene that bears the code for constructing a protein molecule consists of a sequence of several thousand nucleotides, so that each segment of three nucleotides—called a triplet or codon—codes for one particular amino acid in the protein. The nucleotide sequence in the DNA is first transcribed into a molecule of messenger RNA (ribonucleic acid). The RNA, using a slightly different code (represented by the letters A, C, G, and U, the last letter representing the nucleotide base uracil), bears the message that determines which amino acid will be inserted into the protein's chain in the process of translation. Substitutions in the nucleotide sequence of a structural gene may result in changes in the amino acid sequence of the protein, although this is not always the case. The genetic code is redundant in that different triplets may hold the code for the same amino acid. Consider the triplet AUA in messenger RNA, which codes for the amino acid isoleucine. If the last A is replaced by C, the triplet still codes for isoleucine, but if it is replaced by G, it codes for methionine instead.

A nucleotide substitution in the DNA that results in an amino acid substitution in the corresponding protein may or may not severely affect the biological function of the protein. Some nucleotide substitutions change a codon for an amino acid into a signal to terminate translation, and those mutations are likely to have harmful effects. If, for instance, the second U in the triplet UUA, which codes for leucine, is replaced by A, the triplet becomes UAA, a "terminator" codon; the result is that the triplets following this codon in the DNA sequence are not translated into amino acids.

Additions or deletions of nucleotides within the DNA sequence of a structural gene often result in a greatly altered sequence of amino acids in the coded protein. The addition or deletion of one or two nucleotides shifts the "reading frame" of the nucleotide sequence all along the way from the point of the insertion or deletion to the end of the molecule. To illustrate, assume that the DNA segment . . . CATCATCATCATCAT . . . is read in groups of three as . . . CAT-CAT-CAT-CAT-CAT. . . . If a nucleotide base—say, T—is inserted after the first C of the segment, the segment will then be read as . . . CTA-TCA-TCA-TCA-TCA. . . . From the point of the insertion onward, the sequence of encoded amino acids is altered. If, however, a total of three nucleotides is either added or deleted, the original reading frame will be maintained in the rest of the sequence. Additions or deletions of nucleotides in numbers other than three or multiples of three are called frameshift mutations.

Gene mutations can occur spontaneously—that is, without being intentionally caused by humans. They can also be induced by ultraviolet light, X-rays, and other high-frequency electromagnetic radiation, as well as by exposure to certain mutagenic chemicals, such as mustard gas. The consequences of gene mutations may range from negligible to lethal. Mutations that change one or even several amino acids may have a small or undetectable effect on the organism's ability to survive and reproduce if the essential biological function of the coded protein is not hindered. But where an amino acid substitution affects the active site of an enzyme or modifies in some other way an essential function of a protein, the impact may be severe.

Newly arisen mutations are more likely to be harmful than beneficial to their carriers, because mutations are random events with respect to adaptation—that is, their occurrence is independent of any possible consequences.

The allelic variants present in an existing population have already been subject to natural selection. They are present in the population because they improve the adaptation of their carriers, and their alternative alleles have been eliminated or kept at low frequencies by natural selection. A newly arisen mutant is likely to have been preceded by an identical mutation in the previous history of a population. If the previous mutant no longer exists in the population, it is a sign that the new mutant is not beneficial to the organism and is likely also to be eliminated.

This proposition can be illustrated with an analogy. Consider a sentence whose words have been chosen because together they express a certain idea. If single letters or words are replaced with others at random, most changes will be unlikely to improve the meaning of the sentence; very likely they will destroy it. The nucleotide sequence of a gene has been "edited" into its present form by natural selection because it "makes sense." If the sequence is changed at random, the "meaning" rarely will be improved and often will be hampered or destroyed.

Occasionally, however, a new mutation may increase the organism's adaptation. The probability of such an event's happening is greater when organisms colonize a new territory or when environmental changes confront a population with new challenges. In these cases the established adaptation of a population is less than optimal, and there is greater opportunity for new mutations to be better adaptive. The consequences of mutations depend on the environment. Increased melanin pigmentation may be advantageous to inhabitants of tropical Africa, where dark skin protects them from the Sun's ultraviolet radiation, but it is not beneficial in Scandinavia, where the intensity of sunlight is low and light skin facilitates the synthesis of vitamin D.

Mutation rates have been measured in a great variety of organisms, mostly for mutants that exhibit conspicuous effects. Mutation rates are generally lower in bacteria and other microorganisms than in more complex species. In humans and other multicellular organisms, the rate typically ranges from about 1 per 100,000 to 1 per 1,000,000 gametes. There is, however, considerable variation from gene to gene as well as from organism to organism.

Although mutation rates are low, new mutants appear continuously in nature, because there are many individuals in every species and many gene loci in every individual. The process of mutation provides each generation with many new genetic variations. Thus, it is not surprising to see that, when new environmental challenges arise, species are able to adapt to them. More than 200 insect and rodent species, for example, have developed resistance to the pesticide DDT in parts of the world where spraying has been intense. Although these animals had never before encountered this synthetic compound, they adapted to it rapidly by means of mutations that allowed them to survive in its presence. Similarly, many species of moths and butterflies in industrialized regions have shown an increase in the frequency of individuals with dark wings in response to environmental pollution, an adaptation known as industrial melanism.

The resistance of disease-causing bacteria and parasites to antibiotics and other drugs is a consequence of the same process. When an individual receives an antibiotic that specifically kills the bacteria causing the disease — say, tuberculosis — the immense majority of the bacteria die, but one in a million may have a mutation that provides resistance to the antibiotic. These resistant bacteria will survive and multiply, and the antibiotic will no longer cure the disease. This is the reason that modern medicine treats bacterial diseases with cocktails of antibiotics. If the incidence of a mutation conferring resistance for a given antibiotic is one in a million, the incidence of one bacterium carrying three mutations, each conferring resistance to one of three antibiotics, is one in a trillion; such bacteria are far less likely to exist in any infected individual.

CHROMOSOMAL MUTATIONS

Chromosomes, which carry the hereditary material, or DNA, are contained in the nucleus of each cell. Chromosomes come in pairs, with one member of each pair inherited from each parent. The two members of a pair are called homologous chromosomes. Each cell of an organism and all individuals of the same species have, as a rule, the same number of chromosomes. The reproductive cells (gametes) are an exception; they have only half as many chromosomes as the body (somatic) cells. But the number, size, and organization of chromosomes varies between species. The parasitic nematode *Parascaris univalens* has only one pair of chromosomes, whereas many species of butterflies have more than 100 pairs and some ferns more than 600. Even closely related organisms may vary considerably in the number of chromosomes. Species of spiny rats of the South American genus *Proechimys* range from 12 to 31 chromosome pairs.

Changes in the number, size, or organization of chromosomes within a species are termed chromosomal mutations, chromosomal abnormalities, or chromosomal aberrations. Changes in number may occur by the fusion of two chromosomes into one, by fission of one chromosome into two, or by addition or subtraction of one or more whole chromosomes or sets of chromosomes. (The condition in which an organism acquires one or more additional sets of chromosomes is called polyploidy.)

Changes in the structure of chromosomes may occur by inversion, when a chromosomal segment rotates 180 degrees within the same location; by duplication, when a segment is added; by deletion, when a segment is lost; or by translocation, when a segment changes from one location to another in the same or a different chromosome. These are the processes by which chromosomes evolve. Inversions, translocations, fusions, and fissions do not change the amount of DNA. The importance of these mutations in evolution is that they change the linkage relationships between genes. Genes that were closely linked to each other become separated and vice versa; this can affect their expression because genes are often transcribed sequentially, two or more at a time.

THE DYNAMICS OF GENETIC CHANGE

Genetic variation is present throughout natural populations of organisms. This variation is sorted out in new ways in each generation by the process of sexual reproduction, which recombines the chromosomes inherited from the two parents during the formation of the gametes that produce the following generation. Consequently, the frequency of a given gene in a population often differs from one generation to the next.

GENETIC EQUILIBRIUM: THE HARDY-WEINBERG LAW

Heredity by itself does not change gene frequencies. This principle is stated by the Hardy-Weinberg law, so called because it was independently discovered in 1908 by the English mathematician G.H. Hardy and the German physician Wilhelm Weinberg.

The Hardy-Weinberg law describes the genetic equilibrium in a population by means of an algebraic equation. It states that genotypes, the genetic constitution of individual organisms, exist in certain frequencies that are a simple function of the allelic frequencies—namely, the square expansion of the sum of the allelic frequencies.

If there are two alleles, A and a, at a gene locus, three genotypes will be possible: AA, Aa, and aa. If the frequencies of the alleles A and a are p and q, respectively, the equilibrium frequencies of the three genotypes will be given by $(p + q)^2 = p^2 + 2pq + q^2$ for AA, Aa, and aa, respectively. The genotype equilibrium frequencies for any number of alleles are derived in the same way. If there are three alleles, A_1, A_2, and A_3, with frequencies p, q, and r, the equilibrium frequencies corresponding to the six possible genotypes (shown in parentheses) will be calculated as follows:

$$(p + q + r)^2 = p^2(A_1A_1) + q^2(A_2A_2) + r^2(A_3A_3)$$
$$+ 2pq(A_1A_2) + 2pr(A_1A_3) + 2qr(A_2A_3).$$

The probability of genotype AA among the progeny is the probability p that allele A will be present in the paternal gamete multiplied by the probability p that allele A will be present in the maternal gamete, or p^2. Similarly, the probability of the genotype aa is q^2. The genotype Aa can arise when A from the father combines with a from the mother, which will occur with a frequency pq, or when a from the father combines with A from the mother, which also has a probability of pq; the result is a total probability of $2pq$ for the frequency of the Aa genotype in the progeny.

There is no change in the allele equilibrium frequencies from one generation to the next. The frequency of the A allele among the offspring is the frequency of the AA genotype (because all alleles in these individuals are A alleles) plus half the frequency of the Aa genotype (because half the alleles in these individuals are A alleles), or $p^2 + pq = p(p + q) = p$ (because $p + q = 1$). Similarly, the frequency of the a allele among the offspring is given by $q^2 + pq = q(q + p) = q$. These are precisely the frequencies of the alleles in the parents.

The genotype equilibrium frequencies are obtained by the Hardy-Weinberg law on the assumption that there is random mating—that is, the probability of a particular kind of mating is the same as the frequency of the genotypes of the two mating individuals. For example, the probability of an AA female mating with an aa male must be p^2 (the frequency of AA) times q^2 (the frequency of aa). Random mating can occur with respect to most gene loci even though mates may be chosen according to particular characteristics. People, for example, choose their spouses according to all sorts of preferences concerning looks, personality, and the like. But concerning the majority of genes, people's marriages are essentially random.

Assortative, or selective, mating takes place when the choice of mates is not random. Marriages in the United States, for example, are assortative with respect to many social factors, so that members of any one social group tend to marry members of their own group more often, and people from a different group less often, than would be expected from random mating. Consider interracial marriage in a hypothetical community in which 80 percent of the population is white and 20 percent is black. With random mating, 32 percent ($2 \times 0.80 \times 0.20 = 0.32$) of all marriages would be interracial, whereas only 4 percent

WITHDRAWN

(0.20 × 0.20 = 0.04) would be marriages between two blacks. These statistical expectations depart from typical observations even in modern society, as a result of persistent social customs that for evolutionists are examples of assortative mating. The most extreme form of assortative mating is self-fertilization, which occurs rarely in animals but is a common form of reproduction in many plant groups.

The Hardy-Weinberg law assumes that gene frequencies remain constant from generation to generation—that there is no gene mutation or natural selection and that populations are very large. But these assumptions are not correct; indeed, if they were, evolution could not occur. Why, then, is the law significant if its assumptions do not hold true in nature? The answer is that it plays in evolutionary studies a role similar to that of Newton's first law of motion in mechanics. Newton's first law says that a body not acted upon by a net external force remains at rest or maintains a constant velocity. In fact, there are always external forces acting upon physical objects, but the first law provides the starting point for the application of other laws. Similarly, organisms are subject to mutation, selection, and other processes that change gene frequencies, but the effects of these processes can be calculated by using the Hardy-Weinberg law as the starting point.

THE PROCESSES OF GENE-FREQUENCY CHANGE

The frequency of a given gene in a population depends on a number of factors. It may be affected by the rate of mutation occurring within the population and an infusion of new alleles and unique genetic combinations resulting from interbreeding with members of other populations. In addition, gene frequencies in all populations may be affected by random chance, as alleles from gametes join with one another to form genes. In large populations the effects of randomness are often damped by other factors; however, in small populations the effects of randomness, expressed as genetic drift, can be significant and lasting.

MUTATION

The allelic variations that make evolution possible are generated by the process of mutation, but new mutations change gene frequencies very slowly, because mutation rates are low. Assume that the gene allele A_1 mutates to allele A_2 at a rate m per generation and that at a given time the frequency of A_1 is p. In the next generation, a fraction m of all A_1 alleles become A_2 alleles. The frequency of A_1 in the next generation will then be reduced by the fraction of mutated alleles (pm), or $p_1 = p - pm = p(1 - m)$. After t generations the frequency of A_1 will be $p_t = p(1 - m)^t$.

If the mutations continue, the frequency of A_1 alleles will gradually decrease, because a fraction of them change every generation to A_2. If the process continues indefinitely, the A_1 allele will eventually disappear, although the process is slow. If the mutation rate is 10^{-5} (1 in 100,000) per gene per generation, about 2,000 generations will be required for the frequency of A_1 to change from 0.50 to 0.49 and about 10,000 generations for it to change from 0.10 to 0.09.

Moreover, gene mutations are reversible: the allele A_2 may also mutate to A_1. Assume that A_1 mutates to A_2 at a rate m, as before, and that A_2 mutates to A_1 at a rate n per generation. If at a certain time the frequencies of A_1 and A_2 are p and q, respectively, after one generation the frequency of A_1 will be $p_1 = p - pm + qn$. A fraction pm of allele A_1 changes to A_2, but a fraction qn of the A_2 alleles changes to A_1. The conditions for equilibrium occur when $pm = qn$, or $p = n/(m + n)$. Suppose that the mutation rates are $m = 10^{-5}$ and $n = 10^{-6}$; then, at equilibrium, $p = 10^{-6}/(10^{-5} + 10^{-6}) = 1/(10 + 1) = 0.09$, and $q = 0.91$.

Changes in gene frequencies due to mutation occur, therefore, at rates even slower than was suggested above, because forward and backward mutations counteract each other. In any case, allelic frequencies usually are not in mutational equilibrium, because some alleles are favoured over others by natural selection. The equilibrium frequencies are then decided by the interaction between mutation and selection, with selection usually having the greater consequence.

Gene Flow

Gene flow, or gene migration, takes place when individuals migrate from one population to another and interbreed with its members. Gene frequencies are not changed for the species as a whole, but they change locally whenever different populations have different allele frequencies. In general, the greater the difference in allele frequencies between the resident and the migrant individuals, and the larger the number of migrants, the greater effect the migrants have in changing the genetic constitution of the resident population.

Suppose that a proportion of all reproducing individuals in a population are migrants and that the frequency of allele A_1 is p in the population but pm among the migrants. The change in gene frequency, Δp, in the next generation will be $\Delta p = m(pm - p)$. If the migration rate persists for a number t of generations, the frequency of A_1 will be given by $p_t = (1 - m)^t (p - p_m) + p_m$.

Genetic Drift

Gene frequencies can change from one generation to another by a process of pure chance known as genetic drift. This occurs because the number of individuals in any population is finite, and thus the frequency of a gene may change in the following generation by accidents of sampling, just as it is possible to get more or fewer than 50 "heads" in 100 throws of a coin simply by chance.

The magnitude of the gene frequency changes due to genetic drift is inversely related to the size of the population—the larger the number of reproducing individuals, the smaller the effects of genetic drift. This inverse relationship between sample size and magnitude of sampling errors can be illustrated by referring again to tossing a coin. When a penny is tossed twice, two heads are not surprising. But it will be surprising, and suspicious, if 20 tosses all yield heads. The proportion of heads obtained in a series of throws approaches closer to 0.5 as the number of throws grows larger.

The relationship is the same in populations, although the important value here is not the actual number of individuals in the population but the "effective" population size. This is the number of individuals that produce offspring, because only reproducing individuals transmit their genes to the following generation. It is not unusual, in plants as well as animals, for some individuals to have large numbers of progeny while others have none. In marine seals, antelopes, baboons, and many other mammals, for example, a dominant male may keep a large harem of females at the expense of many other males who can find no mates. It often happens that the effective population size is substantially smaller than the number of individuals in any one generation.

The effects of genetic drift in changing gene frequencies from one generation to the next are quite small in most natural populations, which generally consist of thousands of reproducing individuals. The effects over many generations are more important. Indeed, in the absence of other processes of change (such as natural selection and mutation), populations would eventually become fixed, having one allele at each locus after the gradual elimination of all others. With genetic drift as the only force in operation, the probability of a given allele's eventually reaching a frequency of 1 would be precisely the frequency of the allele—that is, an allele with a frequency of 0.8 would have an 80 percent chance of ultimately becoming the only allele present in the population. The process would, however, take a long time, because increases and decreases are likely to alternate with equal probability. More important, natural selection and other processes change gene frequencies in ways not governed by pure chance, so that no allele has an opportunity to become fixed as a consequence of genetic drift alone.

Genetic drift can have important evolutionary consequences when a new population becomes established by only a few individuals—a phenomenon known as the founder principle. Islands, lakes, and other isolated ecological sites are often colonized by one or very few seeds or animals of a species, which are transported there passively by wind, in the fur of larger animals, or in some other way. The allelic frequencies present in these few colonizers are likely to differ at many loci from those in the population they left, and those differences have a lasting impact on the evolution of the new population. The founder principle is one reason that species in neighbouring islands, such as those in the Hawaiian archipelago, are often more heterogeneous than species in comparable continental areas adjacent to one another.

Climatic or other conditions, if unfavourable, may on occasion drastically reduce the number of individuals in a population and even threaten it with extinction. Such occasional reductions are called population bottlenecks. The populations may later recover their typical size, but the allelic frequencies may have been considerably altered and thereby affect the future evolution of the species. Bottlenecks are more likely in relatively large animals and plants than in smaller ones, because populations of large organisms typically consist of fewer individuals. Primitive human populations of the past were subdivided into many small tribes that were time and again decimated by disease, war, and other disasters. Differences among current human populations in the allele frequencies of many genes—such as those determining the ABO and other blood groups—may have arisen at least in part as a consequence of bottlenecks in ancestral populations. Persistent population bottlenecks may reduce the overall genetic variation so greatly as to alter future evolution and endanger the survival of the species. A well-authenticated case is that of the cheetah, where no allelic variation whatsoever has been found among the many scores of gene loci studied.

THE OPERATION OF NATURAL SELECTION IN POPULATIONS

Natural selection occurs at the level of the individual organism; however, its effects must be gauged at the level of the population. A mutation first manifests within the genetic structure of an organism, and such a change may produce a trait that confers an advantage to that organism. If that trait allows the organism greater reproductive success, the frequency of the gene associated with that trait will increase in the population, and the population will evolve.

NATURAL SELECTION AS A PROCESS OF GENETIC CHANGE

Natural selection refers to any reproductive bias favouring some genes or genotypes over others. Natural selection promotes the adaptation of organisms to the environments in which they live; any hereditary variant that improves the ability to survive and reproduce in an environment will increase in frequency over the generations, precisely because the organisms carrying such a variant will leave more descendants than those lacking it. Hereditary variants, favourable or not to the organisms, arise by mutation. Unfavourable ones are eventually eliminated by natural selection; their carriers leave no descendants or leave fewer than those carrying alternative variants. Favourable mutations accumulate over the generations. The process continues indefinitely because the environments that organisms inhabit are forever changing. Environments change physically—in their climate, configuration, and so on—but also biologically, because the predators, parasites, competitors, and food sources with which an organism interacts are themselves evolving.

Mutation, gene flow, and genetic drift are random processes with respect to adaptation; they change gene frequencies without regard for the consequences that such changes may have in the ability of the organisms to survive and reproduce. If these were the only processes of evolutionary change, the organization of living things would gradually disintegrate. The effects of such processes alone would be analogous to those of a mechanic who changed parts in an automobile engine at random, with no regard for the role of the parts in the engine. Natural selection keeps the disorganizing effects of mutation and other processes in check because it multiplies beneficial mutations and eliminates harmful ones.

Natural selection accounts not only for the preservation and improvement of the organization of living beings but also for their diversity. In different localities or in different circumstances, natural selection favours different traits, precisely those that make the organisms well adapted to their particular circumstances and ways of life.

The parameter used to measure the effects of natural selection is fitness, which can be expressed as an absolute or as a relative value. Consider a population consisting at a certain locus of three genotypes: A_1A_1, A_1A_2, and A_2A_2. Assume that on the average each A_1A_1 and each A_1A_2 individual produces one offspring but that each A_2A_2 individual produces two. One could use the average number of progeny left by each genotype as a measure of that genotype's absolute fitness and calculate the changes in gene frequency that would occur over the generations. (This, of course, requires knowing how many of the progeny survive to adulthood and reproduce.) Evolutionists, however, find it mathematically more convenient to use relative fitness values—which they represent with the letter w—in most calculations. They usually assign the value 1 to the genotype with the highest reproductive efficiency and calculate the other relative fitness values proportionally. For the example just used, the relative fitness of the A_2A_2 genotype would be $w = 1$ and that of each of the other two genotypes would be $w = 0.5$. A parameter related to fitness is the selection coefficient, often represented by the letter s, which is defined as $s = 1 - w$. The selection coefficient is a measure of the reduction in fitness of a genotype. The selection coefficients in the example are $s = 0$ for A_2A_2 and $s = 0.5$ for A_1A_1 and for A_1A_2.

The different ways in which natural selection affects gene frequencies are illustrated by the following examples.

SELECTION AGAINST ONE OF THE HOMOZYGOTES

Suppose that one homozygous genotype, A_2A_2, has lower fitness than the other two genotypes, A_1A_1 and A_1A_2. (This is the situation in many human diseases, such as phenylketonuria [PKU] and sickle cell anemia, that are inherited in a recessive fashion and that require the presence of two deleterious mutant alleles for the trait to manifest.) The heterozygotes and the homozygotes for the normal allele (A_1) have equal fitness, higher than that of the homozygotes for the deleterious mutant allele (A_2). Call the fitness of these latter homozygotes $1 - s$ (the fitness of the other two genotypes is 1), and let p be the frequency of A_1 and q the frequency of A_2. It can be shown that the frequency of A_2 will decrease each generation by an amount given by $\Delta q = -spq^2/(1 - sq^2)$. The deleterious allele will continuously decrease in frequency until it has been eliminated. The rate of elimination is fastest when $s = 1$ (i.e., when the relative fitness $w = 0$); this occurs with fatal diseases, such as untreated PKU, when the homozygotes die before the age of reproduction.

Because of new mutations, the elimination of a deleterious allele is never complete. A dynamic equilibrium frequency will exist when the number of new alleles produced by mutation is the same as the number eliminated by selection. If the mutation rate at which the deleterious allele arises is u, the equilibrium frequency for a deleterious allele that is recessive is given approximately by $q = \sqrt{u/s}$, which, if $s = 1$, reduces to $q = \sqrt{u}$.

The mutation rate for many human recessive diseases is about 1 in 100,000 ($u = 10^{-5}$). If the disease is fatal, the equilibrium frequency becomes $q \sqrt{10^{-5}} = 0.003$, or about 1 recessive lethal mutant allele for every 300 normal alleles. That is roughly the frequency in human populations of alleles that in homozygous individuals, such as those with PKU, cause death before adulthood. The equilibrium frequency for a deleterious, but not lethal, recessive allele is much higher. Albinism, for example, is due to a recessive gene. The reproductive efficiency of albinos is, on average, about 0.9 that of normal individuals. Therefore, $s = 0.1$ and $q = \sqrt{u/s} = \sqrt{10^{-5}/10^{-1}} = 0.01$, or 1 in 100 genes rather than 1 in 300 as for a lethal allele.

For deleterious dominant alleles, the mutation-selection equilibrium frequency is given by $p = u/s$, which for fatal genes becomes $p = u$. If the gene is lethal even in single copy, all the genes are eliminated by selection in the same generation in which they arise, and the frequency of the gene in the population is the frequency with which it arises by mutation. One deleterious condition that is caused by a dominant allele present at low frequencies in human populations is achondroplasia, the most common cause of dwarfism. Because of abnormal growth of the long bones, achondroplastics have short, squat, often deformed limbs, along with bulging skulls. The mutation rate from the normal allele to the achondroplasia allele is about 5×10^{-5}. Achondroplastics reproduce only 20 percent as efficiently as normal individuals; hence, $s = 0.8$. The equilibrium frequency of the mutant allele can therefore be calculated as $p = u/s = 6.25 \times 10^{-5}$.

OVERDOMINANCE

In many instances heterozygotes have a higher degree of fitness than homozygotes for one or the other allele. This situation, known as heterosis or overdominance, leads to the stable coexistence of both alleles in the population and hence contributes to the widespread genetic variation found in populations of most organisms. The model situation is:

Genotype	A_1A_1	A_1A_2	A_2A_2
Fitness (w)	$1 - s$	1	$1 - t$

It is assumed that s and t are positive numbers between 0 and 1, so that the fitnesses of the two homozygotes are somewhat less than 1. It is not difficult to show that the change in frequency per generation of allele A_2 is $\Delta q = pq(sp - tq)/(1 - sp^2 - tq^2)$. An equilibrium will exist when $\Delta q = 0$ (gene frequencies no longer change); this will happen when $sp = tq$, at which the numerator of the expression for Δq will be 0. The condition $sp = tq$ can be rewritten as $s(1 - q) = tq$ (when $p + q = 1$), which leads to $q = s/(s + t)$. If the fitnesses of the two homozygotes are known, it is possible to infer the allele equilibrium frequencies.

One of many well-investigated examples of overdominance in animals is the colour polymorphism that exists in the marine copepod crustacean *Tisbe reticulata*. Three populations of colour variants (morphs) are found in the lagoon of Venice; they are known as violacea (homozygous genotype $V^V V^V$), maculata (homozygous genotype $V^M V^M$), and violacea-maculata (heterozygous genotype $V^V V^M$). The colour polymorphism persists in the lagoon because the heterozygotes survive better than either of the two homozygotes. In laboratory experiments, the fitness of the three genotypes depends on the degree of crowding, as shown by the following comparison of their relative fitnesses:

Genotype	Fitness in low crowding	Fitness in high crowding
$V^V V^V$	0.89	0.66
$V^V V^M$	1	1
$V^M V^M$	0.90	0.62

The greater the crowding—with more competition for resources—the greater the superiority of the heterozygotes. (In this example, the colour trait serves a genetic marker—individuals heterozygous for the marker have higher fitness, but whether this is due to the colour per se is not known.)

A particularly interesting example of heterozygote superiority among humans is provided by the gene responsible for sickle cell anemia. Human hemoglobin in adults is for the most part hemoglobin A, a four-component molecule consisting of two α and two β hemoglobin chains. The gene Hb^A codes for the normal β hemoglobin chain, which consists of 146 amino acids. A mutant allele of this gene, Hb^S, causes the β chain to have in the sixth position the amino acid valine instead of glutamic acid. This seemingly minor substitution modifies the properties of hemoglobin so that homozygotes with the mutant allele, $Hb^S Hb^S$, suffer from a severe form of anemia that in most cases leads to death before the age of reproduction.

The Hb^S allele occurs in some African and Asian populations with a high frequency. This formerly was puzzling because the severity of the anemia, representing a strong natural selection against homozygotes, should have eliminated the defective allele. But researchers noticed that the Hb^S allele occurred at high frequency precisely in regions of the world where a particularly severe form of malaria, which is caused by the parasite *Plasmodium falciparum*, was endemic. It was hypothesized that the heterozygotes, $Hb^A Hb^S$, were resistant to malaria, whereas the homozygotes, $Hb^A Hb^A$, were not. In malaria-infested regions then the heterozygotes survived better than either of the homozygotes, which were more likely to die from either malaria ($Hb^A Hb^A$ homozygotes) or anemia ($Hb^S Hb^S$ homozygotes). This hypothesis has been confirmed in various ways. Most significant is that most hospital patients suffering from severe or fatal forms of malaria are homozygotes $Hb^A Hb^A$. In a study of 100 children who died from malaria, only 1 was found to be a heterozygote, whereas 22 were expected to be so according to the frequency of the Hb^S allele in the population.

Fitnesses of the Three Genotypes at the Sickle Cell Anemia Locus in a Population from Nigeria

The table shows how the relative fitness of the three β-chain genotypes can be calculated from their distribution among the Yoruba people of Ibadan, Nigeria. The frequency of the Hb^S allele among adults is estimated as $q = 0.1232$. According to the Hardy-Weinberg law, the three genotypes will be formed at conception in the frequencies p^2, $2pq$, and q^2, which are the expected frequencies given in the table. The ratios of the observed frequencies among adults to the expected frequencies give the relative survival efficiency of the three genotypes. These are divided by their largest value (1.12) in order to obtain the relative fitness of the genotypes. Sickle cell anemia reduces the probability of survival of the $Hb^S Hb^S$ homozygotes to 13 percent of that of the heterozygotes. On the other hand, malaria infection reduces the survival probability of the

	GENOTYPE			TOTAL	FREQUENCY OF Hb^S
	$Hb^A Hb^A$	$Hb^A Hb^S$	$Hb^S Hb^S$		
observed number	9,365	2,993	29	12,387	
observed frequency	0.7560	0.2416	0.0023	1	0.1232
expected frequency	0.7688	0.2160	0.0152	1	0.1232
survival efficiency	0.98	1.12	0.15		
relative fitness	0.88	1	0.13		

homozygotes for the normal allele, $Hb^A Hb^A$, to 88 percent of that of the heterozygotes.

FREQUENCY-DEPENDENT SELECTION

The fitness of genotypes can change when the environmental conditions change. White fur may be protective to a bear living on the Arctic snows but not to one living in a Russian forest; there an allele coding for brown pigmentation may be favoured over one that codes for white. The environment of an organism includes not only the climate and other physical features but also the organisms of the same or different species with which it is associated.

Changes in genotypic fitness are associated with the density of the organisms present. Insects and other short-lived organisms experience enormous yearly oscillations in density. Some genotypes may possess high fitness in the spring, when the population is rapidly expanding, because such genotypes yield more prolific individuals. Other genotypes may be favoured during the summer, when populations are dense, because these genotypes make for better competitors, ones more successful at securing limited food resources. Still others may be at an advantage during the long winter months, because they increase the population's hardiness, or ability to withstand the inclement conditions that kill most members of the other genotypes.

The fitness of genotypes can also vary according to their relative numbers, and genotype frequencies may change as a consequence. This is known as frequency-dependent selection. Particularly interesting is the situation in which genotypic fitnesses are inversely related to their frequencies. Assume that two genotypes, A and B, have fitnesses related to their frequencies in such a way that the fitness of either genotype increases when its frequency decreases and vice versa. When A is rare, its fitness is high, and therefore A increases in frequency. As it becomes more and more common, however, the fitness of A gradually decreases, so that its increase in frequency eventually comes to a halt. A stable polymorphism occurs at the frequency where the two genotypes, A and B, have identical fitnesses.

In natural populations of animals and plants, frequency-dependent selection is very common and may contribute importantly to the maintenance of genetic polymorphism. In the vinegar fly *Drosophila pseudoobscura*, for example, three genotypes exist at the gene locus that codes for the metabolically important enzyme malate dehydrogenase — the homozygous *SS* and *FF* and the heterozygous *SF*. When the *SS* homozygotes represent 90 percent of the population, they have a fitness about two-thirds that of the heterozygotes, *SF*. But when the *SS* homozygotes represent only 10 percent of the population, their fitness is more than double that of the heterozygotes. Similarly, the fitness of the *FF* homozygotes relative to the heterozygotes increases from less than half to nearly double as their frequency goes from 90 to 10 percent. All three genotypes have equal fitnesses when the frequency of the *S* allele, represented by p, is about 0.70, so that there is a stable polymorphism with frequencies $p^2 = 0.49$ for *SS*, $2pq = 0.42$ for *SF*, and $q^2 = 0.09$ for *FF*.

Frequency-dependent selection may arise because the environment is heterogeneous and because different genotypes can better exploit different subenvironments. When a genotype is rare, the subenvironments that it exploits better will be relatively abundant. But as the genotype becomes common, its favoured subenvironment becomes saturated. That genotype must then compete for resources in subenvironments that are optimal for other genotypes. It follows then that a mixture of genotypes exploits the

ANALOGY

In biology, analogy is defined as the similarity of function and superficial resemblance of structures that have different origins. For example, the wings of a fly, a moth, and a bird are analogous because they developed independently as adaptations to a common function—flying. The presence of the analogous structure, in this case the wing, does not reflect evolutionary closeness among the organisms that possess it. Analogy is one aspect of evolutionary biology and is distinct from homology, the similarity of structures as a result of similar embryonic origin and development, considered strong evidence of common descent.

In many cases analogous structures, or analogues, tend to become similar in appearance by a process termed convergence. An example is the convergence of the streamlined form in the bodies of squid, shark, seal, porpoise, penguin, and ichthyosaur, animals of diverse ancestry. Physiological processes and behaviour patterns may also exhibit analogous convergence. Egg-guarding behaviour in the cobra, the stickleback, the octopus, and the spider is thought to have evolved independently among those animals, which are quite distant in their biological relationships.

Many New World cacti and African euphorbias are similar in appearance, being succulent, spiny, water-storing, and adapted to desert conditions generally. They are classified, however, in two separate and distinct families, sharing characteristics that have evolved independently in response to similar environmental challenges.

environmental resources better than a single genotype. This has been extensively demonstrated. When the three *Drosophila* genotypes mentioned above were mixed in a single population, the average number of individuals that developed per unit of food was 45.6. This was greater than the number of individuals that developed when only one of the genotypes was present, which averaged 41.1 for *SS*, 40.2 for *SF*, and 37.1 for *FF*. Plant breeders know that mixed plantings (a mixture of different strains) are more

HOMOLOGY

In biology, homology equates to the similarity in structure, physiology, or development of different species of organisms based upon their descent from a common evolutionary ancestor. Homology is contrasted with analogy, which is a functional similarity of structure based not upon common evolutionary origins but upon mere similarity of use. Thus the forelimbs of such widely differing mammals as humans, bats, and deer are homologous; the form of construction and the number of bones in these varying limbs are practically identical, and represent adaptive modifications of the forelimb structure of their common early mammalian ancestors. Analogous structures, on the other hand, can be represented by the wings of birds and of insects; the structures are used for flight in both types of organisms, but they have no common ancestral origin at the beginning of their evolutionary development. A 19th-century British biologist, Sir Richard Owen, was the first to define both homology and analogy in precise terms.

When two or more organs or structures are basically similar to each other in construction but are modified to perform different functions, they are said to be serially homologous. An example of this is a bat's wing and a whale's flipper. Both originated in the forelimbs of early mammalian ancestors, but they have undergone different evolutionary modifications to perform the radically different tasks of flying and swimming, respectively. Sometimes it is unclear whether similarities in structure in different organisms are analogous or homologous. An example of this is the wings of bats and birds. These structures are homologous in that they are in both cases modifications of the forelimb bone structure of early reptiles. But birds' wings differ from those of bats in the number of digits and in having feathers for flight while bats have none. And most importantly, the power of flight arose independently in these two different classes of vertebrates; in birds while they were evolving from early reptiles, and in bats after their mammalian ancestors had already completely differentiated from reptiles. Thus, the wings of bats and birds can be viewed as analogous rather than homologous upon a more rigorous scrutiny of their morphological differences and evolutionary origins.

Homologies of the forelimb among vertebrates, giving evidence for evolution. The bones correspond, although they are adapted to the specific mode of life of the animal. (Some anatomists interpret the digits in the bird's wing as being 1, 2, and 3, rather than 2, 3, and 4.) Encyclopædia Britannica, Inc.

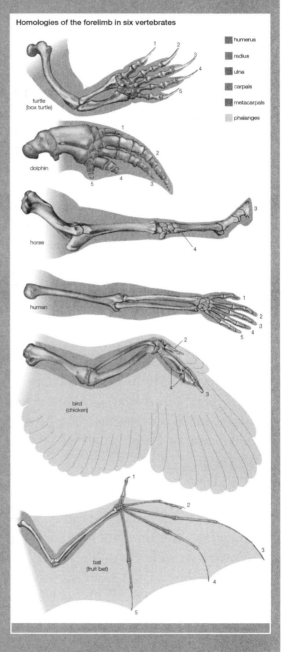

Homologies of the forelimb in six vertebrates

humerus
radius
ulna
carpals
metacarpals
phalanges

turtle (box turtle)

dolphin

horse

human

bird (chicken)

bat (fruit bat)

productive than single stands (plantings of one strain only), although farmers avoid them for reasons such as increased harvesting costs.

Sexual preferences can also lead to frequency-dependent selection. It has been demonstrated in some insects, birds, mammals, and other organisms that the mates preferred are precisely those that are rare. People also appear to experience this rare-mate advantage—blonds may seem attractively exotic to brunets, or brunets to blonds.

TYPES OF SELECTION

Natural selection manifests itself in a variety of ways. All forms bring about some sort of change to a trait or group of traits present in the individuals of a population. For example, considering the trait of body size in a population, stabilizing selection would favour average individuals, whereas directional selection would favour either small or large individuals. Diversifying selection would favour both large and small individuals, whereas average-size members of the population would be selected against. On the surface, sexual and kin selection appear to contradict the theme of maximizing survival; however, in the species that make use of these processes, the survival benefits are indirect.

STABILIZING SELECTION

Natural selection can be studied by analyzing its effects on changing gene frequencies, but it can also be explored by examining its effects on the observable characteristics—or phenotypes—of individuals in a population. Distribution scales of phenotypic traits such as height, weight, number of progeny, or longevity typically show greater numbers of individuals with intermediate values and fewer and fewer

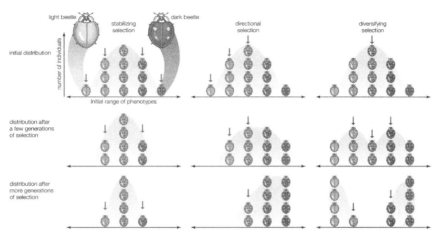

Three types of natural selection, showing the effects of each on the distribution of phenotypes within a population. The downward arrows point to those phenotypes against which selection acts. Stabilizing selection (left column) acts against phenotypes at both extremes of the distribution, favouring the multiplication of intermediate phenotypes. Directional selection (centre column) acts against only one extreme of phenotypes, causing a shift in distribution toward the other extreme. Diversifying selection (right column) acts against intermediate phenotypes, creating a split in distribution toward each extreme.
Encyclopædia Britannica, Inc.

toward the extremes—this is the so-called normal distribution. When individuals with intermediate phenotypes are favoured and extreme phenotypes are selected against, the selection is said to be stabilizing. The range and distribution of phenotypes then remains approximately the same from one generation to another. Stabilizing selection is very common. The individuals that survive and reproduce more successfully are those that have intermediate phenotypic values. Mortality among newborn infants, for example, is highest when they are either very small or very large; infants of intermediate size have a greater chance of surviving.

Stabilizing selection is often noticeable after artificial selection. Breeders choose chickens that produce larger eggs, cows that yield more milk, and corn with higher protein content. But the selection must be continued or reinstated from time to time, even after the desired goals have been achieved. If it is stopped altogether, natural selection gradually takes effect and turns the traits back toward their original intermediate value.

As a result of stabilizing selection, populations often maintain a steady genetic constitution with respect to many traits. This attribute of populations is called genetic homeostasis.

DIRECTIONAL SELECTION

The distribution of phenotypes in a population sometimes changes systematically in a particular direction. The physical and biological aspects of the environment are continuously changing, and over long periods of time the changes may be substantial. The climate and even the configuration of the land or waters vary incessantly. Changes also take place in the biotic conditions—that is, in the other organisms present, whether predators, prey, parasites, or competitors. Genetic changes occur as a consequence, because the genotypic fitnesses may shift so that different sets of alleles are favoured. The opportunity for directional selection also arises when organisms colonize new environments where the conditions are different from those of their original habitat. In addition, the appearance of a new favourable allele or a new genetic combination may prompt directional changes as the new genetic constitution replaces the preexisting one.

The process of directional selection takes place in spurts. The replacement of one genetic constitution with another changes the genotypic fitnesses at other loci, which then change in their allelic frequencies, thereby stimulating additional changes, and so on in a cascade of consequences.

Directional selection is possible only if there is genetic variation with respect to the phenotypic traits under selection. Natural populations contain large stores of genetic variation, and these are continuously replenished by additional new variants that arise by mutation. The nearly universal success of artificial selection and the rapid response of natural populations to new environmental challenges are evidence that existing variation provides the necessary materials for directional selection.

In modern times human actions have been an important stimulus to this type of selection. Human activity transforms the environments of many organisms, which rapidly respond to the new environmental challenges through directional selection. Well-known instances are the many cases of insect resistance to pesticides, which are synthetic substances not present in the natural environment. When a new insecticide is first applied to control a pest, the results are encouraging because a small amount of the insecticide is sufficient to bring the pest organism under control. As time passes, however, the amount required to achieve a certain level of control must be increased again and again until finally it becomes ineffective or economically impractical. This occurs because organisms become resistant to the pesticide through directional selection. The resistance of the housefly, *Musca domestica*, to DDT was first reported in 1947. Resistance to one or more pesticides has since been recorded in several hundred species of insects and mites.

Another example is the phenomenon of industrial melanism (mentioned above in the section Gene Mutations), which is exemplified by the gradual darkening of the wings of many species of moths and butterflies living in woodlands darkened by industrial pollution. The best-investigated case is the peppered moth, *Biston betularia*, of England. Until the middle of the 19th century, these moths were uniformly peppered light gray. Darkly pigmented variants were detected first in 1848 in Manchester and shortly afterward in other industrial regions where the vegetation was blackened by soot and other pollutants. By the middle of the 20th century, the dark varieties had almost completely replaced the lightly pigmented forms in many polluted areas, while in unpolluted regions light moths continued to be the most common. The shift from light to dark moths was an example of directional selection brought about by bird predators. On lichen-covered tree trunks, the light-gray moths are well camouflaged, whereas the dark ones are conspicuously visible and therefore fall victim to the birds. The opposite is the case on trees darkened by pollution.

Over geologic time, directional selection leads to major changes in morphology and ways of life. Evolutionary changes that persist in a more or less continuous fashion over long periods of time are known as evolutionary trends. Directional evolutionary changes increased the cranial capacity of the human lineage from the small brain of *Australopithecus*—human ancestors of three million years ago—which was less than 500 cc in volume (brain weight of 500 grams), to a brain nearly three times as large in modern humans. The evolution of the horse from more than 50 million years ago to modern times is another well-studied example of directional selection.

DIVERSIFYING SELECTION

Two or more divergent phenotypes in an environment may be favoured simultaneously by diversifying selection. No natural environment is homogeneous; rather, the environment of any plant or animal population is a mosaic consisting of more or less dissimilar subenvironments. There is heterogeneity with respect to climate, food resources, and living space. Also, the heterogeneity may be temporal, with change occurring over time, as well as spatial. Species cope with environmental heterogeneity in diverse ways. One strategy is genetic monomorphism, the selection of a generalist genotype that is well adapted to all the subenvironments encountered by the species. Another strategy is genetic polymorphism, the selection of a diversified gene pool that yields different genotypes, each adapted to a specific subenvironment.

There is no single plan that prevails in nature. Sometimes the most efficient strategy is genetic monomorphism to confront temporal heterogeneity but polymorphism to confront spatial heterogeneity. If the environment changes in time or if it is unstable relative to the life span of the organisms, each individual will have to face diverse environments appearing one after the other. A series of genotypes, each well adapted to one or another of the conditions that prevail at various times, will not succeed very well, because each organism will fare well at one period of its life but not at others. A better strategy is to have a population with one or a few genotypes that survive well in all the successive environments.

If the environment changes from place to place, the situation is likely to be different. Although a single genotype, well adapted to the various environmental patches, is a possible strategy, a variety of genotypes, with some individuals optimally adapted to each subenvironment, might fare still better. The ability of the population to exploit the environmental patchiness is thereby increased. Diversifying selection refers to the situation in which natural selection favours different genotypes in different subenvironments.

The efficiency of diversifying natural selection is quite apparent in circumstances in which populations living a short distance apart have become genetically differentiated. In one example, populations of bent grass can be found growing on heaps of mining refuse heavily contaminated with metals such as lead and copper. The soil has become so contaminated that it is toxic to most plants, but the dense stands of bent grass growing over these refuse heaps have been shown to possess genes that make them resistant to high concentrations of lead and copper. But only a few metres from the contaminated soil can be found bent grass plants that are not resistant to these metals. Bent grasses reproduce primarily by cross-pollination, so that the resistant grass receives wind-borne pollen from the neighbouring nonresistant plants. Yet they maintain their genetic differentiation because nonresistant seedlings are unable to grow in the contaminated soil and, in nearby uncontaminated soil, the nonresistant seedlings outgrow the resistant ones. The evolution of these resistant strains has taken place in the fewer than 400 years since the mines were first opened.

Protective morphologies and protective coloration exist in many animals as a defense against predators or as a cover against prey. Sometimes an organism mimics the appearance of a different one for protection. Diversifying selection often occurs in association with mimicry. A species of swallowtail butterfly, *Papilio dardanus*, is endemic in tropical and Southern Africa. Males have yellow and black wings, with characteristic tails in the second pair of wings. But females in many localities are conspicuously different from males; their wings lack tails and have colour patterns that vary from place to place. The explanation for these differences stems from the fact that *P. dardanus* can be eaten safely by birds. Many other butterfly species are noxious to birds, and so they are carefully avoided as food. In localities where *P. dardanus* coexists with noxious butterfly species, the *P. dardanus* females have evolved an appearance that mimics the noxious species. Birds confuse the mimics with their models and do not prey on them. In different localities the females mimic different species; in some areas two or even three different female forms exist, each mimicking different noxious species. Diversifying selection has resulted in different phenotypes of *P. dardanus* as a protection from bird predators.

SEXUAL SELECTION

Mutual attraction between the sexes is an important factor in reproduction. The males and females of many animal species are similar in size and shape except for the sexual organs and secondary sexual characteristics such as the breasts of female mammals. There are, however, species in which the sexes exhibit striking dimorphism. Particularly in birds and mammals, the males are often larger and stronger, more brightly coloured, or endowed with conspicuous adornments. But bright colours make animals more visible to predators — the long plumage of male peacocks and birds of paradise and the enormous antlers of aged male deer are cumbersome loads in the best of cases. Darwin knew that natural selection could not be expected to favour the evolution of disadvantageous traits, and he was able to offer a solution to this problem. He proposed that such traits arise by "sexual selection," which "depends not on a struggle for existence in relation to other organic beings or to external conditions but on a struggle between the individuals of one sex, generally the males, for the possession of the other sex."

The concept of sexual selection as a special form of natural selection is easily explained. Other things being equal, organisms more proficient in securing mates have higher fitness. There are two general circumstances leading to sexual selection. One is the preference shown by one sex (often the females) for individuals of the other sex that

A pair of red deer stags (Cervus elaphus) *competing for possession of a female in the rutting season.* Stefan Meyers GDT/Ardea London.

exhibit certain traits. The other is increased strength (usually among the males) that yields greater success in securing mates.

The presence of a particular trait among the members of one sex can make them somehow more attractive to the opposite sex. This type of "sex appeal" has been experimentally demonstrated in all sorts of animals, from vinegar flies to pigeons, mice, dogs, and rhesus monkeys. When, for example, *Drosophila* flies, some with yellow bodies as a result of spontaneous mutation and others with the normal yellowish gray pigmentation, are placed together, normal males are preferred over yellow males by females with either body colour.

Sexual selection can also come about because a trait—the antlers of a stag, for example—increases prowess in competition with members of the same sex. Stags, rams, and bulls use antlers or horns in contests of strength; a winning male usually secures more female mates. Therefore, sexual selection may lead to increased size and aggressiveness in males. Male baboons are more than twice as large as females, and the behaviour of the docile females contrasts with that of the aggressive males. A similar dimorphism occurs in the northern sea lion, *Eumetopias jubata*, where males weigh about 1,000 kg (2,200 pounds), about three times as much as females. The males fight fiercely in their competition for females; large, battle-scarred males occupy their own rocky islets, each holding a harem of as many as 20 females. Among many mammals that live in packs, troops, or herds—such as wolves, horses, and buffaloes—there usually is a hierarchy of dominance based on age and strength, with males that rank high in the hierarchy doing most of the mating.

KIN SELECTION AND RECIPROCAL ALTRUISM

The apparent altruistic behaviour of many animals is, like some manifestations of sexual selection, a trait that at first seems incompatible with the theory of natural selection. Altruism is a form of behaviour that benefits other individuals at the expense of the one that performs the action; the fitness of the altruist is diminished by its behaviour, whereas individuals that act selfishly benefit from it at no cost to themselves. Accordingly, it might be expected that natural selection would foster the development of selfish behaviour and eliminate altruism. This conclusion is not so compelling when it is noticed that the beneficiaries of altruistic behaviour are usually relatives. They all carry the same genes, including the genes that promote altruistic behaviour. Altruism may evolve by kin selection, which is simply a type of natural selection in which relatives are taken into consideration when evaluating an individual's fitness.

Natural selection favours genes that increase the reproductive success of their carriers, but it is not necessary that all individuals that share a given genotype have higher reproductive success. It suffices that carriers of the genotype reproduce more successfully on the average than those possessing alternative genotypes. A parent shares half of its genes with each progeny, so a gene that promotes parental altruism is favoured by selection if the behaviour's cost to the parent is less than half of its average benefits to the progeny. Such a gene will be more likely to increase in frequency through the generations than an alternative gene that does not promote altruistic behaviour. Parental care is, therefore, a form of altruism readily explained by kin selection. The parent spends some energy caring for the progeny because it increases the reproductive success of the parent's genes.

Kin selection extends beyond the relationship between parents and their offspring. It facilitates the development of altruistic behaviour when the energy invested, or the risk incurred, by an individual is compensated in excess by the benefits ensuing to relatives. The closer the relationship between the beneficiaries and the altruist and the greater the number of beneficiaries, the higher the risks and efforts warranted in the altruist. Individuals that live together in a herd or troop usually are related and often behave toward each other in this way. Adult zebras, for instance, will turn toward an attacking predator to protect the young in the herd rather than fleeing to protect themselves.

Altruism also occurs among unrelated individuals when the behaviour is reciprocal and the altruist's costs are smaller than the benefits to the recipient. This reciprocal altruism is found in the mutual grooming of chimpanzees and other primates as they clean each other of lice and other pests. Another example appears in flocks of birds that post sentinels to warn of danger. A crow sitting in a tree watching for predators while the rest of the flock forages incurs a small loss by not feeding, but this loss is well compensated by the protection it receives when it itself forages and others of the flock stand guard.

A particularly valuable contribution of the theory of kin selection is its explanation of the evolution of social behaviour among ants, bees, wasps, and other social insects. In honeybee populations, for example, the female workers build the hive, care for the young, and gather food, but they are sterile; the queen bee alone produces progeny. It would seem that the workers' behaviour would in no way be promoted or maintained by natural selection. Any genes causing such behaviour would seem likely to be eliminated from the population, because individuals exhibiting the behaviour increase not their own reproductive success but that of the queen. The situation is, however, more complex.

Queen bees produce some eggs that remain unfertilized and develop into males, or drones, having a mother but no father. Their main role is to engage in the nuptial flight during which one of them fertilizes a new queen. Other eggs laid by queen bees are fertilized and develop into females, the large majority of which are workers. A queen typically mates with a single male once during her lifetime; the male's sperm is stored in the queen's spermatheca, from which it is gradually released as she lays fertilized eggs. All the queen's female progeny therefore have the same father, so that workers are more closely related to one another and to any new sister queen than they are to the mother queen. The female workers receive one-half of their genes from the mother and one-half from the father, but they share among themselves three-quarters of their genes. The half of the set from the father is the same in every worker, because the father had only one set of genes rather than two to pass on (the male developed from an unfertilized egg, so all his sperm carry the same set of genes). The other half of the workers' genes come from the mother, and on the average half of them are identical in any two sisters. Consequently, with three-quarters of her genes present in her sisters but only half of her genes able to be passed on to a daughter, a worker's genes are transmitted one and a half times more effectively when she raises a sister (whether another worker or a new queen) than if she produces a daughter of her own.

CHAPTER 3
SPECIES AND SPECIATION

D arwin sought to explain the splendid multiformity of the living world—thousands of organisms of the most diverse kinds, from lowly worms to spectacular birds of paradise, from yeasts and molds to oaks and orchids. His *On the Origin of Species by Means of Natural Selection* (1859) is a sustained argument showing that the diversity of organisms and their characteristics can be explained as the result of natural processes.

Species come about as the result of gradual change prompted by natural selection. Environments are continuously changing in time, and they differ from place to place. Natural selection therefore favours different characteristics in different situations. The accumulation of differences eventually yields different species.

Everyday experience teaches that there are different kinds of organisms and also teaches how to identify them. Everyone knows that people belong to the human species and are different from cats and dogs, which in turn are different from each other. There are differences between people, as well as between cats and dogs, but individuals of the same species are considerably more similar among themselves than they are to individuals of other species.

External similarity is the common basis for identifying individuals as being members of the same species. Nevertheless, there is more to a species than outward appearance. A bulldog, a terrier, and a golden retriever are very different in appearance, but they are all dogs because they can interbreed. People can also interbreed with one another, and so can cats with other cats, but people cannot interbreed with dogs or cats, nor can these with each other. It is clear then that, although species are usually identified by appearance, there is something basic, of great biological significance, behind similarity of appearance—individuals of a species are able to interbreed with one another but not with members of other species. This is expressed in the following definition: Species are groups of interbreeding natural populations that are reproductively isolated from other such groups.

The ability to interbreed is of great evolutionary importance, because it determines that species are independent evolutionary units. Genetic changes originate in single individuals; they can spread by natural selection to all members of the species but not to individuals of other species. Individuals of a species share a common gene pool that is not shared by individuals of other species. Different species have independently evolving gene pools because they are reproductively isolated.

Although the criterion for deciding whether individuals belong to the same species is clear, there may be ambiguity in practice for two reasons. One is lack of knowledge—it may not be known for certain whether individuals living in different sites belong to the same species, because it is not known whether they can naturally interbreed. The other reason for ambiguity is rooted in the nature of evolution as a gradual process. Two geographically separate populations that at one time were members of the same species later may have diverged into two different species. Since the process is gradual, there is no particular point at which it is possible to say that the two populations have become two different species.

A related situation pertains to organisms living at different times. There is no way to test if today's humans could interbreed with those who lived thousands of years ago. It seems reasonable that living people, or living cats, would be able to interbreed with people, or cats, exactly like those that lived a few generations earlier. But what about ancestors removed by a thousand or a million generations? The ancestors of modern humans that lived 500,000 years ago (about 20,000 generations) are classified as the species *Homo erectus*. There is no exact time at which *H. erectus* became *H. sapiens*, but it would not be appropriate to classify remote human ancestors and modern humans in the same species just because the changes from one generation to the next were small. It is useful to distinguish between the two groups by means of different species names, just as it is useful to give different names to childhood and adulthood even though no single moment can separate one from the other. Biologists distinguish species in organisms that lived at different times by means of a commonsense morphological criterion: If two organisms differ from each other in form and structure about as much as do two living individuals belonging to two different species, they are classified in separate species and given different names.

The definition of species given above applies only to organisms able to interbreed. Bacteria and cyanobacteria (blue-green algae), for example, reproduce not sexually but by fission. Organisms that lack sexual reproduction are classified into different species according to criteria such as external morphology, chemical and physiological properties, and genetic constitution.

THE ORIGIN OF SPECIES

New species emerge by different means. Since the ability to reproduce with members of its own kind is the defining characteristic of a species, reproductively isolated populations once belonging to the same species are often recategorized as new ones. Reproductive isolation is thus a key factor in speciation, and it may take many forms. It may be the result of the genetic differences that develop between populations, such as those that might result if two populations are separated from one another by a geographic barrier, or it may occur through natural selection within populations.

REPRODUCTIVE ISOLATION

Among sexual organisms, individuals that are able to interbreed belong to the same species. The biological properties of organisms that prevent interbreeding are called reproductive isolating mechanisms (RIMs). Oaks on different islands, minnows in different rivers, or squirrels in different mountain ranges cannot interbreed because they are physically separated, not necessarily because they are biologically incompatible. Geographic separation, therefore, is not a RIM.

There are two general categories of reproductive isolating mechanisms: prezygotic, or those that take effect before fertilization, and postzygotic, those that take effect afterward. Prezygotic RIMs prevent the formation of hybrids between members of different populations through ecological, temporal, ethological (behavioral), mechanical, and gametic isolation. Postzygotic RIMs reduce the viability or fertility of hybrids or their progeny.

ECOLOGICAL ISOLATION

Populations may occupy the same territory but live in different habitats and so not meet. The *Anopheles maculipennis* group consists of six mosquito species, some of which are involved in the transmission of malaria. Although the species are virtually indistinguishable morphologically, they are isolated reproductively, in part because they breed in different habitats. Some breed in brackish water, others in running fresh water, and still others in stagnant fresh water.

TEMPORAL ISOLATION

Populations may mate or flower at different seasons or different times of day. Three tropical orchid species of the genus *Dendrobium* each flower for a single day; the flowers open at dawn and wither by nightfall. Flowering occurs in response to certain meteorological stimuli, such as a sudden storm on a hot day. The same stimulus acts on all three species, but the lapse between the stimulus and flowering is 8 days in one species, 9 in another, and 10 or 11 in the third. Interspecific fertilization is impossible because, at the time the flowers of one species open, those of the other species have already withered or have not yet matured.

A peculiar form of temporal isolation exists between pairs of closely related species of cicadas, in which one species of each pair emerges every 13 years, the other every 17 years. The two species of a pair may be sympatric (live in the same territory), but they have an opportunity to form hybrids only once every 221 (or 13 × 17) years.

ETHOLOGICAL (BEHAVIORAL) ISOLATION

Sexual attraction between males and females of a given species may be weak or absent. In most animal species, members of the two sexes must first search for each other and come together. Complex courtship rituals then take place, with the male often taking the initiative and the female responding. This in turn generates additional actions by the male and responses by the female, and eventually there is copulation, or sexual intercourse (or, in the case of some aquatic organisms, release of the sex cells for fertilization in the water). These elaborate rituals are specific to a species and play a significant part in species recognition. If the sequence of events in the search-courting-mating process is rendered disharmonious by either of the two

A liger, the result of a mating between a male lion and a female tiger in a captive environment. In nature, interbreeding between these separate species is prevented by prezygotic reproductive isolating mechanisms (RIMs), such as differences in behaviour, and by nonbiologic factors, such as differences in range. Most, if not all, male ligers and many female ligers that arise by accident or intent do not develop functional sex cells. Such hybrid sterility is a postzygotic RIM. Sally Anne Thompson-Animal Photography.

sexes, then the entire process will be interrupted. Courtship and mating rituals have been extensively analyzed in some mammals, birds, and fishes and in a number of insect species.

Ethological isolation is often the most potent RIM to keep animal species from interbreeding. It can be remarkably strong even among closely related species. The vinegar flies *Drosophila serrata*, *D. birchii*, and *D. dominicana* are three sibling species (that is, species nearly indistinguishable morphologically) that are endemic in Australia and on the islands of New Guinea and New Britain. In many areas these three species occupy the same territory, but no hybrids are known to occur in nature. The strength of their ethological isolation has been tested in the laboratory by placing together groups of females and males in various combinations for several days. When the flies were all of the same species but the female and male groups each came from different geographic origins, a large majority of the females (usually 90 percent or more) were fertilized. But no inseminations or very few (less than 4 percent) took place when males and females were of different species, whether from the same or different geographic origins.

It should be added that the rare interspecific inseminations that did occur among the vinegar flies produced hybrid adult individuals in very few instances, and the hybrids were always sterile. This illustrates a common pattern—reproductive isolation between species is maintained by several RIMs in succession; if one breaks down, others are still present. In addition to ethological isolation, the failure of the hybrids to survive and hybrid sterility prevents successful breeding between members of the three *Drosophila* species and between many other animal species as well.

Species recognition during courtship involves stimuli that may be chemical (olfactory), visual, auditory, or tactile. Pheromones are specific substances that play a critical role in recognition between members of a species; they have been chemically identified in such insects as ants, moths, butterflies, and beetles and in such vertebrates as fish, reptiles, and mammals. The "songs" of birds, frogs, and insects (the last of which produce these sounds by vibrating or rubbing their wings) are species recognition signals. Some form of physical contact or touching occurs in many mammals but also in *Drosophila* flies and other insects.

MECHANICAL ISOLATION

Copulation is often impossible between different animal species because of the incompatible shape and size of the genitalia. In plants, variations in flower structure may impede pollination. Two species of sage from California provide an example: The two-lipped flowers of *Salvia mellifera* have stamens and style (respectively, the male structure that produces the pollen and the female structure that bears the pollen-receptive surface, the stigma) in the upper lip, whereas *S. apiana* has long stamens and style and a specialized floral configuration. *S. mellifera* is pollinated by small or medium-size bees that carry pollen on their backs from flower to flower. *S. apiana*, however, is pollinated by large carpenter bees and bumblebees that carry the pollen on their wings and other body parts. Even if the pollinators of one species visit flowers of the other, pollination cannot occur because the pollen does not come into contact with the style of the alternative species.

GAMETIC ISOLATION

Marine animals often discharge their eggs and sperm into the surrounding water, where fertilization takes place. Gametes of different species may fail to attract one another. For example, the sea urchins *Strongylocentrotus purpuratus* and *S. franciscanus* can be induced to release their eggs and sperm simultaneously, but most of the fertilizations that result are between eggs and sperm of the same species. In animals with internal fertilization, sperm cells may be unable to function in the sexual ducts of females of different species. In plants, pollen grains of one species typically fail to germinate on the stigma of another species, so that the pollen tubes never reach the ovary where fertilization would occur.

HYBRID INVIABILITY

Occasionally, prezygotic mechanisms are absent or break down so that interspecific zygotes (fertilized eggs) are formed. These zygotes, however, often fail to develop into mature individuals. The hybrid embryos of sheep and goats, for example, die in the early developmental stages before birth. Hybrid inviability is common in plants, whose hybrid seeds often fail to germinate or die shortly after germination.

HYBRID STERILITY

Hybrid zygotes sometimes develop into adults, such as mules (hybrids between female horses and male donkeys), but the adults fail to develop functional gametes and are sterile.

HYBRID BREAKDOWN

In plants more than in animals, hybrids between closely related species are sometimes partially fertile. Gene exchange may nevertheless be inhibited because the offspring are poorly viable or sterile. Hybrids between the cotton species *Gossypium barbadense*, *G. hirsutum*, and *G. tomentosum* appear vigorous and fertile, but their progenies die in seed or early in development, or they develop into sparse, weak plants.

A MODEL OF SPECIATION

Because species are groups of populations reproductively isolated from one another, asking about the origin of species is equivalent to asking how reproductive isolation arises between populations. Two theories have been advanced to answer this question. One theory considers isolation as an accidental by-product of genetic divergence. Populations that become genetically less and less alike (as a consequence, for example, of adaptation to different environments) may eventually be unable to interbreed because their gene pools are disharmonious. The other theory regards isolation as a product of natural selection. Whenever hybrid individuals are less fit than nonhybrids, natural selection will directly promote the development of RIMs. This occurs because genetic variants interfering with hybridization have greater fitness than those favouring hybridization, given that the latter are often present in hybrids with poor fitness.

These two theories of the origin of reproductive isolation are not mutually exclusive. Reproductive isolation may indeed come about incidentally to genetic divergence between separated populations. Consider, for example, the evolution of many endemic species of plants and animals in the Hawaiian archipelago. The ancestors of these species arrived on these islands several million years ago. There they evolved as they became adapted to the environmental conditions and colonizing opportunities present. Reproductive isolation between the populations evolving in Hawaii and the populations on continents was never directly promoted by natural selection because their geographic remoteness forestalled any opportunities for hybridizing. Nevertheless, reproductive isolation became complete in many cases as a result of gradual genetic divergence over thousands of generations.

Frequently, however, the course of speciation involves the processes postulated by both theories — reproductive isolation starts as a by-product of gradual evolutionary divergence but is completed by natural selection directly promoting the evolution of prezygotic RIMs.

The separate sets of processes identified by the two speciation theories may be seen, therefore, as different stages in the splitting of an evolutionary lineage into two species. The splitting starts when gene flow is somehow interrupted between two populations. It is necessary that gene flow be interrupted, because otherwise the two groups of individuals would still share in a common gene pool and fail to become genetically different. Interruption may be due to geographic separation, or it may be initiated by some genetic change that affects some individuals of the species but not others living in the same territory. The two genetically isolated groups are likely to become more and more different as time goes on. Eventually, some incipient reproductive isolation may take effect because the two gene pools are no longer adapting in concert. Hybrid individuals, which carry genes combined from the two gene pools, will therefore experience reduced viability or fertility.

The circumstances just described may persist for so long that the populations become completely differentiated into separate species. It happens quite commonly, however, in both animals and plants that opportunities for hybridization arise between two populations that are becoming genetically differentiated. Two outcomes are possible. One is that the hybrids manifest little or no reduction of fitness, so that gene exchange between the two populations proceeds freely, eventually leading to their integration into a single gene pool. The second possible outcome is that reduction of fitness in the hybrids is sufficiently large for natural selection to favour the emergence of prezygotic RIMs preventing the formation of hybrids altogether. This situation may be identified as the second stage in the speciation process.

How natural selection brings about the evolution of prezygotic RIMs can be understood in the following way. Beginning with two populations, P1 and P2, assume that there are gene variants in P1 that increase the probability that P1 individuals will choose P1 rather than P2 mates. Such gene variants will increase in frequency in the P1 population, because they are more often present in the progenies of P1 × P1 matings, which have normal fitness. The alternative genetic variants that do not favour P1 × P1 matings will be more often present in the progenies of

P1 × P2 matings, which have lower fitness. The same process will enhance the frequency in the P2 population of genetic variants that lead P2 individuals to choose P2 rather than P1 mates. Prezygotic RIMs may therefore evolve in both populations and lead to their becoming two separate species.

The two stages of the process of speciation can be characterized, finally, by outlining their distinctions. The first stage primarily involves the appearance of postzygotic RIMs as accidental by-products of overall genetic differentiation rather than as express targets of natural selection. The second stage involves the evolution of prezygotic RIMs that are directly promoted by natural selection. The first stage may come about suddenly, in one or a few generations, rather than as a long, gradual process. The second stage follows the first in time but need not always be present.

GEOGRAPHIC SPECIATION

One common mode of speciation is known as geographic, or allopatric (in separate territories), speciation. The general model of the speciation process advanced in the previous section applies well to geographic speciation. The first stage begins as a result of geographic separation between populations. This may occur when a few colonizers reach a geographically separate habitat, perhaps an island, lake, river, isolated valley, or mountain range. Alternately, a population may be split into two geographically separate ones by topographic changes, such as the disappearance of a water connection between two lakes, or by an invasion of competitors, parasites, or predators into the intermediate zone. If these types of geographic separation continue for some time, postzygotic RIMs may appear as a result of gradual genetic divergence.

In the second stage, an opportunity for interbreeding may later be brought about by topographic changes reestablishing continuity between the previously isolated territories or by ecological changes once again making the intermediate territory habitable for the organisms. If postzygotic RIMs that evolved during the separation period sufficiently reduce the fitness of hybrids of the two populations, natural selection will foster the development of prezygotic RIMs, and the two populations may go on to evolve into two species despite their occupying the same geographic territory.

Investigation has been made of many populations that are in the first stage of geographic speciation. There are fewer well-documented instances of the second stage, presumably because this occurs fairly rapidly in evolutionary time.

Both stages of speciation are present in a group of six closely related species of New World *Drosophila* flies that have been extensively studied by evolutionists for several decades. Two of these sibling species, *D. willistoni* and *D. equinoxialis*, each consist of groups of populations in the first stage of speciation and are identified as different subspecies. Two *D. willistoni* subspecies live in continental South America—*D. willistoni quechua* lives west of the Andes and *D. willistoni willistoni* east of the Andes. They are effectively separated by the Andes because the flies cannot live at high altitudes. It is not known whether their geographic separation is as old as the Andes, but it has existed long enough for postzygotic RIMs to have evolved. When the two subspecies are crossed in the laboratory, the hybrid males are completely sterile if the mother came from the *quechua* subspecies, but in the reciprocal cross all hybrids are fertile. If hybridization should occur in nature, selection would favour the evolution of prezygotic RIMs because of the complete sterility of half of the hybrid males.

Another pair of subspecies consists of *D. equinoxialis equinoxialis*, which inhabits continental South America, and *D. equinoxialis caribbensis*, which lives in Central America and the Caribbean. Crosses made in the laboratory between these two subspecies always produce sterile males, irrespective of the subspecies of the mother. Natural selection would, then, promote prezygotic RIMs between these two subspecies more strongly than between those of *D. willistoni*. But, in accord with the speciation model presented above, laboratory experiments show no evidence of the development of ethological isolation or of any other prezygotic RIM, presumably because the geographic isolation of the subspecies has forestalled hybridization between members.

One more sibling species of the group is *D. paulistorum*, a species that includes groups of populations well into the second stage of geographic speciation. Six such groups have been identified as semispecies, or incipient species, two or three of which are sympatric in many localities. Male hybrids between individuals of the different semispecies are sterile; laboratory crosses always yield fertile females but sterile males.

Whenever two or three incipient species of *D. paulistorum* have come into contact in nature, the second stage of speciation has led to the development of ethological isolation, which ranges from incipient to virtually complete. Laboratory experiments show that, when both incipient species are from the same locality, their ethological isolation is complete; only individuals of the same incipient species mate. When the individuals from different incipient species come from different localities, however, ethological isolation is usually present but far from complete. This is precisely as the speciation model predicts. Natural selection effectively promotes ethological isolation in territories where two incipient species live together, but the genes responsible for this isolation have not yet fully spread to populations in which one of the two incipient species is not present.

The eventual outcome of the process of geographic speciation is complete reproductive isolation, as can be observed among the species of the New World *Drosophila* group under discussion. *D. willistoni*, *D. equinoxialis*, *D. tropicalis*, and *D. paulistorum* coexist sympatrically over wide regions of Central and South America while preserving their separate gene pools. Hybrids are not known in nature and are almost impossible to obtain in the laboratory; moreover, all interspecific hybrid males at least are completely sterile. This total reproductive isolation has evolved, however, with very little morphological differentiation. Females from different sibling species cannot be distinguished by experts, while males can be identified only by small differences in the shape of their genitalia, unrecognizable except under a microscope.

ADAPTIVE RADIATION

The geographic separation of populations derived from common ancestors may continue long enough so that the populations become completely differentiated species before ever regaining sympatry and the opportunity to interbreed. As the allopatric populations continue evolving independently, RIMs develop and morphological differences may arise. The second stage of speciation—in which natural selection directly stimulates the evolution of RIMs—never comes about in such situations, because reproductive isolation takes place simply as a consequence of the continued separate evolution of the populations.

This form of allopatric speciation is particularly apparent when colonizers reach geographically remote areas, such as islands, where they find few or no competitors and have an opportunity to diverge as they become adapted to the new environment. Sometimes the new regions offer a multiplicity of environments to the colonizers, giving rise to several different lineages and species. This process of rapid divergence of multiple species from a single ancestral lineage is called adaptive radiation.

Many examples of speciation by adaptive radiation are found in archipelagoes removed from the mainland.

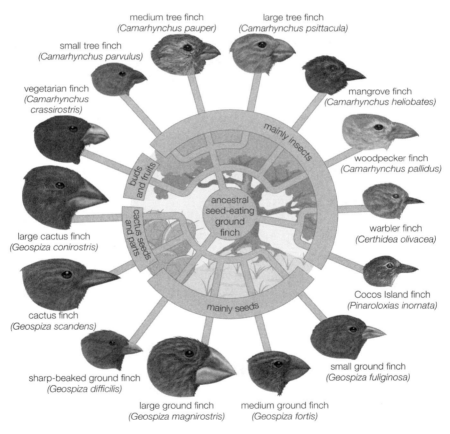

Fourteen species of Galapagos finches that evolved from a common ancestor. The different shapes of their bills, suited to different diets and habitats, show the process of adaptive radiation.
From P.R. Grant, *Ecology and Evolution of Darwin's Finches* (1986).

The Galapagos Islands are about 1,000 km (600 miles) off the west coast of South America. When Charles Darwin arrived there in 1835 during his voyage on the HMS *Beagle*, he discovered many species not found anywhere else in the world—for example, several species of finches, of which 14 are now known to exist (called Galapagos, or Darwin's, finches). These passerine birds have adapted to a diversity of habitats and diets, some feeding mostly on plants, others exclusively on insects. The various shapes of their bills are clearly adapted to probing, grasping, biting, or crushing—the diverse ways in which the different Galapagos species obtain their food. The explanation for such diversity is that the ancestor of Galapagos finches arrived in the islands before other kinds of birds and encountered an abundance of unoccupied ecological niches. Its descendants underwent adaptive radiation, evolving a variety of finch species with ways of life capable of exploiting opportunities that on various continents are already exploited by other species.

The Hawaiian archipelago also provides striking examples of adaptive radiation. Its several volcanic islands, ranging from about 1 million to more than 10 million years in age, are far from any continent or even other large islands. In their relatively small total land area, an astounding number of plant and animal species exist. Most of the species have evolved on the islands, among them about two dozen species (about one-third of them now extinct) of honeycreepers, birds of the family Drepanididae, all derived from a single immigrant form. In fact, all but one of Hawaii's 71 native bird species are endemic; that is, they have evolved there and are found nowhere else. More than 90 percent of the native species of flowering plants, land mollusks, and insects are also endemic, as are two-thirds of the 168 species of ferns.

There are more than 500 native Hawaiian species of *Drosophila* flies—about one-third of the world's total number of known species. Far greater morphological and ecological diversity exists among the species in Hawaii than anywhere else in the world. The species of *Drosophila* in Hawaii have diverged by adaptive radiation from one or a few colonizers, which encountered an assortment of ecological niches that in other lands were occupied by different groups of flies or insects but that were available for exploitation in these remote islands.

Quantum Speciation

In some modes of speciation the first stage is achieved in a short period of time. These modes are known by a variety of names, such as *quantum*, *rapid*, and *saltational* speciation, all suggesting the shortening of time involved. They are also known as *sympatric* speciation, alluding to the fact that quantum speciation often leads to speciation between populations that exist in the same territory or habitat. An important form of quantum speciation, polyploidy, is discussed separately below.

Quantum speciation without polyploidy has been seen in the annual plant genus *Clarkia*. Two closely related species, *Clarkia biloba* and *C. lingulata*, are both native to California. *C. lingulata* is known only from two sites in the central Sierra Nevada at the southern periphery of the distribution of *C. biloba*, from which it evolved starting with translocations and other chromosomal mutations. Such chromosomal rearrangements arise suddenly but reduce the fertility of heterozygous individuals. *Clarkia* species are capable of self-fertilization, which facilitates the propagation of the chromosomal mutants in different sets of individuals even within a single locality. This makes hybridization possible with nonmutant individuals and allows the second stage of speciation to go ahead.

Chromosomal mutations are often the starting point of quantum speciation in animals, particularly in groups such as moles and other rodents that live underground or have little mobility. Mole rats of the species group *Spalax ehrenbergi* in Israel and gophers of the species group *Thomomys talpoides* in the northern Rocky Mountains are well-studied examples.

The speciation process may also be initiated by changes in just one or a few gene loci when these alterations result in a change of ecological niche or, in the case of parasites, a change of host. Many parasites use their host as a place for courtship and mating, so organisms with two different host preferences may become reproductively isolated. If the hybrids show poor fitness because they are not effective parasites in either of the two hosts, natural selection will favour the development of additional RIMs. This type of speciation seems to be common among parasitic insects, a large group comprising tens of thousands of species.

POLYPLOIDY

The multiplication of entire sets of chromosomes is known as polyploidy. Whereas a diploid organism carries in the nucleus of each cell two sets of chromosomes, one inherited from each parent, a polyploid organism has three or more sets of chromosomes. Many cultivated plants are polyploid—bananas are triploid, potatoes are tetraploid, bread wheat is hexaploid, some strawberries are octaploid. These cultivated polyploids do not exist in nature, at least in any significant frequency. Some of them first appeared spontaneously; others, such as octaploid strawberries, were intentionally produced.

In animals polyploidy is relatively rare because it disrupts the balance between the sex chromosome and the other chromosomes, a balance being required for the proper development of sex. Naturally polyploid species are found in hermaphroditic animals—individuals having both male and female organs—which include snails, earthworms, and planarians (a group of flatworms). They are also found in forms with parthenogenetic females (which produce viable progeny without fertilization), such as some beetles, sow bugs, goldfish, and salamanders.

All major groups of plants have naturally polyploid species, but they are most common among angiosperms, or flowering plants, of which about 47 percent are polyploids. Polyploidy is rare among gymnosperms, such as pines, firs, and cedars, although the redwood, *Sequoia sempervirens*, is a polyploid. Most polyploid plants are tetraploids. Polyploids with three, five, or some other odd-number multiple of the basic chromosome number are sterile, because the separation of homologous chromosomes cannot be achieved properly during formation of the sex cells. Some plants with an odd number of chromosome sets persist by means of asexual reproduction, particularly through human cultivation; the triploid banana is one example.

Polyploidy is a mode of quantum speciation that yields the beginnings of a new species in just one or two generations. There are two kinds of polyploids—autopolyploids, which derive from a single species, and allopolyploids, which stem from a combination of chromosome sets from different species. Allopolyploid plant species are much more numerous than autopolyploids.

An allopolyploid species can originate from two plant species that have the same diploid number of chromosomes. The chromosome complement of one species may be symbolized as *AA* and the other *BB*. A hybrid of two different species, represented as *AB*, will usually be sterile because of abnormal chromosome pairing and segregation during formation at meiosis of the gametes, which are haploid (i.e., having only half of the chromosomes, of which in a given gamete some come from the *A* set and some from the *B* set). But chromosome doubling may occur in a diploid cell as a consequence of abnormal mitosis, in which the chromosomes divide but the cell does not. If this happens in the hybrid above, *AB*, the result is a plant cell with four sets of chromosomes, *AABB*. Such a tetraploid cell may proliferate within the plant (which is otherwise constituted of diploid cells) and produce branches and flowers of tetraploid cells. Because the flowers' cells carry two chromosomes of each kind, they can produce functional diploid gametes via meiosis with the constitution *AB*. The union of two such gametes, such as happens during self-fertilization, produces a complete tetraploid individual (*AABB*). In this way, self-fertilization in plants makes possible the formation of a tetraploid individual as the result of a single abnormal cell division.

Autopolyploids originate in a similar fashion, except that the individual in which the abnormal mitosis occurs is not a hybrid. Self-fertilization thus enables a single individual to multiply and give rise to a population. This population is a new species, since polyploid individuals are reproductively isolated from their diploid ancestors. A cross between a tetraploid and a diploid yields triploid progeny, which are sterile.

GENETIC DIFFERENTIATION DURING SPECIATION

Genetic changes underlie all evolutionary processes. In order to understand speciation and its role in evolution, it is useful to know how much genetic change takes place

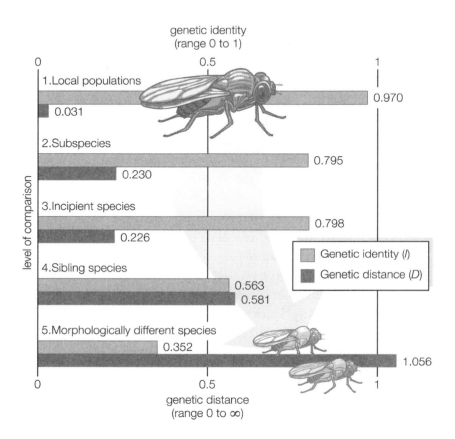

genetic identity
(range 0 to 1)

level of comparison

1. Local populations — 0.970 / 0.031
2. Subspecies — 0.795 / 0.230
3. Incipient species — 0.798 / 0.226
4. Sibling species — 0.563 / 0.581
5. Morphologically different species — 0.352 / 1.056

Genetic identity (*I*)
Genetic distance (*D*)

genetic distance
(range 0 to ∞)

Encyclopædia Britannica, Inc.

during the course of species development. It is of considerable significance to ascertain whether new species arise by altering only a few genes or whether the process requires drastic changes—a genetic "revolution," as postulated by some evolutionists in the past. The issue is best considered separately with respect to each of the two stages of speciation and to the various modes of speciation.

The question of how much genetic differentiation occurs during speciation has become answerable only with the relatively recent development of appropriate methods for comparing genes of different species. Genetic change is measured with two parameters—genetic identity (I), which estimates the proportion of genes that are identical in two populations, and genetic distance (D), which estimates the proportion of gene changes that have occurred in the separate evolution of two populations. The value of I may range between 0 and 1, which correspond to the extreme situations in which no or all genes are identical, respectively; the value of D may range from zero to infinity. D can reach beyond 1 because each gene may change more than once in one or both populations as evolution goes on for many generations.

As a model of geographic speciation, the *Drosophila willistoni* group of flies offers the distinct advantage of exhibiting both stages of the speciation process. The *D. willistoni* group consists of several closely related species, some of which in turn consist of several incipient species, subspecies, or both. About 30 randomly selected genes have been studied in a large number of natural populations of these species. The results are summarized in the figure on page 142. The most significant numbers are those given in the levels of comparison labeled 2 and 3, which represent the first and second stages, respectively, of the process of geographic speciation. The 0.230 value for D (figure, level 2) means that about 23 gene changes have occurred for every 100 gene loci in the separate evolution of two subspecies—that is, the sum of the changes that have occurred in the two separately evolving lineages is 23 percent of all the genes. These are populations well advanced in the first stage of speciation, as manifested by the sterility of the hybrid males.

The genetic distance between incipient species (figure, level 3) is the same, within experimental error, as that between the subspecies, or 22.6 percent. This implies that the development of ethological isolation, as it is found in these populations, does not require many genetic changes beyond those that occurred during the first stage of speciation. Indeed, no additional gene changes were detected in these experiments. The absence of major genetic changes during the second stage of speciation can be understood by considering the role of natural selection, which directly promotes the evolution of prezygotic RIMs during the second stage, so that only genes modifying mate choice need to change. In contrast, the development of postzygotic RIMs during the first stage occurs only after there is substantial genetic differentiation between populations, because it comes about only as an incidental outcome of overall genetic divergence.

Sibling species, such as *D. willistoni* and *D. equinoxialis*, exhibit 58 gene changes for every 100 gene loci after their divergence from a common ancestor (figure, level 4). It is noteworthy that this much genetic evolution has occurred without altering the external morphology of these organisms. In the evolution of morphologically different species (figure, level 5), the number of gene changes is greater yet, as would be expected.

Genetic changes concomitant with one or the other of the two stages in the speciation process have been studied in a number of organisms, from insects and other invertebrates to all sorts of vertebrates, including mammals. The amount of genetic change during geographic speciation varies between organisms, but the two main observations made in the *D. willistoni* group seem to apply quite generally. These are that the evolution of postzygotic mechanisms during the first stage is accompanied by substantial genetic change (a majority of values for genetic distance, D, range between 0.15 and 0.30) and that relatively few additional genetic changes are required during the second stage.

The conclusions drawn from the investigation of geographic speciation make it possible to predict the relative amounts of genetic change expected in the quantum modes of speciation. Polyploid species are a special case — they arise suddenly in one or a few generations, and at first they are not expected to be genetically different from their ancestors. More generally, quantum speciation involves a shortening of the first stage of speciation, so that postzygotic RIMs arise directly as a consequence of specific genetic changes (such as chromosome mutations). Populations in the first stage of quantum speciation, therefore, need not be substantially different in individual gene loci. This has been confirmed by genetic investigations of species recently arisen by quantum speciation. For example, the average genetic distance between four incipient species of the mole rat *Spalax ehrenbergi* is 0.022, and between those of the gopher *Thomomys talpoides* it is 0.078. The second stage of speciation is modulated in essentially the same way as in the geographic mode. Not many gene changes are needed in either case to complete speciation.

PATTERNS AND RATES OF SPECIES EVOLUTION

The pace of evolution is not constant. It is often a gradual process; however, the fossil record also reveals periods of rapid morphological change and speciation. It can be said that all organisms owe their existence to the process of lineage splitting. In some cases, however, it may be difficult to classify species based on structural characteristics alone; the traits of some unrelated species may appear to converge, because of functional similiarities, or to develop in parallel with one another. Although speciation is a significant part of the evolutionary process, the loss of species is also important. Throughout Earth's history several large extinction events have removed many species within a short period of time, but the fossil record has shown that speciation accelerates shortly thereafter.

Evolution Within a Lineage and by Lineage Splitting

Evolution can take place by anagenesis, in which changes occur within a lineage, or by cladogenesis, in which a lineage splits into two or more separate lines. Anagenetic evolution has doubled the size of the human cranium over the course of two million years; in the lineage of the horse it has reduced the number of toes from four to one. Cladogenetic evolution has produced the extraordinary diversity of the living world, with its more than two million species of animals, plants, fungi, and microorganisms.

The most essential cladogenetic function is speciation, the process by which one species splits into two or more species. Because species are reproductively isolated from one another, they are independent evolutionary units; that is, evolutionary changes occurring in one species are not shared with other species. Over time, species diverge more and more from one another as a consequence of anagenetic evolution. Descendant lineages of two related species that existed millions of years ago may now be classified into quite different biological categories, such as different genera or even different families.

The evolution of all living organisms, or of a subset of them, can be seen as a tree, with branches that divide into two or more as time progresses. Such trees are called phylogenies. Their branches represent evolving lineages, some of which eventually die out while others persist in themselves or in their derived lineages down to the present time. Evolutionists are interested in the history of life and hence in the topology, or configuration, of phylogenies. They are concerned as well with the nature of the anagenetic changes within lineages and with the timing of the events.

Phylogenetic relationships are ascertained by means of several complementary sources of evidence. First, there are the discovered remnants of organisms that lived in the past, the fossil record, which provides definitive evidence of relationships between some groups of organisms. The fossil record, however, is far from complete and is often seriously deficient. Second, information about phylogeny comes from comparative studies of living forms. Comparative anatomy contributed the most information in the past, although additional knowledge came from comparative embryology, cytology, ethology, biogeography, and other biological disciplines. In recent years the comparative study of the so-called informational macromolecules—proteins and nucleic acids, whose specific sequences of constituents carry genetic information—has become a powerful tool for the study of phylogeny.

Morphological similarities between organisms have probably always been recognized. In ancient Greece Aristotle and later his followers and those of Plato, particularly Porphyry, classified organisms (as well as inanimate objects) on the basis of similarities. The Aristotelian system of classification was further developed by some medieval Scholastic philosophers, notably Albertus Magnus and Thomas Aquinas. The modern foundations of biological taxonomy, the science of classification of living and extinct organisms, were laid in the 18th century by the Swedish botanist Carolus Linnaeus and the French botanist Michel Adanson. The French naturalist Lamarck dedicated much of his work to the systematic classification of organisms. He proposed that their similarities were due to ancestral relationships—in other words, to the degree of evolutionary proximity.

The modern theory of evolution provides a causal explanation of the similarities between living things. Organisms evolve by a process of descent with modification. Changes, and therefore differences, gradually accumulate over the generations. The more recent the last common ancestor of a group of organisms, the less their differentiation; similarities of form and function reflect phylogenetic propinquity. Accordingly, phylogenetic affinities can be inferred on the basis of relative similarity.

CONVERGENT AND PARALLEL EVOLUTION

A distinction has to be made between resemblances due to propinquity of descent and those due only to similarity of function. As discussed above in the section The Evidence for Evolution: Structural Similarities, correspondence of features in different organisms that is due to inheritance from a common ancestor is called homology. The forelimbs of humans, whales, dogs, and bats are homologous. The skeletons of these limbs are all constructed of bones arranged according to the same pattern because they derive from a common ancestor with similarly arranged forelimbs. Correspondence of features due to similarity of function but not related to common descent is termed analogy. The wings of birds and of flies are analogous. Their wings are not modified versions of a structure present in a common ancestor but rather have developed independently as adaptations to a common function, flying. The similarities between the wings of bats and birds are partially homologous and partially analogous. Their skeletal structure is homologous, due to common descent from the forelimb of a reptilian ancestor; but the modifications for flying are different and independently evolved, and in this respect they are analogous.

Parallel evolution of marsupial mammals in Australia and placental mammals on other continents. Encyclopædia Britannica, Inc.

Features that become more rather than less similar through independent evolution are said to be convergent. Convergence is often associated with similarity of function, as in the evolution of wings in birds, bats, and flies. The shark (a fish) and the dolphin (a mammal) are much alike in external morphology; their similarities are due to convergence, since they have evolved independently as adaptations to aquatic life.

Taxonomists also speak of parallel evolution. Parallelism and convergence are not always clearly distinguishable. Strictly speaking, convergent evolution occurs when descendants resemble each other more than their ancestors did with respect to some feature. Parallel evolution implies that two or more lineages have changed in similar ways, so that the evolved descendants are as similar to each other as their ancestors were. The evolution of marsupials in Australia, for example, paralleled the evolution of placental mammals in other parts of the world. There are Australian marsupials resembling true wolves, cats, mice, squirrels, moles, groundhogs, and anteaters. These placental mammals and the corresponding Australian marsupials evolved independently but in parallel lines by reason of their adaptation to similar ways of life. Some resemblances between a true anteater (genus *Myrmecophaga*) and a marsupial anteater, or numbat (*Myrmecobius*), are due to homology—both are mammals. Others are due to analogy—both feed on ants.

Parallel and convergent evolution are also common in plants. New World cacti and African euphorbias, or spurges, are alike in overall appearance although they belong to separate families. Both are succulent, spiny, water-storing plants adapted to the arid conditions of the desert. Their corresponding morphologies have evolved independently in response to similar environmental challenges.

Homology can be recognized not only between different organisms but also between repetitive structures of the same organism. This has been called serial homology. There is serial homology, for example, between the arms and legs of humans, between the seven cervical vertebrae of mammals, and between the branches or leaves of a tree. The jointed appendages of arthropods are elaborate examples of serial homology. Crayfish have 19 pairs of appendages, all built according to the same basic pattern but serving diverse functions—sensing, chewing, food handling, walking, mating, egg carrying, and swimming. Although serial homologies are not useful in reconstructing the phylogenetic relationships of organisms, they are an important dimension of the evolutionary process.

Relationships in some sense akin to those between serial homologs exist at the molecular level between genes and proteins derived from ancestral gene duplications. The genes coding for the various hemoglobin chains are an example. About 500 million years ago a chromosome segment carrying the gene coding for hemoglobin became duplicated, so that the genes in the different segments thereafter evolved in somewhat different ways, one eventually giving rise to the modern gene coding for the α hemoglobin chain, the other for the β chain. The β chain gene became duplicated again about 200 million years ago, giving rise to the γ hemoglobin chain, a normal component of fetal hemoglobin (hemoblobin F). The genes for the α, β, γ, and other hemoglobin chains are homologous; similarities in their nucleotide sequences occur because they are modified descendants of a single ancestral sequence.

There are two ways of comparing homology between hemoglobins. One is to compare the same hemoglobin chain—for instance, the α chain—in different species of animals. The degree of divergence between the α chains reflects the degree of the evolutionary relationship between the organisms, because the hemoglobin chains have evolved independently of one another since the time of divergence of the lineages leading to the present-day organisms. A second way is to make comparisons between, say, the α and β chains of a single species. The degree of divergence between the different globin chains reflects the degree of relationship between the genes coding for them. The different globins have evolved independently of each other since the time of duplication of their ancestral genes. Comparisons between homologous genes or proteins within a given organism provide information about the phylogenetic history of the genes and hence about the historical sequence of the gene duplication events.

Whether similar features in different organisms are homologous or analogous—or simply accidental—cannot always be decided unambiguously, but the distinction must be made in order to determine phylogenetic relationships. Moreover, the degrees of homology must be quantified in some way so as to determine the propinquity of common descent between species. Difficulties arise here as well. In the case of forelimbs, it is not clear whether the homologies are greater between human and bird than between human and reptile, or between human and reptile than between human and bat. The fossil record sometimes provides the appropriate information, even though the record is deficient. Fossil evidence must be examined together with the evidence from comparative studies of living forms and with the quantitative estimates provided by comparative studies of proteins and nucleic acids.

GRADUAL AND PUNCTUATIONAL EVOLUTION

The fossil record indicates that morphological evolution is by and large a gradual process. Major evolutionary changes are usually due to a building-up over the ages of relatively small changes. But the fossil record is discontinuous. Fossil strata are separated by sharp boundaries; accumulation of fossils within a geologic deposit (stratum) is fairly constant over time, but the transition from one stratum to another may involve gaps of tens of thousands of years. Whereas the fossils within a stratum exhibit little morphological variation, new species—characterized by small but discontinuous morphological changes—typically appear at the boundaries between strata. That is not to say that the transition from one stratum to another always involves sudden changes in morphology; on the contrary, fossil forms often persist virtually unchanged through several geologic strata, each representing millions of years.

The apparent morphological discontinuities of the fossil record are often attributed by paleontologists to the discontinuity of the sediments—that is, to the substantial time gaps encompassed in the boundaries between strata. The assumption is that, if the fossil deposits were more continuous, they would show a more gradual transition of form. Even so, morphological evolution would not always keep progressing gradually, because some forms, at least, remain unchanged for extremely long times. Examples are the lineages known as "living fossils"—for instance, the lamp shell *Lingula*, a genus of brachiopod (a phylum of shelled invertebrates) that appears to have remained essentially unchanged since the Ordovician Period, some 450 million years ago; or the tuatara (*Sphenodon punctatus*), a reptile that has shown little morphological evolution for nearly 200 million years, since the early Mesozoic.

Some paleontologists have proposed that the discontinuities of the fossil record are not artifacts created by gaps in the record but rather reflect the true nature of morphological evolution, which happens in sudden bursts associated with the formation of new species. The lack of morphological evolution, or stasis, of lineages such as *Lingula* and *Sphenodon* is in turn due to lack of speciation within those lineages. The proposition that morphological evolution is jerky, with most morphological change occurring during the brief speciation events and virtually no change during the subsequent existence of the species, is known as the punctuated equilibrium model.

Whether morphological evolution in the fossil record is predominantly punctuational or gradual is a much-debated question. The imperfection of the record makes it unlikely that the issue will be settled in the foreseeable future. Intensive study of a favourable and abundant set of fossils may be expected to substantiate punctuated or gradual evolution in particular cases. But the argument is not about whether only one or the other pattern ever occurs; it is about their relative frequency. Some paleontologists argue that morphological evolution is in most cases gradual and only rarely jerky, whereas others think the opposite is true.

Much of the problem is that gradualness or jerkiness is in the eye of the beholder. Consider the evolution of shell rib strength (the ratio of rib height to rib width) within a lineage of fossil brachiopods of the genus *Eocelia* in the figure on the facing page. One possible interpretation of the data is that rib strength changed little or not at all

Morphological evolution in a lineage of brachiopods, presented as an illustration of the ambiguity in interpreting whether the process is gradual or punctuational. From the statistical analysis of fossil shells detailed in steps A through D, one may conclude that periods of essentially no change in shell rib strength, each lasting millions of years, are interspersed with comparatively short bursts of rapid change. From another point of view, however, one may see the same record as evidence of an unbroken process of evolution in which the rate of change speeds up somewhat at particular times.
Encyclopædia Britannica, Inc.

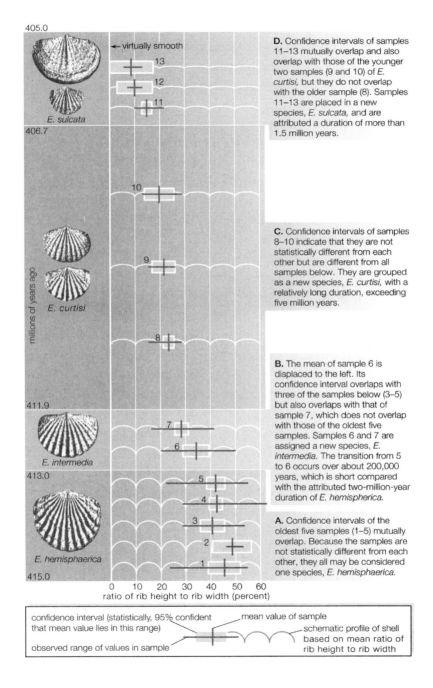

D. Confidence intervals of samples 11–13 mutually overlap and also overlap with those of the younger two samples (9 and 10) of *E. curtisi,* but they do not overlap with the older sample (8). Samples 11–13 are placed in a new species, *E. sulcata,* and are attributed a duration of more than 1.5 million years.

C. Confidence intervals of samples 8–10 indicate that they are not statistically different from each other but are different from all samples below. They are grouped as a new species, *E. curtisi,* with a relatively long duration, exceeding five million years.

B. The mean of sample 6 is displaced to the left. Its confidence interval overlaps with three of the samples below (3–5) but also overlaps with that of sample 7, which does not overlap with those of the oldest five samples. Samples 6 and 7 are assigned a new species, *E. intermedia.* The transition from 5 to 6 occurs over about 200,000 years, which is short compared with the attributed two-million-year duration of *E. hemispherica.*

A. Confidence intervals of the oldest five samples (1–5) mutually overlap. Because the samples are not statistically different from each other, they all may be considered one species, *E. hemisphaerica.*

405.0

E. sulcata
406.7

millions of years ago

E. curtisi

411.9

E. intermedia
413.0

E. hemisphaerica
415.0

← virtually smooth

13
12
11

10

9

8

7
6

5
4

3
2
1

0   10   20   30   40   50   60
ratio of rib height to rib width (percent)

confidence interval (statistically, 95% confident that mean value lies in this range) — mean value of sample

observed range of values in sample — schematic profile of shell based on mean ratio of rib height to rib width from 415 million to 413 million years ago; rapid change ensued for the next 1 million years, followed by virtual stasis from 412 million to 407 million years ago; and then another short burst of change occurred about 406 million years ago, followed by a final period of stasis. On the other hand, the same record may be interpreted as not particularly punctuated but rather a gradual process, with the rate of change somewhat greater at particular times.

The proponents of the punctuated equilibrium model propose not only that morphological evolution is jerky but also that it is associated with speciation events. They argue that phyletic evolution—that is, evolution along lineages of descent—proceeds at two levels. First, there is continuous change through time within a population. This consists largely of gene substitutions prompted by natural selection, mutation, genetic drift, and other genetic processes that operate at the level of the individual organism. The punctualists maintain that this continuous evolution within established lineages rarely, if ever, yields substantial morphological changes in species. Second, they say, there is the process of origination and extinction of species, in which most morphological change occurs. According to the punctualist model, evolutionary trends result from the patterns of origination and extinction of species rather than from evolution within established lineages.

As discussed above in the section The origin of species, speciation involves the development of reproductive isolation between populations previously able to interbreed. Paleontologists discriminate between species by their different morphologies as preserved in the fossil record, but fossils cannot provide evidence of the development of reproductive isolation—new species that are reproductively isolated from their ancestors are often morphologically indistinguishable from them. Speciation as it is seen by paleontologists always involves substantial morphological change. This situation creates an insuperable difficulty for resolving the question of whether morphological evolution is always associated with speciation events. If speciation is defined as the evolution of reproductive isolation, the fossil record provides no evidence that an association between speciation and morphological change is necessary. But if new species are identified in the fossil record by morphological changes, then all such changes will occur concomitantly with the origination of new species.

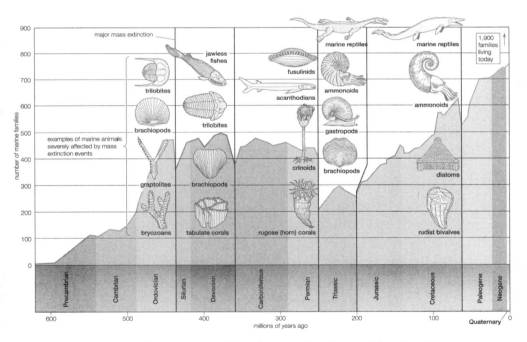

The diversity of marine animal families since late Precambrian time. The data for the curve comprise only those families that are reliably preserved in the fossil record; the 1,900 value for living families also includes those families rarely preserved as fossils. The several pronounced dips in the curve correspond to major mass-extinction events. The most catastrophic extinction took place at the end of the Permian Period. Encyclopædia Britannica, Inc.

DIVERSITY AND EXTINCTION

The current diversity of life is the balance between the species that have arisen through time and those that have become extinct. Paleontologists observe that organisms have continuously changed since the Cambrian Period, more than 500 million years ago, from which abundant animal fossil remains are known. The division of geologic history into a succession of eras and periods is hallmarked by major changes in plant and animal life—the appearance of new sorts of organisms and the extinction of others. Paleontologists distinguish between background extinction, the steady rate at which species disappear through geologic time, and mass extinctions, the episodic events in which large numbers of species become extinct over time spans short enough to appear almost instantaneous on the geologic scale.

Best known among mass extinctions is the one that occurred at the end of the Cretaceous Period, when the dinosaurs and many other marine and land animals disappeared. Most scientists believe that the Cretaceous mass extinction was provoked by the impact of an asteroid or comet on the tip of the Yucatán Peninsula in southeastern Mexico 65.5 million years ago. The object's impact caused an enormous dust cloud, which greatly reduced the Sun's radiation reaching Earth, with a consequent drastic drop in temperature and other adverse conditions. Among animals, about 76 percent of species, 47 percent of genera, and 16 percent of families became extinct. Although the dinosaurs vanished, turtles, snakes, lizards, crocodiles, and other reptiles, as well as some mammals and birds, survived. Mammals that lived prior to the event were small and mostly nocturnal, but during the ensuing Paleogene and Neogene periods they experienced an explosive diversification in size and morphology, occupying ecological niches vacated by the dinosaurs. Most of the orders and families of mammals now in existence originated in the first 10 million to 20 million years after the dinosaurs' extinction. Birds also greatly diversified at that time.

Several other mass extinctions have occurred since the Cambrian. The most catastrophic happened at the end of the Permian Period, about 250 million years ago, when 95 percent of species, 82 percent of genera, and 51 percent of families of animals became extinct. Other large mass extinctions occurred at or near the end of the Ordovician (about 440 million years ago, 85 percent of species extinct), Devonian (about 360 million years ago, 83 percent of species extinct), and Triassic (about 200 million years ago, 80 percent of species extinct). Changes of climate and chemical composition of the atmosphere appear to have caused these mass extinctions; there is no convincing evidence that they resulted from cosmic impacts. Like other mass extinctions, they were followed by the origin or rapid diversification of various kinds of organisms. The first mammals and dinosaurs appeared after the late Permian extinction, and the first vascular plants after the Late Ordovician extinction.

Background extinctions result from ordinary biological processes, such as competition between species, predation, and parasitism. When two species compete for very similar resources—say, the same kinds of seeds or fruits— one may become extinct, although often they will displace one another by dividing the territory or by specializing in slightly different foods, such as seeds of a different size or kind. Ordinary physical and climatic changes also account for background extinctions—for example, when a lake dries out or a mountain range rises or erodes.

New species come about by the processes discussed in previous sections. These processes are largely gradual, yet the history of life shows major transitions in which one kind of organism becomes a very different kind. The earliest organisms were prokaryotes, or bacteria-like cells, whose hereditary material is not segregated into a nucleus. Eukaryotes have their DNA organized into chromosomes that are membrane-bound in the nucleus, have other organelles inside their cells, and reproduce sexually. Eventually, eukaryotic multicellular organisms appeared, in which there is a division of function among cells — some specializing in reproduction, others becoming leaves, trunks, and roots in plants or different organs and tissues such as muscle, nerve, and bone in animals. Social organization of individuals in a population is another way of achieving functional division, which may be quite fixed, as in ants and bees, or more flexible, as in cattle herds or primate groups.

Because of the gradualness of evolution, immediate descendants differ little, and then mostly quantitatively, from their ancestors. But gradual evolution may amount to large differences over time. The forelimbs of mammals are normally adapted for walking, but they are adapted for shoveling earth in moles and other mammals that live mostly underground, for climbing and grasping in arboreal monkeys and apes, for swimming in dolphins and whales, and for flying in bats. The forelimbs of reptiles became wings in their bird descendants. Feathers appear to have served first for regulating temperature but eventually were co-opted for flying and became incorporated into wings.

Eyes, which serve as another example, also evolved gradually and achieved very different configurations, all serving the function of seeing. Eyes have evolved independently at least 40 times. Because sunlight is a pervasive feature of Earth's environment, it is not surprising that organs have evolved that take advantage of it. The simplest "organ" of vision occurs in some single-celled organisms

Steps in the evolution of the eye as reflected in the range of eye complexity in living mollusk species (top to bottom): a pigment spot, as in the limpet Patella; *a pigment cup, as in the slit shell mollusk* Pleurotomaria; *the "pinhole-lens" eye of* Nautilus; *a primitive lensed eye, as in the marine snail* Murex; *and the complex eye— with iris, crystalline lens, and retina—of octopuses and squids.* Encyclopædia Britannica, Inc.

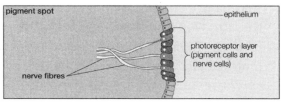

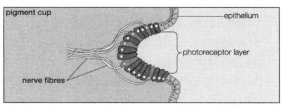

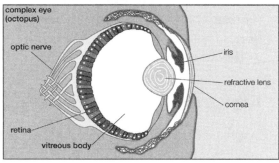

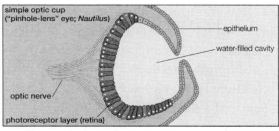

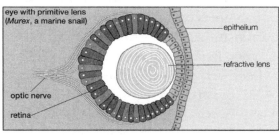

that have enzymes or spots sensitive to light, which helps them move toward the surface of their pond, where they feed on the algae growing there by photosynthesis. Some multicellular animals exhibit light-sensitive spots on their epidermis. Further steps—deposition of pigment around the spot, configuration of cells into a cuplike shape, thickening of the epidermis leading to the development of a lens, development of muscles to move the eyes and nerves to transmit optical signals to the brain—all led to the highly developed eyes of vertebrates and cephalopods (octopuses and squids) and to the compound eyes of insects.

While the evolution of forelimbs—for walking—into the wings of birds or the arms and hands of primates may seem more like changes of function, the evolution of eyes exemplifies gradual advancement of the same function—seeing. In all cases, however, the process is impelled by natural selection's favouring individuals exhibiting functional advantages over others of the same species. Examples of functional shifts are many and diverse. Some transitions at first may seem unlikely because of the difficulty in identifying which possible functions may have been served during the intermediate stages. These cases are eventually resolved with further research and the discovery of intermediate fossil forms. An example of a seemingly unlikely transition is described above in the section The Fossil Record—namely, the transformation of bones found in the reptilian jaw into the hammer and anvil of the mammalian ear.

EVOLUTION AND DEVELOPMENT

Starfish are radially symmetrical, but most animals are bilaterally symmetrical—the parts of the left and right halves of their bodies tend to correspond in size, shape, and position.

Some bilateral animals, such as millipedes and shrimps, are segmented (metameric); others, such as frogs and humans, have a front-to-back (head-to-foot) body plan, with head, thorax, abdomen, and limbs, but they lack the repetitive, nearly identical segments of metameric animals. There are other basic body plans, such as those of sponges, clams, and jellyfish, but their total number is not large—less than 40.

The fertilized egg, or zygote, is a single cell, more or less spherical, that does not exhibit polarity such as anterior and posterior ends or dorsal and ventral sides. Embryonic development is the process of growth and differentiation by which the single-celled egg becomes a multicellular organism.

The determination of body plan from this single cell and the construction of specialized organs, such as the eye, are under the control of regulatory genes. Most notable among these are the *Hox* genes, which produce proteins (transcription factors) that bind with other genes and thus determine their expression—that is, when they will act. The *Hox* genes embody spatial and temporal information. By means of their encoded proteins, they activate or repress the expression of other genes according to the position of each cell in the developing body, determining where limbs and other body parts will grow in the embryo. Since their discovery in the early 1980s, the *Hox* genes have been found to play crucial roles from the first steps of development, such as establishing anterior and posterior ends in the zygote, to much later steps, such as the differentiation of nerve cells.

The critical region of the *Hox* proteins is encoded by a sequence of about 180 consecutive nucleotides (called the homeobox). The corresponding protein region (the homeodomain), about 60 amino acids long, binds to a short stretch of DNA in the regulatory region of the target genes. Genes containing homeobox sequences are found not only in animals but also in other eukaryotes such as fungi and plants.

All animals have *Hox* genes, which may be as few as 1, as in sponges, or as many as 38, as in humans and other mammals. *Hox* genes are clustered in the genome. Invertebrates have only one cluster with a variable number of genes, typically fewer than 13. The common ancestor of the chordates (which include the vertebrates) probably had only one cluster of *Hox* genes, which may have numbered 13. Chordates may have one or more clusters, but not all 13 genes remain in every cluster. The marine animal amphioxus, a primitive chordate, has a single array of 10 *Hox* genes. Humans, mice, and other mammals have 38 *Hox* genes arranged in four clusters, three with 9 genes each and one with 11 genes. The set of genes varies from cluster to cluster, so that out of the 13 in the original cluster, genes designated 1, 2, 3, and 7 may be missing in one set, whereas 10, 11, 12, and 13 may be missing in a different set.

The four clusters of *Hox* genes found in mammals originated by duplication of the whole original cluster and retain considerable similarity between clusters. The 13 genes in the original cluster also themselves originated by repeated duplication, starting from a single *Hox* gene as found in the sponges. These first duplications happened very early in animal evolution, in the Precambrian. The genes within a cluster retain detectable similarity, but they differ more from one another than they differ from the corresponding, or homologous, gene in any of the other sets. There is a puzzling correspondence between the position of the *Hox* genes in a cluster along the chromosome and the patterning of the body—genes located upstream (anteriorly in the direction in which genes are transcribed) in the cluster are expressed earlier and more anteriorly in the body, while those located downstream (posteriorly in the direction of transcription) are expressed later in development and predominantly affect the posterior body parts.

Researchers demonstrated the evolutionary conservation of the *Hox* genes by means of clever manipulations of genes in laboratory experiments. For example, the *ey* gene that determines the formation of the compound eye in *Drosophila* vinegar flies was activated in the developing embryo in various parts of the body, yielding experimental flies with anatomically normal eyes on the legs, wings, and other structures. The evolutionary conservation of the *Hox* genes may be the explanation for the puzzling observation that most of the diversity of body plans within major groups of animals arose early in the evolution of the group. The multicellular animals (metazoans) first found as fossils in the Cambrian already demonstrate all the major body plans found during the ensuing 540 million years, as well as four to seven additional body plans that became extinct and seem bizarre to observers today. Similarly, most of the classes found within a phylum appear early in the evolution of the phylum. For example, all living classes of arthropods are already found in the Cambrian, with body plans essentially unchanged thereafter; in addition, the Cambrian contains a few strange kinds of arthropods that later became extinct.

CHAPTER 4
RECONSTRUCTION OF EVOLUTIONARY HISTORY

The advances of molecular biology have made possible the comparative study of proteins and the nucleic acids, DNA and RNA. DNA is the repository of hereditary (evolutionary and developmental) information. The relationship of proteins to DNA is so immediate that they closely reflect the hereditary information. This reflection is not perfect, because the genetic code is redundant, and, consequently, some differences in the DNA do not yield differences in the proteins. Moreover, this reflection is not complete, because a large fraction of DNA (about 90 percent in many organisms) does not code for proteins. Nevertheless, proteins are so closely related to the information contained in DNA that they, as well as nucleic acids, are called informational macromolecules.

Nucleic acids and proteins are linear molecules made up of sequences of units—nucleotides in the case of nucleic acids, amino acids in the case of proteins—which retain considerable amounts of evolutionary information. Comparing two macromolecules establishes the number of their units that are different. Because evolution usually occurs by changing one unit at a time, the number of differences is an indication of the recency of common ancestry. Changes in evolutionary rates may create difficulties in interpretation, but macromolecular studies have three notable advantages over comparative anatomy and the other classical disciplines. One is that the information is more readily quantifiable. The number of units that are different is readily established when the sequence of units is known for a given macromolecule in different organisms. The second advantage is that comparisons can be made even between very different sorts of organisms.

There is very little that comparative anatomy can say when organisms as diverse as yeasts, pine trees, and human beings are compared, but there are homologous macromolecules that can be compared in all three. Such comparisons allow for the creation of evolutionary trees. The third advantage is multiplicity. Each organism possesses thousands of genes and proteins, which all reflect the same evolutionary history. If the investigation of one particular gene or protein does not resolve the evolutionary relationship of a set of species, additional genes and proteins can be investigated until the matter has been settled.

DNA AND PROTEIN AS INFORMATIONAL MACROMOLECULES

Informational macromolecules provide information not only about the branching of lineages from common ancestors (cladogenesis) but also about the amount of genetic change that has occurred in any given lineage (anagenesis). It might seem at first that quantifying anagenesis for proteins and nucleic acids would be impossible, because it would require comparison of molecules from organisms that lived in the past with those from living organisms. Organisms of the past are sometimes preserved as fossils, but their DNA and proteins have largely disintegrated. Nevertheless, comparisons between living species provide information about anagenesis.

The following is an example of such comparison: Two living species, C and D, have a common ancestor, the extinct species B. If C and D were found to differ by four amino acid substitutions in a single protein, then it could tentatively be assumed that two substitutions (four total changes divided by two species) had taken place in the

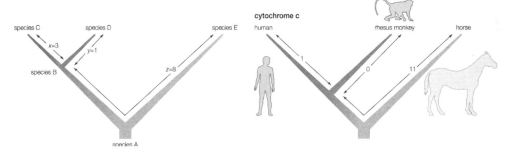

(Left) Amount of change in the evolutionary history of three hypothetical living species (C, D, and E), inferred by comparing amino-acid differences in their myoglobin molecules. All three species have the same earlier ancestor (A). (Right) Phylogeny of the human, the rhesus monkey, and the horse, based on amino-acid substitutions in the evolution of cytochrome c in the lineages of the three species. Encyclopædia Britannica, Inc.

evolutionary lineage of each species. This assumption, however, could be invalidated by the discovery of a third living species, E, that is related to C, D, and their ancestor, B, through an earlier ancestor, A. The number of amino acid differences between the protein molecules of the three living species may be as follows:

$$C \text{ and } D = 4$$
$$C \text{ and } E = 11$$
$$D \text{ and } E = 9$$

Let x denote the number of differences between B and C, y denote the differences between B and D, and z denote the differences between A and B as well as A and E. The following three equations can be produced:

$$x + y = 4$$
$$x + z = 11$$
$$y + z = 9$$

Solving the equations yields $x = 3$, $y = 1$, and $z = 8$.

As a concrete example, consider the protein cytochrome c, involved in cell respiration. The sequence of amino acids in this protein is known for many organisms, from bacteria and yeasts to insects and humans; in animals cytochrome c consists of 104 amino acids. When the amino acid sequences of humans and rhesus monkeys are compared, they are found to be different at position 66 (isoleucine in humans, threonine in rhesus monkeys) but, identical at the other 103 positions. When humans are compared with horses, 12 amino acid differences are found, but, when horses are compared with rhesus monkeys, there are only 11 amino acid differences. Even without knowing anything else about the evolutionary history of mammals, one would conclude that the lineages of humans and rhesus monkeys diverged from each other much more recently than they diverged from the horse lineage. Moreover, it can be concluded that the amino acid difference between humans and rhesus monkeys must have occurred in the human lineage after its separation from the rhesus monkey lineage.

EVOLUTIONARY TREES

Evolutionary trees are models that seek to reconstruct the evolutionary history of taxa—i.e., species or other groups of organisms, such as genera, families, or orders. The trees embrace two kinds of information related to evolutionary change, cladogenesis and anagenesis. The branching relationships of the trees reflect the relative relationships of ancestry, or cladogenesis. For example, humans and rhesus monkeys are seen to be more closely related to each other than either is to the horse. Stated another way, it is thought that the last common ancestor to all three species lived in a more remote past than the last common ancestor to humans and monkeys.

Evolutionary trees may also indicate the changes that have occurred along each lineage, or anagenesis. Thus, in the evolution of cytochrome c since the last common ancestor of humans and rhesus monkeys, one amino acid changed in the lineage going to humans but none in the lineage going to rhesus monkeys.

There exist several methods for constructing evolutionary trees. Some were developed for interpreting morphological data, others for interpreting molecular data; some can be used with either kind of data. The main methods currently in use are called distance, parsimony, and maximum likelihood.

DISTANCE METHODS

A "distance" is the number of differences between two taxa. The differences are measured with respect to certain traits (i.e., morphological data) or to certain macromolecules (primarily the sequence of amino acids in proteins or the sequence of nucleotides in DNA or RNA). The two trees illustrated in the figure on page 168 were obtained by taking into account the distance, or number of amino acid differences, between three organisms with respect to a particular protein. The amino acid sequence of a protein contains more information than is reflected in the number of amino acid differences. This is because in some cases the replacement of one amino acid by another requires no more than one nucleotide substitution in the

DNA that codes for the protein, whereas in other cases it requires at least two nucleotide changes.

The relationships between species as shown in the figure on the following pages correspond fairly well to the relationships determined from other sources, such as the fossil record. According to the figure, chickens are less closely related to ducks and pigeons than to penguins, and humans and monkeys diverged from the other mammals before the marsupial kangaroo separated from the nonprimate placentals. Although these examples are known to be erroneous relationships, the power of the method is apparent in that a single protein yields a fairly accurate reconstruction of the evolutionary history of 20 organisms that started to diverge more than one billion years ago.

Morphological data also can be used for constructing distance trees. The first step is to obtain a distance matrix, such as that making up the nucleotide differences table, but one based on a set of morphological comparisons between species or other taxa. For example, in some insects one can measure body length, wing length, wing width, number and length of wing veins, or another trait. The most common procedure to transform a distance matrix into a phylogeny is called cluster analysis. The distance matrix is scanned for the smallest distance element, and the two taxa involved (say, A and B) are joined at an internal node, or branching point. The matrix is scanned again for the next smallest distance, and the two new taxa (say, C and D) are clustered. The procedure is continued until all taxa have been joined. When a distance involves a taxon that is already part of a previous cluster (say, E and A), the average distance is obtained between the new taxon and the preexisting cluster (say, the average distance between E to A and E to B). This simple procedure, which can also be used with molecular data, assumes that the rate of evolution is uniform along all branches.

Minimum Number of Nucleotide Differences in Genes Coding for Cytochrome C in 20 Different Organisms

	ORGANISM	1	2	3	4	5	6	7	8	9
1.	*human*		1	13	17	16	13	12	12	17
2.	*monkey*			12	16	15	12	11	13	16
3.	*dog*				10	8	4	6	7	12
4.	*horse*					1	5	11	11	16
5.	*donkey*						4	10	12	15
6.	*pig*							6	7	13
7.	*rabbit*								7	10
8.	*kangaroo*									14
9.	*duck*									
10.	*pigeon*									
11.	*chicken*									
12.	*penguin*									
13.	*turtle*									
14.	*rattlesnake*									
15.	*tuna*									
16.	*screwworm*									
17.	*moth*									
18.	*neurospora (mold)*									
19.	*Saccharomyces (yeast)*									
20.	*Candida (yeast)*									

10	11	12	13	14	15	16	17	18	19	20
16	18	18	19	20	31	33	36	63	56	66
15	17	17	28	21	32	32	35	62	57	65
12	14	14	13	30	29	24	28	64	61	66
16	16	17	16	32	27	24	33	64	60	68
15	15	16	15	31	26	26	32	64	59	67
13	13	14	13	30	25	26	31	64	59	67
8	11	11	11	25	26	23	29	62	59	67
14	15	13	14	30	27	26	31	66	58	68
3	3	3	7	24	26	25	29	61	62	66
	4	4	8	24	27	26	30	59	62	66
		2	8	28	26	26	31	61	62	66
			8	28	27	28	30	62	61	65
				30	27	30	33	65	64	67
					38	40	41	61	61	69
						34	41	72	66	69
							16	58	63	65
								59	60	61
									57	61
										41

Source: Walter M. Fitch, *Science*, vol. 155, Jan. 20, 1967, p. 281, © 1967 by the AAAS

Other distance methods relax the condition of uniform rate and allow for unequal rates of evolution along the branches. One of the most extensively used methods of this kind is called neighbour-joining. The method starts, as before, by identifying the smallest distance in the matrix and linking the two taxa involved. The next step is to remove these two taxa and calculate a new matrix in which their distances to other taxa are replaced by the distance between the node linking the two taxa and all other taxa. The smallest distance in this new matrix is used for making the next connection, which will be between two other taxa or between the previous node and a new taxon. The procedure is repeated until all taxa have been connected with one another by intervening nodes.

Maximum Parsimony Methods

Maximum parsimony methods seek to reconstruct the tree that requires the fewest (i.e., most parsimonious) number of changes summed along all branches. This is a reasonable assumption, because it usually will be the most likely. But evolution may not necessarily have occurred following a minimum path, because the same change instead may have occurred independently along different branches, and some changes may have involved intermediate steps. Consider three species — C, D, and E. If C and D differ by two amino acids in a certain protein and either one differs by three amino acids from E, parsimony will lead to a tree with the structure shown in the left side of the figure illustrating the two simple phylogenies. It may be the case, however, that in a certain position at which C and D both have amino acid g while E has h, the ancestral amino acid was g. Amino acid g did not change in the lineage going to C but changed to h in a lineage going to the ancestor of D and E and then changed again, back to g, in the lineage going to D. The correct phylogeny would lead then from the common ancestor of all three species to C in one branch (in which no amino acid changes occurred), and to the last common ancestor of D and E in the other branch (in which g changed to h) with one additional change (from h to g) occurring in the lineage from this ancestor to E.

Not all evolutionary changes, even those that involve a single step, may be equally probable. For example, among the four nucleotide bases in DNA, cytosine (C) and thymine (T) are members of a family of related molecules called pyrimidines; likewise, adenine (A) and guanine (G) belong to a family of molecules called purines. A change within a DNA sequence from one pyrimidine to another (C # T) or from one purine to another (A # G), called a transition, is more likely to occur than a change from a purine to a pyrimidine or the converse (G or A # C or T), called a transversion. Parsimony methods take into account different probabilities of occurrence if they are known.

Maximum parsimony methods are related to cladistics, a very formalistic theory of taxonomic classification, extensively used with morphological and paleontological data. The critical feature in cladistics is the identification of derived shared traits, called synapomorphic traits. A synapomorphic trait is shared by some taxa but not others because the former inherited it from a common ancestor that acquired the trait after its lineage separated from the lineages going to the other taxa. In the evolution of carnivores, for example, domestic cats, tigers, and leopards are clustered together because of their possessing retractable claws, a trait acquired after their common ancestor branched off from the lineage leading to the dogs, wolves, and coyotes. It is important to ascertain that the shared traits are homologous rather than analogous. For example, mammals and birds, but not lizards, have a four-chambered heart. Yet birds are more closely related to lizards than to mammals; the four-chambered heart evolved independently in the bird and mammal lineages, by parallel evolution.

Maximum Likelihood Methods

Maximum likelihood methods seek to identify the most likely tree, given the available data. They require that an evolutionary model be identified, which would make it possible to estimate the probability of each possible individual change. For example, as is mentioned in the preceding section, transitions are more likely than transversions among DNA nucleotides, but a particular probability must be assigned to each. All possible trees are considered. The probabilities for each individual change are multiplied for each tree. The best tree is the one with the highest probability (or maximum likelihood) among all possible trees.

Maximum likelihood methods are computationally expensive when the number of taxa is large, because the number of possible trees (for each of which the probability must be calculated) grows factorially with the number of taxa. With 10 taxa, there are about 3.6 million possible trees; with 20 taxa, the number of possible trees is about 2 followed by 18 zeros (2×10^{18}). Even with powerful computers, maximum likelihood methods can be prohibitive if the number of taxa is large. Heuristic methods exist in which only a subsample of all possible trees is examined and thus an exhaustive search is avoided.

Evaluation of Evolutionary Trees

The statistical degree of confidence of a tree can be estimated for distance and maximum likelihood trees. The most common method is called bootstrapping. It consists of taking samples of the data by removing at least one data point at random and then constructing a tree for the new data set. This random sampling process is repeated hundreds or thousands of times. The bootstrap value for each node is defined by the percentage of cases in which all species derived from that node appear together in the trees. Bootstrap values above 90 percent are regarded as statistically strongly reliable; those below 70 percent are considered unreliable.

MOLECULAR EVOLUTION

Since the middle of the 20th century, several advancements have increased the scientific understanding of evolution and have allowed the creation of evolutionary histories. The development of gene-sequencing techniques have enabled scientists to explore the complexities and the evolutionary patterns revealed in gene duplications. Today the sequencing of complete genomes of complex organisms occurs.

Furthermore, comparisons of homologous proteins on two given species may enable scientists to create a type of molecular clock. Although statistical studies have determined that the calibration of such a clock to other methods of time-tracking and dating is problematic, it is thought that a molecular clock could calculate the approximate time in which two given species diverged from one another. Some scientists argue that the theoretical foundation of a molecular clock might be supported by the neutrality theory of molecular evolution.

MOLECULAR PHYLOGENY OF GENES

The methods for obtaining the nucleotide sequences of DNA have enormously improved since the 1980s and have become largely automated. Many genes have been sequenced in numerous organisms, and the complete genome has been sequenced in various species ranging from humans to viruses. The use of DNA sequences has been particularly rewarding in the study of gene duplications. The genes that code for the hemoglobins in humans and other mammals provide a good example.

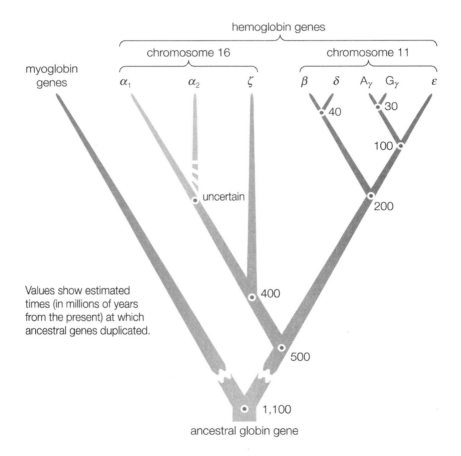

Encyclopædia Britannica, Inc.

Knowledge of the amino acid sequences of the hemo-globin chains and of myoglobin, a closely related protein, has made it possible to reconstruct the evolutionary history of the duplications that gave rise to the corresponding genes. But direct examination of the nucleotide sequences in the genes coding for these proteins has shown that the situation is more complex, and also more interesting, than it appears from the protein sequences.

DNA sequence studies on human hemoglobin genes have shown that their number is greater than previously thought. Hemoglobin molecules are tetramers (molecules made of four subunits), consisting of two polypeptides (relatively short protein chains) of one kind and two of another kind. In embryonic hemoglobin E, one of the two kinds of polypeptide is designated ε; in fetal hemoglogin F, it is γ; in adult hemoglobin A, it is β; and in adult hemo-globin A_2, it is δ. (Hemoglobin A makes up about 98 percent of human adult hemoglobin, and hemoglobin A_2 about 2 percent). The other kind of polypeptide in embry-onic hemoglobin is ζ; in both fetal and adult hemoglobin, it is α. The genes coding for the first group of polypeptides (ε, γ, β, and δ) are located on chromosome 11; the genes coding for the second group of polypeptides (ζ and α) are located on chromosome 16.

There are yet additional complexities. Two γ genes exist (known as Gγ and Aγ), as do two α genes (α_1 and α_2). Furthermore, there are two β pseudogenes ($\psi\beta_1$ and $\psi\beta_2$) and two α pseudogenes ($\psi\alpha_1$ and $\psi\alpha_2$), as well as a ζ pseudo-gene. These pseudogenes are very similar in nucleotide sequence to the corresponding functional genes, but they include terminating codons and other mutations that make it impossible for them to yield functional hemoglobins.

The similarity in the nucleotide sequence of the poly-peptide genes, and pseudogenes, of both the α and β gene families indicates that they are all homologous — that is, that they have arisen through various duplications and subsequent evolution from a gene ancestral to all. Moreover, homology also exists between the nucleotide sequences that separate one gene from another.

MULTIPLICITY AND RATE HETEROGENEITY

Cytochrome c consists of only 104 amino acids, encoded by 312 nucleotides. Nevertheless, this short protein stores enormous evolutionary information, which made possible the fairly good approximation to the evolutionary history of 20 very diverse species over a period longer than one billion years. But cytochrome c is a slowly evolving protein. Widely different species have in common a large proportion of the amino acids in their cytochrome c, which makes possible the study of genetic differences between organisms only remotely related. For the same reason, however, comparing cytochrome c molecules cannot determine evolutionary relationships between closely related species. For example, the amino acid sequence of cytochrome c in humans and chimpanzees is identical, although they diverged about 6 million years ago; between humans and rhesus monkeys, which diverged from their common ancestor 35 million to 40 million years ago, it differs by only one amino acid replacement.

Proteins that evolve more rapidly than cytochrome c can be studied in order to establish phylogenetic relationships between closely related species. Some proteins evolve very fast; the fibrinopeptides — small proteins involved in the blood-clotting process — are suitable for reconstructing the phylogeny of recently evolved species, such as closely related mammals. Other proteins evolve at intermediate rates; the hemoglobins, for example, can be

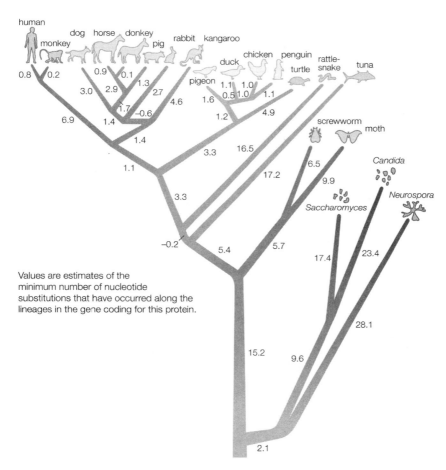

human
dog   horse   donkey
monkey   pig   rabbit   kangaroo
                        duck   chicken   penguin   rattle-
                                              turtle   snake   tuna
0.8   0.2   0.9   0.1   pigeon   1.1   1.0
          3.0   2.9   1.3   1.6   0.5 1.0   1.1
                     1.7   2.7   4.6   1.1
6.9   1.4   -0.6   4.9
                                    1.2
          1.4
                                        3.3   16.5   screwworm
     1.1   moth
                                              17.2   6.5   Candida
          3.3   9.9
                                                        Neurospora
                    -0.2   Saccharomyces
                              5.4   5.7
                                              17.4   23.4

Values are estimates of the
minimum number of nucleotide
substitutions that have occurred along the
lineages in the gene coding for this protein.

28.1

15.2   9.6

2.1

Encyclopædia Britannica, Inc.

used for reconstructing evolutionary history over a fairly
broad range of time (see chart, p. 182).

One great advantage of molecular evolution is its multiplicity, as noted above in the section DNA and protein as
informational macromolecules. Within each organism are
thousands of genes and proteins; these evolve at different
rates, but every one of them reflects the same evolutionary

RATES OF EVOLUTION FOR THREE DIFFERENT PROTEINS

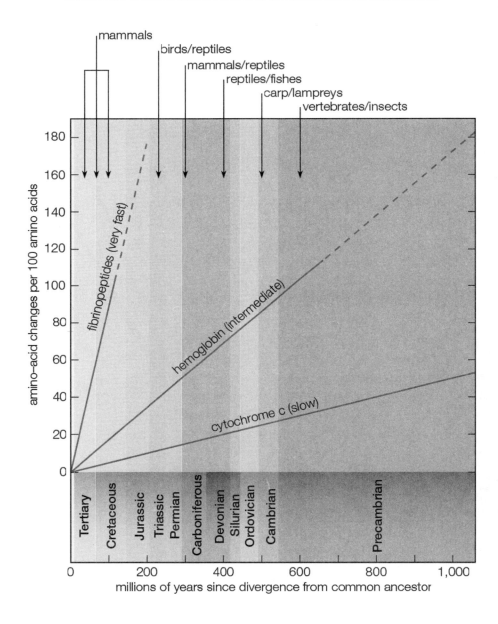

Encyclopædia Britannica, Inc.

events. Scientists can obtain greater and greater accuracy in reconstructing the evolutionary phylogeny of any group of organisms by increasing the number of genes investigated. The range of differences in the rates of evolution between genes opens up the opportunity of investigating different sets of genes for achieving different degrees of resolution in the tree, relying on slowly evolving ones for remote evolutionary events. Even genes that encode slowly evolving proteins can be useful for reconstructing the evolutionary relationships between closely related species, by examination of the redundant codon substitutions (nucleotide substitutions that do not change the encoded amino acids), the introns (noncoding DNA segments interspersed among the segments that code for amino acids), or other noncoding segments of the genes (such as the sequences that precede and follow the encoding portions of genes); these generally evolve much faster than the nucleotides that specify the amino acids.

THE MOLECULAR CLOCK OF EVOLUTION

One conspicuous attribute of molecular evolution is that differences between homologous molecules can readily be quantified and expressed, as, for example, proportions of nucleotides or amino acids that have changed. Rates of evolutionary change can therefore be more precisely established with respect to DNA or proteins than with respect to phenotypic traits of form and function. Studies of molecular evolution rates have led to the proposition that macromolecules may serve as evolutionary clocks.

It was first observed in the 1960s that the numbers of amino acid differences between homologous proteins of any two given species seemed to be nearly proportional to the time of their divergence from a common ancestor. If the rate of evolution of a protein or gene were approximately the same in the evolutionary lineages leading to different species, proteins and DNA sequences would provide a molecular clock of evolution. The sequences could then be used to reconstruct not only the sequence of branching events of a phylogeny but also the time when the various events occurred.

Consider, for example, a 20-organism phylogeny. If the substitution of nucleotides in the gene coding for cytochrome c occurred at a constant rate through time, one could determine the time elapsed along any branch of the phylogeny simply by examining the number of nucleotide substitutions along that branch. One would need only to calibrate the clock by reference to an outside source, such as the fossil record, that would provide the actual geologic time elapsed in at least one specific lineage.

The molecular evolutionary clock, of course, is not expected to be a metronomic clock, like a watch or other timepiece that measures time exactly, but a stochastic clock like radioactive decay. In a stochastic clock the probability of a certain amount of change is constant (for example, a given quantity of atoms of radium-226 is expected, through decay, to be reduced by half in 1,620 years), although some variation occurs in the actual amount of change. Over fairly long periods of time a stochastic clock is quite accurate. The enormous potential of the molecular evolutionary clock lies in the fact that each gene or protein is a separate clock. Each clock "ticks" at a different rate—the rate of evolution characteristic of a particular gene or protein—but each of the thousands and thousands of genes or proteins provides an independent measure of the same evolutionary events.

Evolutionists have found that the amount of variation observed in the evolution of DNA and proteins is greater than is expected from a stochastic clock—in other words, the clock is erratic. The discrepancies in evolutionary rates along different lineages are not excessively large, however. So it is possible, in principle, to time phylogenetic events with as much accuracy as may be desired, but more genes or proteins (about two to four times as many) must be examined than would be required if the clock was stochastically constant. The average rates obtained for several proteins taken together become a fairly precise clock, particularly when many species are studied and the evolutionary events involve long time periods (on the order of 50 million years or longer).

This conclusion is illustrated in the figure on page 181, which plots the cumulative number of nucleotide changes in seven proteins against the dates of divergence of 17 species of mammals (16 pairings) as determined from the fossil record. The overall rate of nucleotide substitution is fairly uniform. Some primate species (the pairs represented by triangular points in the figure) appear to have evolved at a slower rate than the average for the rest of the species. This anomaly occurs because the more recent the divergence of any two species, the more likely it is that the changes observed will depart from the average evolutionary rate. As the length of time increases, periods of rapid and slow evolution in any lineage are likely to cancel one another out.

Evolutionists have discovered, however, that molecular time estimates tend to be systematically older than estimates based on other methods and, indeed, to be older than the actual dates. This is a consequence of the statistical properties of molecular estimates, which are asymmetrically distributed. Because of chance, the number of molecular differences between two species may be larger or smaller than expected. But overestimation errors are unbounded, whereas underestimation errors are bounded, since they cannot be smaller than zero. Consequently, a graph of a typical distribution of estimates of the age when two species diverged, gathered from a number of different genes, is skewed from the normal bell shape, with a large number of estimates of younger age clustered together at one end and a long "tail" of older-age estimates trailing away toward the other end. The average of the estimated times thus will consistently overestimate the true date. The overestimation bias becomes greater when the rate of molecular evolution is slower, the sequences used are shorter, and the time becomes increasingly remote.

THE NEUTRALITY THEORY OF MOLECULAR EVOLUTION

In the late 1960s it was proposed that at the molecular level most evolutionary changes are selectively "neutral," meaning that they are due to genetic drift rather than to natural selection. Nucleotide and amino acid substitutions appear in a population by mutation. If alternative alleles (alternative DNA sequences) have identical fitness—if they are identically able to perform their function—changes in allelic frequency from generation to generation will occur only by genetic drift. Rates of allelic substitution will be stochastically constant—that is, they will occur with a constant probability for a given gene or protein. This constant rate is the mutation rate for neutral alleles.

According to the neutrality theory, a large proportion of all possible mutants at any gene locus are harmful to their carriers. These mutants are eliminated by natural selection, just as standard evolutionary theory postulates. The neutrality theory also agrees that morphological, behavioral, and ecological traits evolve under the control of natural selection. What is distinctive in the theory is the claim that at each gene locus there are several favourable mutants, equivalent to one another with respect to adaptation, so that they are not subject to natural selection among themselves. Which of these mutants increases or decreases in frequency in one or another species is purely a matter of chance, the result of random genetic drift over time.

Neutral alleles are those that differ so little in fitness that their frequencies change by random drift rather than by natural selection. This definition is formally stated as $4N_e s < 1$, where N_e is the effective size of the population and s is the selective coefficient that measures the difference in fitness between the alleles.

Assume that k is the rate of substitution of neutral alleles per unit time in the course of evolution. The time units can be years or generations. In a random-mating population with N diploid individuals, $k = 2Nux$, where u is the neutral mutation rate per gamete per unit time (time measured in the same units as for k) and x is the probability of ultimate fixation of a neutral mutant. The derivation of this equation is straightforward: there are $2Nu$ mutants per time unit, each with a probability x of becoming fixed. In a population of N diploid individuals there are $2N$ genes at each locus, all of them, if they are neutral, with an identical probability, $x = 1/(2N)$, of becoming fixed. If this value of x is substituted in the equation above ($k = 2Nux$), the result is $k = u$. In terms of the theory, then, the rate of substitution of neutral alleles is precisely the rate at which the neutral alleles arise by mutation, independently of the number of individuals in the population or of any other factors.

If the neutrality theory of molecular evolution is strictly correct, it will provide a theoretical foundation for the hypothesis of the molecular evolutionary clock, since the rate of neutral mutation would be expected to remain constant through evolutionary time and in different lineages. The number of amino acid or nucleotide differences between species would, therefore, simply reflect the time elapsed since they shared the last common ancestor.

Evolutionists debate whether the neutrality theory is valid. Tests of the molecular clock hypothesis indicate that the variations in the rates of molecular evolution are substantially larger than would be expected according to the neutrality theory. Other tests have revealed substantial discrepancies between the amount of genetic polymorphism found in populations of a given species and the amount predicted by the theory. But defenders of the theory argue that these discrepancies can be assimilated by modifying the theory somewhat—by assuming, for example, that alleles are not strictly neutral but their differences in selective value are quite small. Be that as it may, the neutrality theory provides a "null hypothesis," or point of departure, for measuring molecular evolution.

CHAPTER 5
NOTABLE EVOLUTIONARY THINKERS

Throughout history many scientists have considered questions of speciation and evolution. The most well-known of these thinkers is Charles Darwin, who developed the modern theory along with fellow British scientist Alfred Russel Wallace. Nevertheless, several other scientists have made notable contributions. Some, such as Jean-Baptiste Lamarck, developed alternative theories of evolution, whereas the work of others, such as T.H. Huxley, helped to mainstream Darwin's theory of evolution. Later, the contributions of Julian Huxley, Theodosius Dobzhansky, Ernst Mayr, and others further solidified Darwin's theory in the sciences by adding evidence from genetics, embryology, and paleontology.

CHARLES DARWIN

(b. Feb. 12, 1809, Shrewsbury, Shropshire, Eng.—d. Apr. 19, 1882, Downe, Kent)

Charles Robert Darwin was an English naturalist whose theory of evolution by natural selection became the foundation of modern evolutionary studies. An affable country gentleman, Darwin at first shocked religious Victorian society by suggesting that animals and humans shared a common ancestry. However, his nonreligious biology appealed to the rising class of professional scientists, and by the time of his death evolutionary imagery had spread through all of science, literature, and politics. Darwin, himself an agnostic, was accorded the ultimate British accolade of burial in Westminster Abbey, London.

Darwin formulated his bold theory in private in 1837–39, after returning from a voyage around the world aboard

Pictured here in this 1887 portrait is British naturalist Charles Darwin (1809—82). Henry Guttmann/Hulton Archive/Getty Images.

HMS *Beagle*, but it was not until two decades later that he finally gave it full public expression in *On the Origin of Species* (1859), a book that has deeply influenced modern Western society and thought.

EARLY LIFE AND EDUCATION

Darwin was the second son of society doctor Robert Waring Darwin and of Susannah Wedgwood, daughter of the Unitarian pottery industrialist Josiah Wedgwood. Darwin's other grandfather, Erasmus Darwin, a freethinking physician and poet fashionable before the French Revolution, was author of *Zoonomia; or, The Laws of Organic Life* (1794–96). Darwin's mother died when he was eight, and he was cared for by his three elder sisters. The boy stood in awe of his overbearing father, whose astute medical observations taught him much about human psychology. But he hated the rote learning of classics at the traditional Anglican Shrewsbury School, where he studied between 1818 and 1825. Science was then considered dehumanizing in English public schools, and for dabbling in chemistry Darwin was condemned by his headmaster (and nicknamed "Gas" by his schoolmates).

His father, considering the 16-year-old a wastrel interested only in game shooting, sent him to study medicine at Edinburgh University in 1825. Later in life, Darwin gave the impression that he had learned little during his two years at Edinburgh. In fact, it was a formative experience. There was no better science education in a British university. He was taught to understand the chemistry of cooling rocks on the primitive Earth and how to classify plants by the modern "natural system." In Edinburgh Museum he was taught to stuff birds by a freed South American slave and to identify the rock strata and colonial flora and fauna.

More crucially, the university's radical students exposed the teenager to the latest Continental sciences. Edinburgh attracted English Dissenters who were barred from graduating at the Anglican universities of Oxford and Cambridge, and at student societies Darwin heard freethinkers deny the divine design of human facial anatomy and argue that animals shared all the human mental faculties. One talk, on the mind as the product of a material brain, was officially censored, for such materialism was considered subversive in the conservative decades after the French Revolution. Darwin was witnessing the social penalties of holding deviant views. As he collected sea slugs and sea pens on nearby shores, he was accompanied by Robert Edmond Grant, a radical evolutionist and disciple of the French biologist Jean-Baptiste Lamarck. An expert on sponges, Grant became Darwin's mentor, teaching him about the growth and relationships of primitive marine invertebrates, which Grant believed held the key to unlocking the mysteries surrounding the origin of more complex creatures. Darwin, encouraged to tackle the larger questions of life through a study of invertebrate zoology, made his own observations on the larval sea mat (*Flustra*) and announced his findings at the student societies.

The young Darwin learned much in Edinburgh's rich intellectual environment, but not medicine: he loathed anatomy, and (pre-chloroform) surgery sickened him. His freethinking father, shrewdly realizing that the church was a better calling for an aimless naturalist, switched him to Christ's College, Cambridge, in 1828. In a complete change of environment, Darwin was now educated as an Anglican gentleman. He took his horse, indulged his drinking, shooting, and beetle-collecting passions with other squires' sons, and managed 10th place in the bachelor of arts degree in 1831. Here he was shown the conservative side of botany by a young professor, the Reverend John Stevens Henslow, while that doyen of providential design in the animal world, the Reverend Adam Sedgwick, took Darwin to Wales in 1831 on a geologic field trip.

Fired by Alexander von Humboldt's account of the South American jungles in his *Personal Narrative of Travels*, Darwin jumped at Henslow's suggestion of a voyage to Tierra del Fuego, at the southern tip of South America, aboard a rebuilt brig, HMS *Beagle*. Darwin would not sail as a lowly surgeon-naturalist but as a self-financed gentleman companion to the 26-year-old captain, Robert Fitzroy, an aristocrat who feared the loneliness of command. Fitzroy's was to be an imperial-evangelical voyage: he planned to survey coastal Patagonia to facilitate British trade and return three "savages" previously brought to England from Tierra del Fuego and Christianized. Darwin equipped himself with weapons, books (Fitzroy gave him the first volume of *Principles of Geology*, by Charles Lyell), and advice on preserving carcasses from London Zoo's experts. The *Beagle* sailed from England on Dec. 27, 1831.

THE *BEAGLE* VOYAGE

The circumnavigation of the globe would be the making of the 22-year-old Darwin. Five years of physical hardship and mental rigour, imprisoned within a ship's walls, offset by wide-open opportunities in the Brazilian jungles and the Andes Mountains, were to give Darwin a new seriousness. As a gentleman naturalist, he could leave the ship for extended periods, pursuing his own interests. As a result, he spent only 18 months of the voyage aboard the ship.

The hardship was immediate: a tormenting seasickness. And so was his questioning: on calm days Darwin's plankton-filled townet left him wondering why beautiful creatures teemed in the ocean's vastness, where no human could appreciate them. On the Cape Verde Islands (January 1832), the sailor saw bands of oyster shells running through local rocks, suggesting that Lyell was right in his geologic speculations and that the land was rising in places, falling in others. At Bahia (now Salvador), Brazil, the luxuriance of the rainforest left Darwin's mind in "a chaos of delight." But that mind, with its Wedgwood-abolitionist characteristics, was revolted by the local slavery. For Darwin, so often alone, the tropical forests seemed to compensate for human evils: months were spent in Rio de Janeiro amid this shimmering tropical splendour, full of "gaily-coloured" flatworms, and the collector himself became "red-hot with Spiders." But nature had its own evils, and Darwin always remembered with a shudder the parasitic ichneumon wasp, which stored caterpillars to be eaten alive by its grubs. He would later consider this evidence against the beneficent design of nature.

On the River Plate (Río de la Plata) in July 1832, he found Montevideo, Uruguay, in a state of rebellion and joined armed sailors to retake the rebel-held fort. At Bahía Blanca, Argentina, gauchos told him of their extermination of the Pampas "Indians." Beneath the veneer of human civility, genocide seemed the rule on the frontier, a conclusion reinforced by Darwin's meeting with General Juan Manuel de Rosas and his "villainous Banditti-like army," in charge of eradicating the natives. For a sensitive young man, fresh from Christ's College, this was disturbing. His contact with "untamed" humans on Tierra del Fuego in December 1832 unsettled him more. How great, wrote Darwin, the "difference between savage & civilized man is.—It is greater than between a wild & [a] domesticated animal." God had evidently created humans in a vast cultural range, and yet, judging by the Christianized savages aboard, even the "lowest" races were capable of improvement. Darwin was tantalized, and always he niggled for explanations.

His fossil discoveries raised more questions. Darwin's periodic trips over two years to the cliffs at Bahía Blanca and farther south at Port St. Julian yielded huge bones of extinct mammals. Darwin manhandled skulls, femurs, and armour plates back to the ship—relics, he assumed, of rhinoceroses, mastodons, cow-size armadillos, and giant ground sloths. He unearthed a horse-size mammal with a long face like an anteater's, and he returned from a 550-km (340-mile) ride to Mercedes near the Uruguay River with a skull 71 cm (28 inches) long strapped to his horse. Fossil extraction became a romance for Darwin. It pushed him into thinking of the primeval world and what had caused these giant beasts to die out.

The land was evidently changing, rising; Darwin's observations in the Andes Mountains confirmed it. After the *Beagle* surveyed the Falkland Islands, and after Darwin had packed away at Port Desire (Puerto Deseado), Argentina, the partially gnawed bones of a new species of small rhea, the ship sailed up the west coast of South America to Valparaíso, Chile. Here Darwin climbed 1,200 metres (4,000 feet) into the Andean foothills and marveled at the forces that could raise such mountains. The forces themselves became tangible when he saw volcanic Mount Osorno erupt on Jan. 15, 1835. Then in Valdivia, Chile, on February 20, as he lay on a forest floor, the ground shook: the violence of the earthquake and ensuing tidal wave was enough to destroy the great city of Concepción, whose rubble Darwin walked through. But what intrigued him was the seemingly insignificant: the local mussel beds, all dead, were now lying above high tide. The land had risen: Lyell, taking the uniformitarian position, had argued that geologic formations were the result of steady cumulative forces of the sort we see today. And Darwin had seen them. The continent was thrusting itself up, a few feet at a time. He imagined the eons it had taken to raise the fossilized trees in sandstone (once seashore mud) to 2,100 metres (7,000 feet), where he found them. Darwin began thinking in terms of deep time.

They left Peru on the circumnavigation home in September 1835. First Darwin landed on the "frying hot" Galapagos Islands. These were volcanic prison islands, crawling with marine iguanas and giant tortoises. (Darwin and the crew brought small tortoises aboard as pets, to join their coatis from Peru.) Contrary to legend, these islands never provided Darwin's "eureka" moment. Although he noted that the mockingbirds differed on four islands and tagged his specimens accordingly, he failed to label his other birds—what he thought were wrens, "gross-beaks," finches, and oriole-relatives—by island. Nor did Darwin collect tortoise specimens, even though local prisoners believed that each island had its distinct race.

The "home-sick heroes" returned via Tahiti, New Zealand, and Australia. By April 1836, when the *Beagle* made the Cocos (Keeling) Islands in the Indian Ocean—Fitzroy's brief being to see if coral reefs sat on mountain tops—Darwin already had his theory of reef formation. He imagined (correctly) that these reefs grew on sinking mountain rims. The delicate coral built up, compensating for the drowning land, so as to remain within optimal heat and lighting conditions. At the Cape of Good Hope, Darwin talked with the astronomer Sir John Herschel, possibly about Lyell's gradual geologic evolution and perhaps about how it entailed a new problem, the "mystery of mysteries," the simultaneous change of fossil life.

On the last leg of the voyage Darwin finished his 770-page diary, wrapped up 1,750 pages of notes, drew up 12 catalogs of his 5,436 skins, bones, and carcasses—and still he wondered: Was each Galapagos mockingbird a naturally produced variety? Why did ground sloths become extinct? He sailed home with problems enough to last him a lifetime. When he landed in October 1836, the vicarage had faded, the gun had given way to the notebook, and the supreme theorizer—who would always move from small causes to big outcomes—had the courage to look beyond the conventions of his own Victorian culture for new answers.

Evolution by Natural Selection: The London Years, 1836–42

With his voyage over and with a £400 annual allowance from his father, Darwin now settled down among the urban gentry as a gentleman geologist. He befriended Lyell, and he discussed the rising Chilean coastline as a new fellow of the Geological Society in January 1837 (he was secretary of the society by 1838). Darwin became well known through his diary's publication as *Journal of Researches into the Geology and Natural History of the Various Countries Visited by H.M.S. Beagle* (1839). With a £1,000 Treasury grant, obtained through the Cambridge network, he employed the best experts and published their descriptions of his specimens in his *Zoology of the Voyage of H.M.S. Beagle* (1838–43). Darwin's star had risen, and he was now lionized in London.

It was in these years of civil unrest following the First Reform Act (1832) that Darwin devised his theory of evolution. Radical Dissenters were denouncing the church's monopoly on power—attacking an Anglican status quo that rested on miraculous props: the supposed supernatural creation of life and society. Darwin had Unitarian roots, and his breathless notes show how his radical Dissenting understanding of equality and antislavery framed his image of mankind's place in nature: "Animals—whom we have made our slaves we do not like to consider our equals.—Do not slave holders wish to make the black man

THE

ZOOLOGY

OF

THE VOYAGE OF H.M.S. BEAGLE,

UNDER THE COMMAND OF CAPTAIN FITZROY, R.N.,

DURING THE YEARS

1832 TO 1836.

PUBLISHED WITH THE APPROVAL OF
THE LORDS COMMISSIONERS OF HER MAJESTY'S TREASURY.

Edited and Superintended by
CHARLES DARWIN, ESQ. M.A. F.R.S. SEC. G.S.
NATURALIST TO THE EXPEDITION.

PART I.

FOSSIL MAMMALIA:

BY
RICHARD OWEN, ESQ. F.R.S.
PROFESSOR OF ANATOMY AND PHYSIOLOGY TO THE ROYAL COLLEGE OF SURGEONS IN LONDON ;
CORRESPONDING MEMBER OF THE INSTITUTE OF FRANCE, ETC. ETC.

LONDON:

PUBLISHED BY SMITH, ELDER AND CO. 65, CORNHILL.
MDCCCXL.

Zoology: The Voyage of H.M.S. Beagle Under the Command of Captain Fitzroy, R.N. *was edited by Charles Darwin, who eventually went on to write the groundbreaking* On the Origin of Species. SSPL via Getty Images.

other kind?" Some radicals questioned whether each animal was uniquely "designed" by God when all vertebrates shared a similar structural plan. The polymathic Charles Babbage—of calculating machine fame—made God a divine programmer, preordaining life by means of natural law rather than ad hoc miracle. It was the ultra-Whig way, and in 1837 Darwin, an impeccable Whig reformer who enjoyed Babbage's soirees, likewise accepted that "the Creator creates by . . . laws."

The experts' findings sent Darwin to more heretical depths. At the Royal College of Surgeons, the eminent anatomist Richard Owen found that Darwin's Uruguay River skull belonged to *Toxodon*, a hippotamus-size antecedent of the South American capybara. The Pampas fossils were nothing like rhinoceroses and mastodons; they were huge extinct armadillos, anteaters, and sloths, which suggested that South American mammals had been replaced by their own kind according to some unknown "law of succession." At the Zoological Society, ornithologist John Gould announced that the Galapagos birds were not a mixture of wrens, finches, and "gross-beaks" but were all ground finches, differently adapted. When Gould diagnosed the Galapagos mockingbirds as three species, unique to different islands, in March 1837, Darwin examined Fitzroy's collection to discover that each island had its representative finch as well. But how had they all diverged from mainland colonists? By this time Darwin was living near his freethinking brother, Erasmus, in London's West End, and their dissident dining circle, which included the Unitarian Harriet Martineau, provided the perfect milieu for Darwin's ruminations. Darwin adopted "transmutation" (evolution, as it is now called), perhaps because of his familiarity with it through the work of his grandfather and Robert Grant. Nonetheless, it was abominated by the Cambridge clerics as a bestial, if not blasphemous, heresy that would corrupt mankind and destroy the spiritual safeguards of the social order. Thus began Darwin's double life, which would last for two decades.

For two years he filled notebooks with jottings. There was an intensity and doggedness to it. He searched for the causes of extinction, accepted life as a branching tree (not a series of escalators, the old idea), tackled island isolation, and wondered whether variations appeared gradually or at a stroke. He dismissed a Lamarckian force driving life inexorably upward with the cavalier joke, "If all men were dead then monkeys make men. — Men make angels," which showed how little the failed ordinand shared his Cambridge mentors' hysteria about an ape ancestry. Indeed, there was no "upward": he became relativistic, sensing that life was spreading outward into niches, not standing on a ladder. There was no way of ranking humans and bees, no yardstick of "highness": man was no longer the crown of creation.

Heart palpitations and stomach problems were affecting him by September 1837. Stress sent him to the Highlands of Scotland in 1838, where he diverted himself studying the "parallel roads" of Glen Roy, so like the raised beaches in Chile. But the sickness returned as he continued chipping at the scientific bedrock of a cleric-dominated society. The "whole [miraculous] fabric totters & falls," he jotted. Darwin had a right to be worried. Were his secret discovered, he would stand accused of social abandon. At Edinburgh he had seen censorship; other materialists were being publicly disgraced. His notes began mooting disarming ploys: "Mention persecution of early astronomers." Behind his respectable facade at the Geological Society lay a new contempt for the divines' providential shortsightedness. The president, the Reverend William Whewell, "says length of days adapted to duration of sleep of man.!!!" he jotted. What "arrogance!!"

Mankind: there was the crux. Darwin wrote humans and society into the evolutionary equation from the start. He saw the social instincts of troop animals developing into morality and studied the humanlike behaviour of orangutans at the zoo. With avant-garde society radicalized, Darwin moved into his own ultraradical phase in 1838 — even suggesting that belief in God was an ingrained tribal survival strategy: "love of [the] deity [is an] effect of [the brain's] organization. Oh you Materialist!" he mocked himself. In a day when a gentleman's character had to be above reproach, Darwin's notes had a furtive ring. None of this could become known—yet. The rich careerist— admitted to the prestigious Athenaeum Club in 1838 and the Royal Society in 1839 — had too much to lose.

As a sporting gent from the shires, Darwin queried breeders about the way they changed domestic dogs and fancy pigeons by spotting slight variations and accentuating them through breeding. But he only saw the complete congruity between the way nature operated and the way fanciers produced new breeds upon reading the economist Thomas Malthus's *Essay on the Principle of Population* in September 1838. This was a seminal moment—even if Malthusian ideas had long permeated his Whig circle. Darwin was living through a workhouse revolution. Malthus had said that there would always be too many mouths to feed—population increases geometrically, whereas food production rises arithmetically—and that charity was useless. So the Whigs had passed a Malthusian Poor Law in 1834 and were incarcerating sick paupers in workhouses (separating men from women to stop them from breeding). Darwin's dining companion Harriet Martineau (whom many expected to marry his brother, Erasmus), was the Whigs' poor law propagandist. (Her novelistic Malthusian pamphlets had been sent to Darwin while he was on the *Beagle*.) Darwin realized that

NEW THINKING ABOUT EVOLUTION

population explosions would lead to a struggle for resources and that the ensuing competition would weed out the unfit. It was an idea he now applied to nature (he had previously thought that animal populations remained stable in the wild). Darwin called his modified Malthusian mechanism "natural selection." Nature was equally uncharitable, went the argument: overpopulated, it experienced a fierce struggle, and from all manner of chance variations, good and bad, the best, "the surviving one of ten thousand trials," won out, endured, and thus passed on its improved trait. This was the way a species kept pace with the Lyellian evolution of the Earth.

Darwin was a born list maker. In 1838 he even totted up the pros and cons of taking a wife—and married his cousin Emma Wedgwood (1808–96) in 1839. He rashly confided his thoughts on evolution, evidently shocking her. By now, Darwin accepted the notion that even mental traits and instincts were randomly varying, that they were the stuff for selection. But he saw from Emma's reaction that he must publicly camouflage his views. Although the randomness and destructiveness of his evolutionary system—with thousands dying so that the "fittest" might survive—left little room for a personally operating benign deity, Darwin still believed that God was the ultimate lawgiver of the universe. In 1839 he shut his last major evolution notebook, his theory largely complete.

THE SQUIRE NATURALIST IN DOWNE

Darwin drafted a 35-page sketch of his theory of natural selection in 1842 and expanded it in 1844, but he had no immediate intention of publishing it. He wrote Emma a letter in 1844 requesting that, if he died, she should pay an editor £400 to publish the work. Perhaps he wanted to die first. In 1842, Darwin, increasingly shunning society, had moved the family to the isolated village of Downe, in Kent, at the "extreme edge of [the] world." (It was in fact only 26 km [16 miles] from central London.) Here, living in a former parsonage, Down House, he emulated the lifestyle of his clerical friends. Fearing prying eyes, he even lowered the road outside his house. His seclusion was complete: from now on he ran his days like clockwork, with set periods for walking, napping, reading, and nightly backgammon. He fulfilled his parish responsibilities, eventually helping to run the local Coal and Clothing Club for the labourers. His work hours were given over to bees, flowers, and barnacles and to his books on coral reefs and South American geology, three of which in 1842–46 secured his reputation as a career geologist.

He rarely mentioned his secret. When he did, notably to the Kew Gardens botanist Joseph Dalton Hooker, Darwin said that believing in evolution was "like confessing a murder." The analogy with this capital offense was not so strange: seditious atheists were using evolution as part of their weaponry against Anglican oppression and were being jailed for blasphemy. Darwin, nervous and nauseous, trying spas and quack remedies (even tying plate batteries to his heaving stomach), understood the conservative clerical morality. He was sensitive to the offense he might cause. He was also immensely wealthy: by the late 1840s the Darwins had £80,000 invested; he was an absentee landlord of two large Lincolnshire farms; and in the 1850s he plowed tens of thousands of pounds into railway shares. Even though his theory, with its capitalist and meritocratic emphasis, was quite unlike anything touted by the radicals and rioters, these turbulent years were no time to break cover.

From 1846 to 1854, Darwin added to his credibility as an expert on species by pursuing a detailed study of all known barnacles. Intrigued by their sexual differentiation, he discovered that some females had tiny degenerate males clinging to them. This sparked his interest in the evolution of diverging male and female forms from an original hermaphrodite creature. Four monographs on such an obscure group made him a world expert and gained him the Royal Society's Royal Medal in 1853. No longer could he be dismissed as a speculator on biological matters.

ON THE ORIGIN OF SPECIES

England became quieter and more prosperous in the 1850s, and by mid-decade the professionals were taking over, instituting exams and establishing a meritocracy. The changing social composition of science—typified by the rise of the freethinking biologist Thomas Henry Huxley—promised a better reception for Darwin. Huxley, the philosopher Herbert Spencer, and other outsiders were opting for a secular nature in the rationalist *Westminster Review* and deriding the influence of "parsondom." Darwin had himself lost the last shreds of his belief in Christianity with the tragic death of his oldest daughter, Annie, from typhoid in 1851.

The world was becoming safer for Darwin and his theory: mid-Victorian England was stabler than the "hungry Thirties" or turbulent 1840s. In 1854 he solved his last major problem, the forking of genera to produce new evolutionary branches. He used an industrial analogy familiar from the Wedgwood factories, the division of labour: competition in nature's overcrowded marketplace would favour variants that could exploit different aspects of a niche. Species would diverge on the spot, like tradesmen in the same tenement. Through 1855 Darwin experimented with seeds in seawater, to prove that they could survive ocean crossings to start the process of speciation on islands. Then he kept fancy pigeons, to see if the chicks were more like the ancestral rock dove than their own bizarre parents. Darwin perfected his analogy of natural selection with the fancier's "artificial selection," as he called it. He was preparing his rhetorical strategy, ready to present his theory.

After speaking to Huxley and Hooker at Downe in April 1856, Darwin began writing a triple-volume book, tentatively called *Natural Selection*, which was designed to crush the opposition with a welter of facts. Darwin now had immense scientific and social authority, and his place in the parish was assured when he was sworn in as a justice of the peace in 1857. Encouraged by Lyell, Darwin continued writing through the birth of his 10th and last child, the mentally retarded Charles Waring Darwin (born in 1856, when Emma was 48). Whereas in the 1830s Darwin had thought that species remained perfectly adapted until the environment changed, he now believed that every new variation was imperfect, and that perpetual struggle was the rule. He also explained the evolution of sterile worker bees in 1857. These could not be selected because they did not breed, so he opted for "family" selection (kin selection, as it is known today): the whole colony benefited from their retention.

Darwin had finished a quarter of a million words by June 18, 1858. That day he received a letter from Alfred Russel Wallace, an English socialist and specimen collector working in the Malay Archipelago, sketching a similar-looking theory. Darwin, fearing loss of priority, accepted Lyell's and Hooker's solution: they read joint extracts from Darwin's and Wallace's works at the Linnean Society on July 1, 1858. Darwin was away, sick, grieving for his tiny son who had died from scarlet fever, and thus he missed the first public presentation of the theory of natural selection. It was an absenteeism that would mark his later years.

An abstract of an Essay
on the

Origin
of
Species and Varieties

Through natural Selection
by

Charles Darwin M. A

Fellow of the Royal, Geological & Linn. Soc.

London

1859

Darwin hastily began an "abstract" of *Natural Selection*, which grew into a more accessible book, *On the Origin of Species by Means of Natural Selection, or the Preservation of Favoured Races in the Struggle for Life*. Suffering from a terrible bout of nausea, Darwin, now 50, was secreted away at a spa on the desolate Yorkshire moors when the book was sold to the trade on Nov. 22, 1859. He still feared the worst and sent copies to the experts with self-effacing letters ("how you will long to crucify me alive"). It was like "living in Hell," he said about these months.

The book did distress his Cambridge patrons, but they were marginal to science now. However, radical Dissenters were sympathetic, as were the rising London biologists and geologists, even if few actually adopted Darwin's cost-benefit approach to nature. The newspapers drew the one conclusion that Darwin had specifically avoided: that humans had evolved from apes, and that Darwin was denying mankind's immortality. A sensitive Darwin, making no personal appearances, let Huxley, by now a good friend, manage this part of the debate. The pugnacious Huxley, who loved public argument as much as Darwin loathed it, had his own reasons for taking up the cause, and did so with enthusiasm. He wrote three reviews of *Origin of Species*, defended human evolution at the Oxford meeting of the British Association for the Advancement of Science in 1860 (when Bishop Samuel Wilberforce jokingly asked whether the apes were on Huxley's grandmother's or grandfather's side), and published his own book on human evolution, *Evidence as to Man's Place in Nature* (1863). What

The facing page, written in Charles Darwin's own hand, reads "An Abstract on an Essay on the Origin of Species and Varieties through Natural Selection." The abstract eventually became Darwin's most influential work.
Hulton Archive/Getty Images.

Huxley championed was Darwin's evolutionary naturalism, his nonmiraculous assumptions, which pushed biological science into previously taboo areas and increased the power of Huxley's professionals. And it was they who gained the Royal Society's Copley Medal for Darwin in 1864.

Huxley's reaction, with its enthusiasm for evolution and cooler opinion of natural selection, was typical. Natural selection—the "law of higgledy-piggledy" in Herschel's dismissive words—received little support in Darwin's day. By contrast, evolution itself ("descent," Darwin called it—the word *evolution* would only be introduced in the last, 1872, edition of the *Origin*) was being acknowledged from British Association platforms by 1866. That year, too, Darwin met his German admirer, the zoologist Ernst Haeckel, whose proselytizing would spread *Darwinismus* through the Prussian world. Two years later the king of Prussia conferred on Darwin the order *Pour le Mérite*.

The Patriarch in His Home Laboratory

Long periods of debilitating sickness in the 1860s left the craggy, bearded Darwin thin and ravaged. He once vomited for 27 consecutive days. Down House was an infirmary where illness was the norm and Emma the attendant nurse. She was a shield, protecting the patriarch, cosseting him. Darwin was a typical Victorian in his racial and sexual stereotyping—however dependent on his redoubtable wife, he still thought women inferior; and although a fervent abolitionist, he still considered blacks a lower race. But few outside of the egalitarian socialists challenged these prejudices—and Darwin, immersed in a competitive Whig culture, and enshrining its values in his science, had no time for socialism.

The house was also a laboratory, where Darwin continued experimenting and revamping the *Origin* through six editions. Although quietly swearing by "my deity 'Natural Selection,'" he answered critics by reemphasizing other causes of change—for example, the effects of continued use of an organ—and he bolstered the Lamarckian belief that such alterations through excessive use might be passed on. In *Variation of Animals and Plants under Domestication* (1868) he marshaled the facts and explored the causes of variation in domestic breeds. The book answered critics such as George Douglas Campbell, the eighth duke of Argyll, who loathed Darwin's blind, accidental process of variation and envisaged the appearance of "new births" as goal directed. By showing that fanciers picked from the gamut of naturally occurring variations to produce the tufts and topknots on their fancy pigeons, Darwin undermined this providential explanation.

In 1867 the engineer Fleeming Jenkin argued that any single favourable variation would be swamped and lost by back-breeding within the general population. No mechanism was known for inheritance, and so in the *Variation* Darwin devised his hypothesis of "pangenesis" to explain the discrete inheritance of traits. He imagined that each tissue of an organism threw out tiny "gemmules," which passed to the sex organs and permitted copies of themselves to be made in the next generation. But Darwin's cousin Francis Galton failed to find these gemmules in rabbit blood, and the theory was dismissed.

Darwin was adept at flanking movements in order to get around his critics. He would take seemingly intractable subjects—like orchid flowers—and make them test cases for "natural selection." Hence the book that appeared after the *Origin* was, to everyone's surprise, *The Various Contrivances by which British and Foreign Orchids are Fertilised by Insects* (1862). He showed that the orchid's beauty was not a piece of floral whimsy "designed" by God to please humans but honed by selection to attract insect cross-pollinators.

The petals guided the bees to the nectaries, and pollen sacs were deposited exactly where they could be removed by a stigma of another flower.

But why the importance of cross-pollination? Darwin's botanical work was always subtly related to his evolutionary mechanism. He believed that cross-pollinated plants would produce fitter offspring than self-pollinators, and he used considerable ingenuity in conducting thousands of crossings to prove the point. The results appeared in *The Effects of Cross and Self Fertilization in the Vegetable Kingdom* (1876). His next book, *The Different Forms of Flowers on Plants of the Same Species* (1877), was again the result of long-standing work into the way evolution in some species favoured different male and female forms of flowers to facilitate outbreeding. Darwin had long been sensitive to the effects of inbreeding because he was himself married to a Wedgwood cousin, as was his sister Caroline. He agonized over its debilitating consequence for his five sons. Not that he need have worried, for they fared well: William became a banker, Leonard an army major, George the Plumian Professor of Astronomy at Cambridge, Francis a reader in botany at Cambridge, and Horace a scientific instrument maker. Darwin also studied insectivorous plants, climbing plants, and the response of plants to gravity and light (sunlight, he thought, activated something in the shoot tip, an idea that guided future work on growth hormones in plants).

THE PRIVATE MAN AND THE PUBLIC DEBATE

Through the 1860s natural selection was already being applied to the growth of society. A.R. Wallace saw cooperation strengthening the moral bonds within primitive tribes. Advocates of social Darwinism, in contrast, complained that modern civilization was protecting the "unfit" from natural selection. Francis Galton argued that particular character traits—even drunkenness and genius—were inherited and that "eugenics," as it would come to be called, would stop the genetic drain. The trend to explain the evolution of human races, morality, and civilization was capped by Darwin in his two-volume *The Descent of Man, and Selection in Relation to Sex* (1871). The book was authoritative, annotated, and heavily anecdotal in places. The two volumes were discrete, the first discussing the evolution of civilization and human origins among the Old World monkeys. (Darwin's depiction of a hairy human ancestor with pointed ears led to a spate of caricatures.) The second volume responded to critics like Argyll, who doubted that the iridescent hummingbird's plumage had any function—or any Darwinian explanation. Darwin argued that female birds were choosing mates for their gaudy plumage. Darwin as usual tapped his huge correspondence network of breeders, naturalists, and travelers worldwide to produce evidence for this. Such "sexual selection" happened among humans too. With primitive societies accepting diverse notions of beauty, aesthetic preferences, he believed, could account for the origin of the human races.

Darwin's explanation was also aimed partly at Wallace. Like so many disillusioned socialists, Wallace had become engaged in spiritualism. He argued that an overdeveloped human brain had been provided by the spirit forces to move humanity toward millennial perfection. Darwin had no time for this. Even though he eventually attended a séance with Galton and the novelist George Eliot (Marian Evans) at his brother's house in 1874, he was appalled at "such rubbish," and in 1876 he sent £10 toward the costs of the prosecution of the medium Henry Slade.

Darwin finished another long-standing line of work. Since studying the moody orangutans at London Zoo in 1838, through the births of his 10 children (whose facial contortions he duly noted), Darwin had been fascinated by expression. As a student he had heard the attacks on the idea that peoples' facial muscles were designed by God to express their unique thoughts. Now his photographically illustrated *The Expression of the Emotions in Man and Animals* (1872) expanded the subject to include the rages and grimaces of asylum inmates, all to show the continuity of emotions and expressions between humans and animals.

The gentle Darwin elicited tremendous devotion. A protective circle formed around him, locked tight by Huxley and Hooker. It was they who ostracized detractors, particularly the Roman Catholic zoologist St. George Jackson Mivart. Nor did Darwin forget it: he helped raise £2,100 to send a fatigued Huxley on holiday in 1873, and his pestering resulted in the impecunious Wallace being added to the Civil List in 1881. Darwin was held in awe by many, the more so because he was rarely seen. And when he was seen—for example, by the Harvard philosopher John Fiske, a privileged visitor to Down House in 1873— he was found to be "the dearest, sweetest, loveliest old grandpa that ever was."

Darwin wrote his autobiography between 1876 and 1881. It was composed for his grandchildren, rather than for publication, and it was particularly candid on his dislike of Christian myths of eternal torment. To people who inquired about his religious beliefs, however, he would only say that he was an agnostic.

The treadmill of experiment and writing gave so much meaning to his life. But as he wrapped up his final, long-term interest, publishing *The Formation of Vegetable Mould, Through the Action of Worms* (1881), the future looked bleak. Such an earthy subject was typical Darwin: just as he had shown that today's ecosystems were built by infinitesimal degrees and the mighty Andes by tiny uplifts, so he ended on the monumental transformation of landscapes by the Earth's humblest denizens.

Suffering from angina, he looked forward to joining the worms, contemplating "Down graveyard as the sweetest place on earth." He had a seizure in March 1882 and died of a heart attack on April 19. Influential groups wanted a grander commemoration than a funeral in Downe, something better for the gentleman naturalist who had delivered the "new Nature" into the new professionals' hands. Galton had the Royal Society request the family's permission for a state burial. Huxley, who by taking over the public debate had preserved Darwin's reputation of "sweet and gentle nature blossomed into perfection," as a newspaper put it, convinced the canon of Westminster Abbey to bury the diffident agnostic there. And so Darwin was laid to rest with full ecclesiastical pomp on Apr. 26, 1882, attended by the new nobility of science and the state.

RICHARD DAWKINS

(b. Mar. 26, 1941, Nairobi, Kenya)

Clinton Richard Dawkins, a British evolutionary biologist and popular-science writer, emphasized the gene as the driving force of evolution and generated significant controversy with his enthusiastic advocacy of atheism.

Dawkins spent his early childhood in Kenya, where his father was stationed during World War II. The family returned to England in 1949. In 1959 Dawkins entered Balliol College, University of Oxford, where he received a bachelor's degree in zoology in 1962. He remained at Oxford, earning his master's and doctorate degrees in zoology in 1966 under famed ethologist Nikolaas Tinbergen. Dawkins assisted Tinbergen before becoming an assistant professor of zoology (1967–69) at the University of California, Berkeley. He returned to Oxford to lecture in zoology in 1970.

In 1976 he published his first book, *The Selfish Gene*, in which he tried to rectify what he maintained was a widespread misunderstanding of Darwinism. Dawkins argued that natural selection takes place at the genetic rather than the species or individual level, as was often assumed. Genes, he maintained, use the bodies of living things to further their own survival. He also introduced the concept of "memes," the cultural equivalent of genes. Ideas and concepts, from fashion to music, take on a life of their own within society and, by propagating and mutating from mind to mind, affect the progress of human evolution. Dawkins named the concept after the Greek word *mimeme*, meaning "to imitate." It later spawned an entire field of study called memetics. The book was notable not just because of what it espoused but also because of its approachable style, which made it accessible to a popular audience.

More books followed, including *The Extended Phenotype* (1982), *The Blind Watchmaker* (1986), which won the Royal Society of Literature Award in 1987, and *River Out of Eden* (1995). Dawkins particularly sought to address a growing misapprehension of what exactly Darwinian natural selection entailed in *Climbing Mount Improbable* (1996). Stressing the gradual nature of response to selective pressures, Dawkins took care to point out that intricate structures such as the eye do not manifest randomly but instead successively increase in sophistication. He also released *The Evolution of Life* (1996), an interactive CD-ROM with which users could create "biomorphs," computer-simulated examples of evolution first introduced in *The Blind Watchmaker*.

Dawkins was named the first Charles Simonyi Professor of Public Understanding of Science at Oxford

British biological theorist Richard Dawkins.
Jens-Ulrich Koch/AFP/Getty Images.

(1995–2008). In that capacity he continued to publish pro-lifically and produced an array of television programs. His 1996 documentary *Break the Science Barrier* featured Dawkins conversing with an array of prominent scientists about their discoveries. In *Unweaving the Rainbow* (1998), Dawkins contended that evolutionary theory is aestheti-cally superior to supernatural explanations of the world. *The Ancestor's Tale* (2004), structured after Geoffrey Chaucer's *The Canterbury Tales*, traced the human branch of the phylogenetic tree back to points where it converges with the evolution of other species.

Though much of Dawkins's oeuvre generated debate for asserting the supremacy of science over religion in explaining the world, nothing matched the response to the polemical *The God Delusion* (2006). The book relentlessly points out the logical fallacies in religious belief and ulti-mately concludes that the laws of probability preclude the existence of an omnipotent creator. Dawkins used the book as a platform to launch the Richard Dawkins Foundation for Reason and Science (2006), an organiza-tion that, in dual American and British incarnations, sought to foster the acceptance of atheism and championed scientific answers to existential questions. Along with fellow atheists Christopher Hitchens, Sam Harris, and Daniel C. Dennett, he embarked on a campaign of lectures and public debates proselytizing and defending a secular worldview. Dawkins launched the Out Campaign in 2007 in order to urge atheists to publicly declare their beliefs.

In addition to promoting his organization through its Web site and YouTube channel, Dawkins produced several more television documentaries, variously declaiming the problems created by religion and superstition in *The Root of All Evil* (2006) and *The Enemies of Reason* (2007) and celebrating the achievements of Darwin in *The Genius of Charles Darwin* (2008). Dawkins was named a fellow of the

Royal Society in 2001. He also edited *The Oxford Book of Modern Science Writing* (2008).

THEODOSIUS DOBZHANSKY

(b. Jan. 25, 1900, Nemirov, Ukraine, Russian Empire [now in Ukraine]—d. Dec. 18, 1975, Davis, Calif., U.S.)

The work of Ukrainian-American geneticist and evolutionist Theodosius Dobzhansky had a major influence on 20th-century thought and research on genetics and evolutionary theory.

The son of a mathematics teacher, Dobzhansky (original name Feodosy Grigorevich Dobrzhansky) attended the University of Kiev (1917–21), where he remained to teach. In 1924 he moved to Leningrad (now St. Petersburg).

In 1927 Dobzhansky went to Columbia University in New York City as a Rockefeller Fellow to work with the geneticist Thomas Hunt Morgan. He accompanied Morgan to the California Institute of Technology in Pasadena and, on being offered a teaching position there, decided to remain in the United States, becoming a citizen in 1937. He returned to Columbia as a professor of zoology in 1940, remaining until 1962, and then moved to Rockefeller Institute (later Rockefeller University). After his official retirement, Dobzhansky went in 1971 to the University of California at Davis.

Between 1920 and 1935, mathematicians and experimentalists began laying the groundwork for a theory combining Darwinian evolution and Mendelian genetics. Starting his career about this time, Dobzhansky was involved in the project almost from its inception. His book *Genetics and the Origin of Species* (1937) was the first substantial synthesis of the subjects and established evolutionary genetics as an independent discipline. Until the 1930s, the commonly held view was that natural selection produced something close to the best of all possible worlds and that changes would be rare and slow and not apparent over one life span, in agreement with the observed constancy of species over historical time.

Dobzhansky's most important contribution was to change this view. In observing wild populations of the vinegar fly *Drosophila pseudo obscura,* he found extensive genetic variability. Furthermore, about 1940 evidence accumulated that in a given local population some genes would regularly change in frequency with the seasons of the year. For example, a certain gene might appear in 40 percent of all individuals in the population in the spring, increase to 60 percent by late summer at the expense of other genes at the same locus, and return to 40 percent in overwintering flies. Compared to a generation time of about one month, these changes were rapid and effected very large differences in reproductive fitness of the various types under different climatic conditions. Other experiments showed that, in fact, flies of mixed genetic makeup (heterozygotes) were superior in survival and fertility to pure types.

It was already known that these superiorities of such heterozygotes would ensure the preservation of both sets of genes in the population. Dobzhansky pointed out that newly arisen genes are rare at first and that an individual is exceedingly unlikely to receive such a gene from both parents. Hence, in the beginning, the only genes that can "get ahead" and become more widespread in the population are those that are "good mixers"—that is, those that produce superior genotypes when combined with a random gene from the population.

A genetic system of the kind proposed by Dobzhansky can change rapidly, in response to natural selection, if environmental conditions should change. Among the myriad genotypes appearing in each generation would be many that were adapted to the changed conditions and that would leave more descendants; thus, these genes would be more common in the next generation. In contrast, under the older idea of a fairly uniform population in which most gene variants occurred rarely, much more time would be needed before variants adapted to new conditions could arise and become common. Meanwhile, local populations of the species could be in danger of becoming very reduced in numbers or even extinct.

Other important work of Dobzhansky dealt with speciation: the process by which a species does not merely change its characteristics over time but actually splits into two or more species. In extension of his work in human genetics and in human paleontology, Dobzhansky also wrote on the "descent of man" in *Mankind Evolving* (1962). Finally, his interest in the direction that human evolution might take in the future, added to a natural philosophical inclination, led him into thought on the nature of humans and the purpose of life and death, as shown in his works *The Biological Basis of Human Freedom* (1956) and *The Biology of Ultimate Concern* (1967). *Genetics of the Evolutionary Process* (1970) reflects 33 years of scientific progress in the study of evolution, largely by Dobzhansky or under his influence.

Although preeminently a laboratory biologist and writer, Dobzhansky never lost his liking for fieldwork; he boasted of having collected specimens from Alaska to Tierra del Fuego and in every continent except Antarctica. An inspiring teacher and lecturer, he received over the years a steady stream of scientists from other countries, who came to spend time in his laboratory to learn his approach to research.

Beginning in 1918, Dobzhansky published well over 400 research papers that provide an important part of the factual evidence for modern evolutionary theory. His preeminence, however, lay even more in the rare talent for synthesizing the masses of experimental and theoretical data in the literature into a broad, comprehensive view of the subject.

SIR JULIAN HUXLEY

(b. June 22, 1887, London, Eng. — d. Feb. 14, 1975, London)

Sir Julian Sorell Huxley was an English biologist, philosopher, educator, and author who greatly influenced the modern development of embryology, systematics, and studies of behaviour and evolution.

Julian, a grandson of the prominent biologist T.H. Huxley, a brother of novelist Aldous Huxley, and the oldest son of the biographer and man of letters Leonard Huxley, was educated at Eton and Balliol College, Oxford. His scientific research included important work on hormones, developmental processes, ornithology, and ethology. He developed and headed the biology department at the newly formed Rice University in Houston, Texas, before serving in the British Army Intelligence Corps between 1916 and the end of World War I. He later became professor of zoology at King's College, London University; served for seven years as secretary to the Zoological Society of London, transforming the zoo at Regent's Park and being actively involved in the development of that at Whipsnade in Bedfordshire; and became a Fellow of the Royal Society. He is perhaps best known among biologists for coining the term "evolutionary synthesis" to refer to the unification of taxonomy, genetics, and Darwinian theory in the 1940s. He was the first director general of the United Nations Educational, Scientific and Cultural Organization (UNESCO) in 1946–48. He was knighted in 1958. In 1961 he cofounded the World

Sir Julian Huxley with the skull of an elephant, 1967.
Horst Tappe/EB Inc.

Wildlife Fund for Nature. A biography *The Huxleys* by
Ronald W. Clark was published in 1968.

In 1919 Huxley married Marie Juliette Baillot, daughter
of a Swiss lawyer, by whom he had two sons: Anthony
Julian Huxley, who conducted valuable operational
research on aircraft, became an authority on exotic garden
plants, and produced the standard encyclopaedia on
mountains, and Francis Huxley, who became a lecturer in
social anthropology at Oxford.

T.H. HUXLEY

(b. May 4, 1825, Ealing, Middlesex, Eng.—d. June 29, 1895,
Eastbourne, Sussex)

Thomas Henry Huxley was an English biologist, educator,
and advocate of agnosticism (he coined the word).
Huxley's vigorous public support of Charles Darwin's

evolutionary naturalism earned him the nickname "Darwin's bulldog," while his organizational efforts, public lectures, and writing helped elevate the place of science in modern society.

STUDENT LIFE

T.H. Huxley, born above a butcher's shop, was the youngest of the six surviving children of schoolmaster George Huxley and his wife, Rachel. Although Huxley received only two years (1833–35) of formal education at his father's declining Ealing School, its evangelicalism later marked his scientific rhetoric. From 1835 his father tried managing a bank in his native Coventry, which left Huxley footloose in the ribbon-weaving city. Huxley's parents were Anglicans (members of the Church of England), but the boy sympathized with the town's Nonconformist (or Dissenting) weavers, who wanted religious equality and an end to the Anglicans' control of public institutions. Fascinated by science and religion, he studied Unitarian works, whose cause-and-effect explanations and denial of the duality of spirit and matter challenged the socially conservative views dominant in natural history and natural theology. Thomas Carlyle's books taught Huxley that the religious feeling of awe was distinct from theology, which dealt with gods and miraculous events. The teenager speculated (as did radical Dissenters) that morality was a cultural product, which left it open to a scientific explanation. These were the seeds of Huxley's agnosticism, scientific enthusiasm, and understanding of sectarian power play.

The longhaired student was apprenticed (c. 1838–41) to his sister Ellen's beer-swilling husband, John Charles Cooke, a medical materialist. Transferred to a London dockside practitioner early in 1841, Huxley was shaken by the lives of his pauper patients. Even at the back-street anatomy school where Huxley took the botany prize in 1842 — Sydenham College, off Gower Street in London — there was no escaping sectarian politics and science; Sydenham's owner, Marshall Hall, was studying mechanistic reflex arcs while haranguing the Royal College of Physicians for excluding Dissenters from its fellowship.

On a free scholarship (1842–45) to Charing Cross Hospital, London, Huxley won medals in physiology and organic chemistry. His own mechanistic bent showed as he sought to explain living processes by physicochemical laws, and his superb microscopy was revealed in his discovery in 1845 of a new membrane, now known as Huxley's layer, in the human hair sheath.

THE *RATTLESNAKE* VOYAGE

To repay his debts, he entered the navy and served (1846–50) as assistant surgeon on HMS *Rattlesnake* surveying Australia's Great Barrier Reef and New Guinea. With his microscope lashed to a table in the chart room, he studied the structure and growth of sea anemones, hydras, jellyfish, and sea nettles such as the Portuguese man-of-war, which decomposed too quickly to be studied anywhere except on the high seas. He grouped them together as Nematophora (named for their stinging cells), although they were later classified as the phylum Cnidaria (or Coelenterata). Demonstrating that they were all composed of two "foundation membranes" (shortly to be called endoderm and ectoderm), he even suggested that these membranes were related to the two original cell layers in the vertebrate embryo. The aristocratic Captain Owen Stanley, commander of the *Rattlesnake,* posted Huxley's papers to his father, the bishop of Norwich, for London publication; but such old-style patronage galled Huxley, who insisted that science no longer needed aristocratic sanction.

A whirlwind romance in Sydney in 1847 left the sailor engaged to a brewer's daughter, Henrietta ("Nettie") Anne Heathorn. By now Huxley considered it a moral duty to weigh the evidence before believing church dogmas, and his skepticism worried Nettie. He sailed to the Great Barrier Reef and southern coast of New Guinea, sketched Papuans, and suffered terrible mental collapses in the broiling heat of the Coral Sea as he worried about the worth of his scientific work. But he continued his path-breaking observations, noting that the larval sea squirt has tail muscles like a tadpole's. This, in later years, would be part of the proof that sea squirts, or ascidians, are the ancestors of the vertebrates.

Huxley returned home in 1850, hoping to earn enough to bring Nettie to England. His success at the Royal Society of London testified to the meteoric rise of his scientific reputation: elected a fellow in 1851, he was its Royal Medal winner in 1852 and a councillor in 1853. But it was all praise and no pudding, he fumed. Although the British Treasury put him on half pay to finish his research (which appeared in 1859 as *The Oceanic Hydrozoa*), Huxley could not find an academic post in science. Such jobs were rare when Britain's Oxbridge-trained leaders studied classics and when the public (privately funded) schools considered science dehumanizing. This led Huxley to more crushing depressions and a desire to raise science to a paying profession. Huxley took sides on the controversial issues of the day. He insisted that sea nettles were individual organisms, not colonies. He denied that the skull was composed of vertebrae, as his rival, the comparative anatomist Richard Owen, believed. Following the geologist Sir Charles Lyell, Huxley challenged the view that fossils showed a progression through the rocks, and he went on to repudiate a Christian-based geology that made humans the culmination of Creation. Marian Evans (the novelist George Eliot), writing alongside Huxley on the rationalist *Westminster Review,* an influential magazine at the cutting edge of 19th-century literary Britain, saw his brilliance as counterpoised by a love of provocation.

After four increasingly difficult years, Huxley's professional fortunes improved in 1854. He began teaching natural history and paleontology at the Government School of Mines in Piccadilly, central London. With a new professional ethos sweeping the country, Huxley trained schoolmasters in science and fostered a meritocratic, exam-based approach to education and professional advancement. He simultaneously occupied chairs at the Royal Institution and the Royal College of Surgeons, and he organized public lectures for workers, themselves looking for a new, liberating science. His situation stabilized, he brought Nettie to England, and their eight-year engagement ended with their marriage in 1855.

"DARWIN'S BULLDOG"

Charles Darwin, about to start writing his *On the Origin of Species* (1859), saw Huxley's star rising. A visit to Darwin's Down House in 1856 laid the foundation for a long relationship between the two men and their families (Nettie recuperated at Down after the death of her firstborn, Noel, in 1860; she and Emma Darwin shared concerns over their husbands' scientific theorizing and its theological consequences; and the Darwins stood as godparents to two of the Huxleys' eight children). Charles Darwin and

T.H. Huxley, meanwhile, complemented each other perfectly. The reclusive Darwin needed a public champion and defender. Huxley had initial difficulty with natural selection itself and opted for an internal source of variation that could produce new species at a stroke. Nonetheless, he saw Darwin's naturalistic (i.e., nonmiraculous) approach as a valuable aid in his campaign to build an independent scientific elite unfettered by the constraints of the old order. Therefore, rather than shy away from the controversial aspects of evolutionary theory, Huxley played them up, using Darwin's *Origin of Species* as a "Whitworth gun in the armoury of liberalism." Unlike some contemporaries (such as St. George Jackson Mivart) who sought a reconciliation between science and theology, he framed the debate over Creation and evolution in black-and-white, either/or terms and was unforgiving of colleagues who straddled the fence.

A defining moment in this professional campaign came early, in an exchange with the conservative bishop of Oxford, Samuel Wilberforce, at the British Association for the Advancement of Science meeting in 1860. Wilberforce apparently asked whether the apes were on his grandmother's or grandfather's line (a tasteless joke by Victorian standards), to which Huxley—exuding Puritan virtue—replied that he would rather have an ape as an ancestor than a wealthy bishop who prostituted his gifts. Although Darwinian propagandists, in continually recounting this episode, helped to put the men of science on an intellectual par with the powerful clergy, the reality was more complicated. At Oxford, Huxley was supported by some liberal Anglican clergy who disliked the hard-line bishop, and Wilberforce himself subsequently worked alongside Huxley at the Zoological Society. Nor did Huxley shy away from appropriating religious authority when it suited his purposes; he spoke of developing a "church scientific" and arranged for Darwin to be buried at Westminster Abbey.

Huxley carried the standard of scientific naturalism and evolution on a number of battlefields. He challenged the notion of supernatural creation, informing his democratic artisans that humans had risen from animals—a lowly-ancestor-bright-future image that appealed to the downtrodden—and that Darwin's Nature was a book open for all to read, rather than the prerogative of priests. He plunged headlong into the inflammatory issue of human ancestry; Darwin avoided it, but Huxley made it his specialty. In 1861 he denied that human and ape brains differ significantly, sparking a raging dispute with Richard Owen that brought human evolution to public attention. He discussed ape ancestry and the new fossil Neanderthal man in *Evidence as to Man's Place in Nature* (1863). Huxley also turned to fossils, working first on crossopterygians (Devonian lobe-fin fishes, the ancestors of amphibians) and the crocodile-shaped amphibians disinterred in Britain's coal pits. But his coup came in 1867–68, as he achieved a better understanding of phylogeny, or life's fossil pathway, when after reclassifying birds according to their palate bones, he proceeded to show that all birds were descended from small carnivorous dinosaurs.

POWER AND "POPE HUXLEY"

Huxley's controversial positions in the 1860s and '70s won the support of an increasing number of his contemporaries, while his research established him as one of the leading scientists of his era. As a scientific popularizer he was without peer, and he was an energetic organizer and political infighter. These qualities gave Huxley the levers necessary to elevate the position of science in British society, and he helped to build a social order in which science and professionalism replaced classics and patronage.

He did not fight alone. With the Kew Gardens botanist Joseph Dalton Hooker, the philosopher Herbert Spencer, the physicist John Tyndall, and other former outsiders, Huxley formed the X-Club in 1864 to advance science. Within a decade they were parceling out Royal Society posts. Their mouthpiece was the *Reader*—in which Huxley, answering Conservative leader Benjamin Disraeli's criticism of Darwinism, notoriously claimed that science would achieve "domination over the whole realm of the intellect"— and *Nature* (founded in 1869 by Huxley's team). Huxley also served as president of the Geological Society (1869– 71), the Ethnological Society (1868–71), the British Association for the Advancement of Science (1870), the Marine Biological Association (1884–90), and the Royal Society (1883–85). With seats on 10 Royal Commissions, deliberating on everything from fisheries to diseases to vivisection, he had clearly penetrated the labyrinthine corridors of power.

Those corridors shuddered at the growing strength of the rival industrial powers Germany and the United States. Huxley and his circle argued that better scientific educa- tion and support for scientific research would produce the workers and innovations necessary to maintain British supremacy. Huxley spent much of the 1860s and '70s immersed in educational reform and institution building. He joined the Eton College governing board and the London School Board (1870–72), devising a modern cur- riculum suitable for both the sons of privilege and the capital's "street arabs." He likewise served as rector (1872–74) of the ancient University of Aberdeen and principal (1868–80) of the new Working Men's College in south London. As a member (1870–75) of the Royal Commission on Scientific Instruction, he recommended the fusion of his Government School of Mines with the Royal College of Chemistry; they were moved to South Kensington and renamed the Normal School of Science (ultimately the Imperial College of Science and Technology, now part of the University of London). He advised on the founding of a vocational Central Institution for Technical Education (opened in London in 1884), for which he was made a freeman of the City of London in 1883. To fill the demand for science teachers (driven in part by the Education Act of 1870), he taught courses at South Kensington for school-masters and mistresses (the latter did so well that he was inspired to fight for the admission of women to universities), and he set the Department of Science and Art's public exams. His exam invigilators were Royal Engineers (the construction workers at South Kensington), which gave his "warfare" image of science with theology its deeper military aura. Not for nothing did the students nickname him "the General."

His popularity grew with his political influence. Huxley's talks were headline grabbers. The provocation and the handsome looks drew enormous crowds; once, in 1866, as he gave a talk on blind faith as the ultimate sin, the evangelist of science saw 2,000 people turned away from the crammed hall. A bequest of £1,000 from a Quaker supporter financed Huxley's American tour in 1876, on which he gave talks about the birds' dinosaur ancestry, made the succession of fossil horses in America the "Demonstrative Evidence of Evolution," and was dubbed "Huxley Eikonoklastes" by a New York City paper. (Huxley's whistle-stop tours led his children to call him "the lodger" at home.) No less popular were his writings. He took readers through time tunnels to experience exotic past worlds. An essay on protoplasm as the substrate of life sent the *Fortnightly Review* into seven editions in 1869. His numerous introductory textbooks were well received.

Such prodigious activity on so many fronts led to continual breakdowns and recuperations in Egypt, Germany, Italy, and France. In addition, his pay never quite sufficed, as he financed the children of his broken-down brother James and drunken sister Ellen. And the more he upheld family values and denied that skepticism and evolutionism led to debauchery, the more he worried about scandals breaking around his ne'er-do-well relations.

In 1869 he coined the word *agnostic,* meaning that one could know nothing of ultimate reality, whether spiritual or material. For him morality rested not in reciting creeds but in weighing evidence for events; it was a consecration of doubt that vested his new professionals with the priests' old power. (For such messianic pronouncements he was nicknamed "Pope Huxley.") His research, meanwhile, became increasingly influenced by evolution. He used the fishlike lancelet (amphioxus) to plumb the origin of all vertebrates, tackled crayfish evolution, showed that Mesozoic crocodiles progressively developed a secondary palate (which allowed them to drown newly evolved mammalian prey), and wrote the section on evolution in biology in the article "Evolution" for the ninth edition of the *Encyclopædia Britannica* (published 1878). Finally, in creating a package that the teachers could take to their hometowns, Huxley forged the discipline of biology—based on structural (rather than evolutionary) anatomy, stripped down to a few exemplary animal and plant "types."

THE OLD LION

With a radical home secretary making Huxley an inspector of fisheries in 1881, his pay was finally augmented. But so was the strain. The final blow came as his talented daughter Marian went mad after 1882 (she died in Paris, under the care of the renowned neurologist Jean-Martin Charcot, in 1887). A distraught, overworked Huxley resigned his professorship at the Normal School of Science (the future novelist H.G. Wells sat his last course) and the presidency of the Royal Society in 1885. He was awarded a state pension of £1,200 a year by the Liberal prime minister William Ewart Gladstone, even though Huxley—ever the polemicist—struck out against Gladstone's Irish Home Rule policy, dissected his scriptural literalism, and refuted his attempt to reconcile the fossil evidence with the order of Creation listed in the book of Genesis.

Grieving for his daughter, Huxley in "The Struggle for Existence in Human Society" (1887) adopted a bitter social Darwinism—a term that would itself be introduced about 1890. Accepting Darwin's Malthusian belief that over-population was the rule, Huxley maintained that the inevitable struggle and death undermined any possibility of socialist cooperation, which was back in contention after the socialist revival of 1886. He was answered by the anarchist prince Peter Kropotkin in *Mutual Aid* (1902). Huxley also nationalized the Darwinian struggle; he saw the industrial powers competing, making workforce training obligatory to win the economic "battle." His last major talk, "Evolution and Ethics," was held at the University of Oxford in 1893. Mellower now, six years after Marian's death, Huxley used the occasion to detach benign human ethics from natural competition. Darwin's "war"—between animals or industrial nations—had no place in our personal lives, he said. Society grows as we curb these "anti-social" animal instincts—it advances through the selection of individuals who are ethically the best, rather than physically the fittest.

Huxley suffered from pleurisy and heart disease in London's smog, and the family moved to Eastbourne, on the Sussex coast, in 1890. Huxley was now an elder statesman of science, his once-radical ideas the foundations of the new Establishment. Agnosticism was equated with nonsectarianism; a lord chief justice in 1883 declared that Christianity was no longer the law of the land in England, with the caveat that while Huxley's reverent questioning was now legal, vulgar working-class attacks on Christian beliefs were still indictable. Huxley's brand of national Darwinism turned science against socialism and made naturalism synonymous with patriotism. The professions, including those in science, were accumulating power. He was also patriarch of an expanding intellectual dynasty. His son Leonard was a prominent editor, and three grandchildren would earn their own fame: Julian and Andrew as biologists and Aldous as a writer. It was this Huxley, as much a Unionist and nationalist as a brilliant propagandist for science, who was appointed to the Privy Council by the Conservative prime minister Robert Cecil, 3rd marquis of Salisbury, in 1892.

And so it was the Right Honourable T.H. Huxley who died of a heart attack on June 29, 1895—typically, midway through a defense of agnosticism. Huxley was buried on July 4, 1895, next to his tiny son Noel in St. Marylebone Cemetery, in Finchley, north London, his funeral being attended by a constellation of the greatest Victorian scientists.

JEAN-BAPTISTE LAMARCK

(b. Aug. 1, 1744, Bazentin-le-Petit, Picardy, France—d. Dec. 18, 1829, Paris)

Jean-Baptiste-Pierre-Antoine de Monet, chevalier de Lamarck was a French biologist who is best known for his idea that acquired characters are inheritable, an idea known as Lamarckism, which is controverted by modern genetics and evolutionary theory.

EARLY LIFE AND CAREER

Lamarck was the youngest of 11 children in a family of the lesser nobility. His family intended him for the priesthood, but, after the death of his father and the expulsion of the Jesuits from France, Lamarck embarked on a military career in 1761. As a soldier garrisoned in the south of France, he became interested in collecting plants. An injury forced him to resign in 1768, but his fascination for botany endured, and it was as a botanist that he first built his scientific reputation.

Lamarck gained attention among the naturalists in Paris at the Jardin et Cabinet du Roi (the king's garden and natural history collection, known informally as the Jardin du Roi) by claiming he could create a system for identifying the plants of France that would be more efficient than any system currently in existence, including that of the great Swedish naturalist Carolus Linnaeus. This project appealed to Georges-Louis Leclerc, comte de Buffon, who was the director of the Jardin du Roi and Linnaeus's greatest rival. Buffon arranged to have Lamarck's work published at government expense, and Lamarck received the proceeds from the sales. The work appeared in three volumes under the title *Flore française* (1778; "French Flora"). Lamarck designed the *Flore française* specifically for the task of plant identification and used dichotomous keys, which are classification tools that allow the user to choose between opposing pairs of morphological characters to achieve this end.

With Buffon's support, Lamarck was elected to the Academy of Sciences in 1779. Two years later, Buffon named Lamarck "correspondent" of the Jardin du Roi, evidently to give Lamarck additional status while he escorted Buffon's son on a scientific tour of Europe. This provided Lamarck with his first official connection, albeit an unsalaried one, with the Jardin du Roi. Shortly after Buffon's death in 1788, his successor, Flahault de la Billarderie, created a salaried position for Lamarck with the title of "botanist of the King and keeper of the King's herbaria."

Between 1783 and 1792 Lamarck published three large botanical volumes for the *Encyclopédie méthodique* ("Methodical Encyclopaedia"), a massive publishing enterprise begun by French publisher Charles-Joseph Panckoucke in the late 18th century. Lamarck also published botanical papers in the *Mémoires* of the Academy of Sciences. In 1792 he cofounded and coedited a short-lived journal of natural history, the *Journal d'histoire naturelle*.

PROFESSORSHIP AT THE NATIONAL MUSEUM OF NATURAL HISTORY

Lamarck's career changed dramatically in 1793 when the former Jardin du Roi was transformed into the Muséum National d'Histoire Naturelle ("National Museum of Natural History"). In the changeover, all 12 of the scientists who had been officers of the previous establishment were named as professors and coadministrators of the new institution; however, only two professorships of botany were created. The botanists Antoine-Laurent de Jussieu and René Desfontaines held greater claims to these positions, and Lamarck, in a striking shift of responsibilities, was made professor of the "insects, worms, and microscopic animals." Although this change of focus was remarkable, it was not wholly unjustified, as Lamarck was an ardent shell collector. Lamarck then set out to classify this large and poorly analyzed expanse of the animal kingdom. Later he would name this group "animals without vertebrae" and invent the term *invertebrate*. By 1802 Lamarck had also introduced the term *biology*.

This challenge would have been enough to occupy the energies of most naturalists; however, Lamarck's intellectual aspirations ran well beyond that of reforming invertebrate classification. In the 1790s he began promoting the broad theories of physics, chemistry, and meteorology that he had been nurturing for almost two decades. He also began thinking about Earth's geologic history and developed notions that he would eventually publish under the title of *Hydrogéologie* (1802). In his physico-chemical writings, he advanced an old-fashioned, four-element theory that was self-consciously at odds with the revolutionary advances of the emerging pneumatic chemistry of Antoine-Laurent Lavoisier. His colleagues at the Institute of France (the successor to the Academy of Sciences) saw Lamarck's broad theorizing as unscientific "system building." Lamarck in turn became increasingly scornful of scientists who preferred "small facts" to "larger," more important ones. He began to characterize himself as a "naturalist-philosopher," a person more concerned with the broader processes of nature than the details of the chemist's laboratory or naturalist's closet.

THE INHERITANCE OF ACQUIRED CHARACTERS

In 1800 Lamarck first set forth the revolutionary notion of species mutability during a lecture to students in his invertebrate zoology class at the National Museum of Natural History. By 1802 the general outlines of his broad theory of organic transformation had taken shape. He presented the theory successively in his *Recherches sur l'organisation des corps vivans* (1802; "Research on the Organization of Living Bodies"), his *Philosophie zoologique* (1809; "Zoological Philosophy"), and the introduction to his great multivolume work on invertebrate classification, *Histoire naturelle des animaux sans vertèbres* (1815–22; "Natural

History of Invertebrate Animals"). Lamarck's theory of organic development included the idea that the very simplest forms of plant and animal life were the result of spontaneous generation. Life became successively diversified, he claimed, as the result of two very different sorts of causes. He called the first "the power of life," or the "cause that tends to make organization increasingly complex," whereas he classified the second as the modifying influence of particular circumstances (that is, the effects of the environment). He explained this in his *Philosophie zoologique*: "The state in which we now see all the animals is on the one hand the product of the increasing composition of organization, which tends to form a regular gradation, and on the other hand that of the influences of a multitude of very different circumstances that continually tend to destroy the regularity in the gradation of the increasing composition of organization."

With this theory, Lamarck offered much more than an account of how species change. He also explained what he understood to be the shape of a truly "natural" system of classification of the animal kingdom. The primary feature of this system was a single scale of increasing complexity composed of all the different classes of animals, starting with the simplest microscopic organisms, or "infusorians," and rising up to the mammals. The species, however, could not be arranged in a simple series. Lamarck described them as forming "lateral ramifications" with respect to the general "masses" of organization represented by the classes. Lateral ramifications in species resulted when they underwent transformations that reflected the diverse, particular environments to which they had been exposed.

By Lamarck's account, animals, in responding to different environments, adopted new habits. Their new habits caused them to use some organs more and some organs less, which resulted in the strengthening of the former and the weakening of the latter. New characters thus acquired by organisms over the course of their lives were passed on to the next generation (provided, in the case of sexual reproduction, that both of the parents of the offspring had undergone the same changes). Small changes that accumulated over great periods of time produced major differences. Lamarck thus explained how the shapes of giraffes, snakes, storks, swans, and numerous other creatures were a consequence of long-maintained habits. The basic idea of "the inheritance of acquired characters" had originated with Anaxagoras, Hippocrates, and others, but Lamarck was essentially the first naturalist to argue at length that the long-term operation of this process could result in species change.

Later in the century, after English naturalist Charles Darwin advanced his theory of evolution by natural selection, the idea of the inheritance of acquired characters came to be identified as a distinctively "Lamarckian" view of organic change (though Darwin himself also believed that acquired characters could be inherited). The idea was not seriously challenged in biology until the German biologist August Weismann did so in the 1880s. In the 20th century, since Lamarck's idea failed to be confirmed experimentally and the evidence commonly cited in its favour was given different interpretations, it became thoroughly discredited.

Lamarck made his most important contributions to science as a botanical and zoological systematist, as a founder of invertebrate paleontology, and as an evolutionary theorist. In his own day, his theory of evolution was generally rejected as implausible, unsubstantiated, or heretical. Today he is primarily remembered for his notion of the inheritance of acquired characteristics. Nonetheless,

Lamarck stands out in the history of biology as the first writer to set forth—both systematically and in detail—a comprehensive theory of organic evolution that accounted for the successive production of all the different forms of life on Earth.

ERNST MAYR

(b. July 5, 1904, Kempten, Ger.—d. Feb. 3, 2005, Bedford, Mass., U.S.)

German-born American biologist Ernst Walter Mayr is known for his work in avian taxonomy, population genetics, and evolution. Considered one of the world's leading evolutionary biologists, he was sometimes referred to as the "Darwin of the 20th century."

Two years after receiving a Ph.D. degree in ornithology from the University of Berlin (1926), Mayr, then a member of the university staff, led the first of three expeditions to New Guinea and the Solomon Islands, where he was profoundly impressed with the effects of geographic distribution among various animal species. His early studies of the ability of one species to separate or subdivide into daughter species (speciation) and of those populations that were established by a small number of founders (founder populations) made him one of the leaders in the development of the modern synthetic theory of evolution. The theory, an integration of the work of Charles Darwin (natural selection) and Gregor Mendel (genetics), encompassed the biological processes of gene mutation and recombination, changes in the structure and function of chromosomes, reproductive isolation, and natural selection. Mayr presented his ideas in the seminal book *Systematics and the Origin of Species* (1942).

Mayr continued his studies as the curator of the ornithological department at the American Museum of Natural History in New York (1932–53), where he wrote more than 100 papers on avian taxonomy, including *Birds of the Southwest*

Pacific (1945). He proposed in 1940 a definition of species that won wide acceptance in scientific circles and led to the discovery of a number of previously unknown species; by the time of his death, he had named some 25 new bird species and 410 subspecies. In 1953 he became Alexander Agassiz Professor of Zoology at Harvard University, and from 1961 to 1970 he served as director of the university's Museum of Comparative Zoology. He became professor emeritus at Harvard in 1975. Mayr's works include *Methods and Principles of Systemic Zoology* (with E.G. Linsley and R.L. Usinger; 1953), *Animal Species and Evolution* (1963), *The Growth of Biological Thought* (1982), and *What Evolution Is* (2001).

GEORGE GAYLORD SIMPSON

(b. June 16, 1902, Chicago, Ill., U.S.—d. Oct. 6, 1984, Tucson, Ariz.)

American paleontologist George Gaylord Simpson was known for his contributions to evolutionary theory and to the understanding of intercontinental migrations of animal species in past geological times.

Simpson received a doctorate from Yale University in 1926. He chose for the subject of his thesis the mammals of the Mesozoic Era, which are important for the understanding of mammalian evolution, although evidence of their existence consists mainly of tantalizing fragments of jaws and teeth. The materials were located chiefly in the Peabody Museum at Yale and the British Museum in London. Simpson produced substantial quarto monographs on the two collections, making his reputation as an able worker in mammalian paleontology.

In 1927 he joined the staff of the American Museum of Natural History, New York City, where he was to continue research in paleontology for three decades. The first 15 years were highly productive; he published about 150 scientific papers, many of considerable importance. A few dealt with lower vertebrates, but nearly all were on mammalian paleon-tology. In his first years in New York City he was interested in the fauna of Florida of the Neogene Period and the Pleistocene Epoch (the Pleistocene, which followed the Neogene Period, began about 2.6 million years ago and ended about 11,700 years ago). He published a number of works on this topic. For the most part, however, his interests were in the early history of mammals, and most of his publica-tions in the 1930s were concerned with this field. He studied the Cretaceous mammals of Mongolia and North America, especially the Paleocene fauna of the latter continent (the Paleocene Epoch began about 65.5 million years ago and ended about 55.8 million years ago). This resulted in a major work on the Paleocene fauna of the Fort Union Formation of Montana, in which about 50 mammals of a variety of primi-tive types were found. The breadth of his studies of mammalian evolution led to the writing of a detailed classification of mammals that is standard in the field.

In the early Cenozoic a series of mammalian fauna lived in South America that were quite unlike those of any other continent. Those of the Neogene and Pleistocene forms were fairly well known, but little was known of the earlier history of the peculiar South American groups. Hence, in the early 1930s he made three expeditions to Patagonia to collect new material and re-study specimens already described; as a result of these efforts, the early history of the Neogene mammals of South America became vastly better known. He published several dozen papers on these forms in the late 1930s and afterward two volumes summarizing their early history.

During World War II Simpson did staff work for the U.S. Army, principally in North Africa. On his return to the American Museum, he became curator in charge of the active department of paleontology, as well as a professor at Columbia University. This restricted the time available for research, but his scientific productivity remained undiminished. While his descriptive work in paleontology continued, his interests spread to other fields. The possibility of applying mathematical methods to paleontology had already led to his coauthorship of a work on quantitative zoology. A consideration of the successive faunas of the various continental areas led to studies of the problems of the intercontinental migrations of animal species. Problems of taxonomy and classification are intimately connected with evolutionary studies, and, in addition to giving a thorough consideration of principles of classification in his work on mammalian classification, he published in 1961 a volume on *The Principles of Animal Taxonomy*. In a series of lectures that appeared in book form as *The Meaning of Evolution* in 1949, he discussed the philosophical implications of the acceptance of evolutionary theory, which attracted worldwide attention. In the postwar period there was a renewed study of evolutionary theory by geneticists, systematists, and paleontologists. Simpson took a major part in such studies; his principal publications in the area were his volumes *Tempo and Mode in Evolution* (1944; reissued 1984) and *Major Features of Evolution* (1953).

In 1958 Simpson left New York City to spend a decade as an Alexander Agassiz Professor of Vertebrate Paleontology at the Harvard Museum of Comparative Zoology. After that he moved to Tucson, Ariz., where he became professor of geosciences at the University of Arizona, a post from which he retired in 1982. He continued to publish widely. Later works include *Splendid Isolation: The Curious History of South American Mammals* (1980), *Why and How: Some Problems and Methods in Historical Biology* (1980), and *Fossils and the History of Life* (1983).

GEORGE LEDYARD STEBBINS, JR.

(b. Jan. 6, 1906, Lawrence, N.Y., U.S.—d. Jan. 19, 2000, Davis, Calif.)

American botanist and geneticist George Ledyard Stebbins, Jr., was known for his application of the modern synthetic theory of evolution to plants. Called the father of evolutionary botany, he was the first scientist to synthesize artificially a species of plant that was capable of thriving under natural conditions.

Stebbins was educated at Harvard University, receiving a Ph.D. in biology in 1931. He taught at Colgate University in Hamilton, New York, and until 1973 was a member of the faculty at the University of California, Berkeley. In 1950 he transferred to the Davis campus of the University of California, where he founded the Department of Genetics. He made an extensive study of the distribution of plants in that area.

Stebbins shares the credit for formulating and applying the modern synthetic theory of evolution to higher organisms. This theory distinguishes the basic processes of gene mutation and recombination, natural selection, changes in structure and number of chromosomes, and reproductive isolation. The publication of his *Variation and Evolution in Plants* (1950) established Stebbins as one of the first biologists to apply this theory to plant evolution. Working with several species of flowering plants, Stebbins and his coworker, Ernest B. Babcock, studied polyploid plants, which are new species of plants that have originated from a spontaneous doubling of the chromosomes of an existing species. When a technique was developed for doubling a plant's chromosomal number artificially, Stebbins used it to produce polyploids from several species of wild grass, of which the new species *Ehrharta erecta* was established in a natural environment in 1944.

Stebbins wrote numerous books, including *Processes of Organic Evolution* (1966), as well as some 250 journal articles. Among his later works are *Flowering Plants: Evolution Above the Species Level* (1974) and *Evolution* (1977; with T. Dobzhansky, F. Ayala, and J. Valentine).

HUGO DE VRIES

(b. Feb. 16, 1848, Haarlem, Neth.—d. May 21, 1935, near Amsterdam)

Dutch botanist and geneticist Hugo de Vries introduced the experimental study of organic evolution. His rediscovery in 1900 (simultaneously with the botanists Carl Correns and Erich Tschermak von Seysenegg) of Gregor Mendel's principles of heredity and his theory of biological mutation, though considerably different from a modern understanding of the phenomenon, resolved ambiguous concepts concerning the nature of variation of species that, until then, had precluded the universal acceptance and active investigation of Charles Darwin's system of organic evolution.

Educated at the universities of Leiden, Heidelberg, and Würzburg, de Vries became a professor at the University of Amsterdam in 1878, serving there until 1918. In 1886 de Vries noticed wild varieties of the evening primrose (*Oenothera lamarckiana*) that differed markedly from the cultivated species. This suggested to de Vries that evolution might be studied by a new, experimental method rather than by the old method of observation and inference. He discovered in his cultivation of the evening primrose new forms or varieties appearing randomly among the host of ordinary specimens. He gave the name mutations to these phenomena, which he showed to arise suddenly, as distinct from Darwin's variation of species through natural selection. De Vries believed these varieties to be an example of an evolution that could be studied experimentally and conceived of evolution as a series of abrupt changes radical enough to bring new species into existence in a single leap.

De Vries's research into the nature of mutations, summarized in his *Die Mutationstheorie* (1901–03; *The Mutation Theory*), led him to begin a program of plant breeding in 1892, and eight years later he drew up the same laws of heredity that Mendel had. While surveying literature on the subject, de Vries discovered the Austrian monk's paper of 1866 on the breeding of garden peas, and he was careful to attribute the original discovery of the laws of heredity to Mendel in his subsequent publications.

De Vries also contributed to knowledge of the role played in plant physiology by osmosis, and in 1877 he demonstrated a relation between osmotic pressure and the molecular weight of substances in plant cells. Among de Vries's other works are *Intracellular Pangenesis* (1889) and *Plant Breeding* (1907).

ALFRED RUSSEL WALLACE

(b. Jan. 8, 1823, Usk, Monmouthshire, Wales—d. Nov. 7, 1913, Broadstone, Dorset, Eng.)

British humanist, naturalist, geographer, and social critic, Alfred Russel Wallace became a public figure in England during the second half of the 19th century, known for his courageous views on scientific, social, and spiritualist subjects. His formulation of the theory of evolution by natural selection, which predated Charles Darwin's published contributions, is his most outstanding legacy, but it was just one of many controversial issues he studied and wrote about during his lifetime. Wallace's wide-ranging interests—from socialism to spiritualism, from island biogeography to life on Mars, from evolution to land nationalization—stemmed from his profound concern with the moral, social, and political values of human life.

EARLY LIFE AND WORK

The eighth of nine children born to Thomas Vere Wallace and Mary Anne Greenell, Alfred Russel Wallace grew up in modest circumstances in rural Wales and then in Hertford, Hertfordshire, England. His formal education was limited to six years at the one-room Hertford Grammar School. Although his education was curtailed by the family's worsening financial situation, his home was a rich source of books, maps, and gardening activities, which Wallace remembered as enduring sources of learning and pleasure. Wallace's parents belonged to the Church of England, and as a child Wallace attended services. His lack of enthusiasm for organized religion became more pronounced when he was exposed to secular teachings at a London mechanics' institute, the "Hall of Science" off Tottenham Court Road. Living in London with his brother John, an apprentice carpenter, the 14-year-old Wallace became familiar with the lives of tradesmen and labourers, and he shared in their efforts at self-education. Here Wallace read treatises and attended lectures by Robert Owen and his son Robert Dale Owen that formed the basis of his religious skepticism and his reformist and socialist political philosophy.

In 1837 Wallace became an apprentice in the surveying business of his eldest brother, William. New tax laws (Tithe Commutation Act, 1836) and the division of public land among landowners (General Enclosures Act, 1845) created a demand for accurate surveys and maps of farmlands, public lands, and parishes, as surveys and maps made according to regulations were legal documents in

British naturalist, explorer, and biologist Alfred Wallace circa 1894.
Hulton Archive/Getty Images.

executing these laws. For approximately 8 of the next 10 years, Wallace surveyed and mapped in Bedfordshire and then in Wales. He lived among farmers and artisans and saw the injustices suffered by the poor as a result of the new laws. Wallace's detailed observations of their habits are recorded in one of his first writing efforts, an essay on "the South Wales Farmer," which is reproduced in his autobiography. When surveying work could not be found as a result of violent uprisings by the Welsh farmers, Wallace spent a year (1844) teaching at a boys' school, the Collegiate School in Leicester, Leicestershire, England. After his brother William died in early 1845, Wallace worked in London and Wales, saw to his brother's business, surveyed for a proposed railway line, and built a mechanics' institute at Neath, Wales, with his brother John.

THE CAREER OF A NATURALIST

As a surveyor, Wallace spent a great deal of time outdoors, both for work and pleasure. An enthusiastic amateur naturalist with an intellectual bent, he read widely in natural history, history, and political economy, including works by William Swainson, Charles Darwin, Alexander von Humboldt, and Thomas Malthus. He also read works and attended lectures on phrenology and mesmerism, forming an interest in nonmaterial mental phenomena that grew increasingly prominent later in his life. Inspired by reading about organic evolution in Robert Chambers's controversial *Vestiges of the Natural History of Creation* (1844), unemployed, and ardent in his love of nature, Wallace and his naturalist friend Henry Walter Bates, who had introduced Wallace to entomology four years earlier, traveled to Brazil in 1848 as self-employed specimen collectors. Wallace and Bates participated in the culture of natural history collecting, honing practical skills to identify, collect, and send back to England biological objects that were highly valued in the flourishing trade in natural specimens. The two young men amicably parted ways after several joint collecting ventures; Bates spent 11 years in the region, while Wallace spent a total of 4 years traveling, collecting, mapping, drawing, and writing in unexplored regions of the Amazon River basin. He studied the languages and habits of the peoples he encountered; he collected butterflies, other insects, and birds; and he searched for clues to solve the mystery of the origin of plant and animal species. Except for one shipment of specimens sent to his agent in London, however, most of Wallace's collections were lost on his voyage home when his ship went up in flames and sank. Nevertheless, he managed to save some of his notes before his rescue and return journey. From these he published several scientific articles, two books (*Palm Trees of the Amazon and Their Uses* and *Narrative of Travels on the Amazon and Rio Negro,* both 1853), and a map depicting the course of the Negro River. These won him acclaim from the Royal Geographical Society, which helped to fund his next collecting venture, in the Malay Archipelago.

Wallace spent eight years in the Malay Archipelago, from 1854 to 1862, traveling among the islands, collecting biological specimens for his own research and for sale, and writing scores of scientific articles on mostly zoological subjects. Among these were two extraordinary articles dealing with the origin of new species. The first of these, published in 1855, concluded with the assertion that "every species has come into existence coincident both in space and time with a preexisting closely allied species." Wallace then proposed that new species arise by the progression and continued divergence of varieties that outlive the parent species in the struggle for existence. In early 1858 he sent a paper outlining these ideas to Darwin, who saw such a striking coincidence to his own theory that he consulted his closest colleagues, the geologist Charles Lyell and the botanist Joseph Dalton Hooker. The three men decided to present two extracts of Darwin's previous writings, along with Wallace's paper, to the Linnean Society. The resulting set of papers, with both Darwin's and Wallace's names, was published as a single article entitled "On the Tendency of Species to Form Varieties; and on the Perpetuation of Varieties and Species by Natural Means of Selection" in the *Proceedings of the Linnean Society* in 1858. This compromise sought to avoid a conflict of priority interests and was reached without Wallace's knowledge. Wallace's research on the geographic distribution of animals among the islands of the Malay Archipelago provided crucial evidence for his evolutionary theories and led him to devise what soon became known as Wallace's Line, the boundary that separates the fauna of Australia from that of Asia.

Wallace returned to England in 1862 an established natural scientist and geographer, as well as a collector of more than 125,000 animal specimens. He married Annie Mitten (1848–1914), with whom he raised three children (Herbert died at age 4, whereas Violet and William survived their father); published a highly successful narrative of his journey, *The Malay Archipelago: The Land of the Orang-Utan, and the Bird of Paradise* (1869); and wrote *Contributions to the Theory of Natural Selection* (1870). In the latter volume and in several articles from this period on human evolution and spiritualism, Wallace parted from the scientific naturalism of many of his friends and colleagues in claiming that natural selection could not account for the higher faculties of human beings.

The Wallace family moved several times, from Inner London to the outer borough of Barking, to Grays in Essex, and then south to Dorking, Surrey, to the outer borough of Croydon, to Godalming, Surrey, then to Parkstone and finally Broadstone, both in Dorset. Wallace built three of his family's houses, and at each he and his wife kept gardens. Although he applied for several jobs, Wallace never held a permanent position. He lost the profits from his collections through bad investments and other financial misfortunes. His income was limited to earnings from his writings, from grading school exams (which he did for some 25 years), and from a small inheritance from a relative. In 1881 he was added to the Civil List, thanks largely to the efforts of Darwin and T.H. Huxley.

Wallace's two-volume *Geographical Distribution of Animals* (1876) and *Island Life* (1880) became the standard authorities in zoogeography and island biogeography, synthesizing knowledge about the distribution and dispersal of living and extinct animals in an evolutionary framework. For the ninth edition of *Encyclopædia Britannica* (1875–89), he wrote the article "Acclimatisation" (adaptation) and the animal life section of the article "Distribution." He also lectured in the British Isles and in the United States and traveled on the European continent. In addition to his major scientific works, Wallace actively pursued a variety of social and political interests. In writings and public appearances he opposed vaccination, eugenics, and vivisection while strongly supporting women's rights and land nationalization. Foremost among these commitments was an increasing engagement with spiritualism in his personal and public capacities.

Wallace received several awards, including the Royal Society of London's Royal Medal (1868), Darwin Medal (1890; for his independent origination of the origin of species by natural selection), Copley Medal (1908), and Order of Merit (1908); the Linnean Society of London's Gold Medal (1892) and Darwin-Wallace Medal (1908); and the Royal Geographical Society's Founder's Medal (1892). He was also awarded honorary doctorates from the Universities of Dublin (1882) and Oxford (1889) and won election to the Royal Society (1893).

Wallace published 21 books, and the list of his articles, essays, and letters in periodicals contains more than 700 items. Yet his career eludes simple description or honorifics. He was keenly intellectual but no less spiritual, a distinguished scientist and a spokesman for unpopular causes, a gifted naturalist who never lost his boyish enthusiasm for nature, a prolific and lucid writer, a committed socialist, a seeker of truth, and a domestic, modest individual. His engagement with progressive politics and spiritualism likely contributed to his lack of employment and to his somewhat peripheral status in the historical record. What touched those who knew him was his compassion, his humanness and sympathy, and his lack of pretense or acquired pride. Wallace died in his 91st year and was buried in Broadstone, to be joined there by his widow the following year. A commemorative medallion in his honour was unveiled at Westminster Abbey in 1915.

CHAPTER 6
RELATED EVOLUTIONARY CONCEPTS

A number of terms are used in the study of evolution. Some of the more helpful concepts are described below.

ACQUIRED CHARACTER

Any modification in structure or function acquired by an organism during its life, caused by environmental factors, is called an acquired character. With respect to higher organisms, there is no evidence that such changes are transmissible genetically—the view associated with Lamarckism—but, among protozoans and bacteria, certain induced changes are heritable.

ADAPTATION

In biology, adaptation is the process by which an animal or plant species becomes fitted to its environment; it is the result of natural selection's acting upon heritable variation. Even the simpler organisms must be adapted in a great variety of ways: in their structure, physiology, and genetics, in their locomotion or dispersal, in their means of defense and attack, in their reproduction and development, and in other respects.

The word *adaptation* does not stem from its current usage in evolutionary biology but rather dates back to the early 17th century, when it was used to indicate a relation between design and function or how something fits into something else. In biology this general idea has been co-opted so that it has three meanings. First, in a physiological sense, an animal or plant can adapt by adjusting to its immediate environment—for instance, by changing its temperature or metabolism with an increase in altitude. Second, and more commonly, the word refers either to the process of becoming adapted or to the features of organisms that promote reproductive success relative to other possible features. Here the process of adaptation is driven by genetic variations among individuals that become adapted to—that is, have greater success in—a specific environmental context. A classic example is shown by the melanistic (dark) phenotype of the peppered moth (*Biston betularia*), which increased in numbers in Britain following the Industrial Revolution as dark-coloured moths appeared cryptic against soot-darkened trees and escaped predation by birds. The process of adaptation occurs through an eventual change in the gene frequency relative to advantages conferred by a particular characteristic, as with the coloration of wings in the moths.

The third and more popular view of adaptation is in regard to the form of a feature that has evolved by natural selection for a specific function. Examples include the long necks of giraffes for feeding in the tops of trees, the streamlined bodies of aquatic fish and mammals, the light bones of flying birds and mammals, and the long dagger-like canine teeth of carnivores.

All biologists agree that organismal traits commonly reflect adaptations. However, much disagreement has arisen over the role of history and constraint in the appearance of traits as well as the best methodology for showing that a trait is truly an adaptation. A trait may be a function of history rather than adaptation. The so-called panda's thumb, or radial sesamoid bone, is a wrist bone that now functions as an opposable thumb, allowing giant pandas to grasp and manipulate bamboo stems with dexterity. The ancestors of giant pandas and all closely related species, such as black bears, raccoons, and red pandas, also have sesamoid bones, though the latter species do not feed on bamboo or use the bone for feeding behaviour. Therefore, this bone is not an adaptation for bamboo feeding.

The English naturalist Charles Darwin, in *On the Origin of Species by Means of Natural Selection* (1859), recognized the problem of determining whether a feature evolved for the function it currently serves:

> *The sutures of the skulls of young mammals have been advanced as a beautiful adaptation for aiding parturition [birth], and no doubt they facilitate, or may be indispensable for this act; but as sutures occur in the skulls of young birds and reptiles, which only have to escape from a broken egg, we may infer that this structure has arisen from the laws of growth, and has been taken advantage of in the parturition of the higher animals.*

Thus, before explaining that a trait is an adaptation, it is necessary to identify whether it is also shown in ancestors and therefore may have evolved historically for different functions from those that it now serves.

Another problem in designating a trait as an adaptation is that the trait may be a necessary consequence, or constraint, of physics or chemistry. One of the most common forms of constraint involves the function of anatomical traits that differ in size. For example, canine teeth are larger in carnivores than in herbivores. This difference in size is often explained as an adaptation for predation. However, the size of canine teeth is also related to overall body size (such scaling is known as allometry), as shown by large carnivores such as leopards that have bigger canines than do small carnivores such as weasels. Thus, differences in many animal and plant characteristics, such as the sizes of young, duration of developmental periods (e.g., gestation, longevity), or patterns and sizes of tree leaves, are related to physical size constraints.

Adaptive explanations in biology are difficult to test because they include many traits and require different methodologies. Experimental approaches are important for showing that any small variability, as in many physiological or behavioral differences, is an adaptation. The most rigorous methods are those that combine experimental approaches with information from natural settings—for example, in showing that the beaks of different species of Galapagos finch are shaped differently because they are adapted to feed on seeds of different sizes.

The comparative method, using comparisons across species that have evolved independently, is an effective means for studying historical and physical constraints. This approach involves using statistical methods to account for differences in size (allometry) and evolutionary trees (phylogenies) for tracing trait evolution among lineages.

ADAPTIVE RADIATION

The evolution of an animal or plant group into a wide variety of types adapted to specialized modes of life is called adaptive radiation. Adaptive radiations are best exemplified in closely related groups that have evolved in a relatively short time. A striking example is the radiation, beginning in the Paleogene Period (beginning 65.5 million years ago), of basal mammalian stock into forms adapted to running, leaping, climbing, swimming, and flying. Other examples include Australian marsupials, cichlid fish, and Darwin's finches (also known as Galapagos finches).

CEPHALIZATION

Cephalization is the differentiation of the anterior (front) end of an organism into a definite head. Considered an evolutionary advance, cephalization is accompanied by a concentration of nervous tissue (cephalic ganglion or brain) and feeding mechanisms in the head region that serves to integrate the activities of the nervous system. Some groups of organisms show full cephalization, but because their bodies are not divided into distinct trunks and heads, they cannot be said to possess a distinct anatomical head.

DARWINISM

Darwinism is the theory of the evolutionary mechanism propounded by Charles Darwin as an explanation of organic change. It denotes Darwin's specific view that evolution is driven mainly by natural selection.

Beginning in 1837, Darwin proceeded to work on the now well-understood concept that evolution is essentially brought about by the interplay of three principles: (1) variation—a liberalizing factor, which Darwin did not attempt to explain, present in all forms of life; (2) heredity—the conservative force that transmits similar organic form from one generation to another; and (3) the struggle for existence—which determines the variations that will confer advantages in a given environment, thus altering species through a selective reproductive rate.

On the basis of newer knowledge, neo-Darwinism has superseded the earlier concept and purged it of Darwin's lingering attachment to the Lamarckian theory of inheritance of acquired characters. Present knowledge of the mechanisms of inheritance are such that modern scientists can distinguish more satisfactorily than Darwin between non-inheritable bodily variation and variation of a genuinely inheritable kind.

DISPERSION

In biology, the dissemination, or scattering, of organisms over periods within a given area or over the Earth is called dispersion.

The disciplines most intimately intertwined with the study of dispersion are systematics and evolution. Systematics is concerned with the relationships between organisms and includes the classification of life into ordered groups, providing the detailed information essential to all biology. The study of evolution grew from a combination of systematics and dispersion, or distribution, as both Charles Darwin and Alfred Russel Wallace, pioneers in evolutionary biology, attested; and, in turn, an understanding of the process of natural selection has illuminated the reasons for changes in distribution in the history of the Earth.

A specific type of organism can establish one of three possible patterns of dispersion in a given area: a random pattern; an aggregated pattern, in which organisms gather in clumps; or a uniform pattern, with a roughly equal spacing of individuals. The type of pattern often results from the nature of the relationships within the population. Social animals, such as chimpanzees, tend to gather in groups, while territorial animals, such as birds, tend to assume uniform spacing. Close attention must be paid to the scale of study in order to get an accurate reading of these patterns. If a group of monkeys occupies three widely separated trees, their spacing will obviously be aggregate; yet in each tree, their spacing may appear to be uniform.

Distribution can be affected by time of day, month, or year. The most common form of distributional change occurs among migratory animals, which may be plentiful in the summer months and virtually absent in the winter. The forces governing the dispersal of organisms are either vectorial (directed motion), that is, caused by wind, water, or some other environmental motion, or stochastic (random), as in the case of the change in seasons, which gives no indication of where the dispersing organisms may ultimately settle. Dispersion may also be affected by the interrelationship of species with one another or with nutrients. Competition between species that depend on the same food types often leads to the elimination of one species, just as the extent of plant life often determines the boundaries of a species' territory.

The irregularities of most distribution patterns are simplified in the case of life forms dependent upon relatively restricted habitats, like that of intertidal mollusks, which have an almost linear distribution along rocky seacoasts. A few species, most notably humans and the animals dependent upon them, have a worldwide distribution.

Among both plants and animals, dispersal usually takes place at the time of reproduction. Dispersal is defined as the movement of individual organisms from their birthplace to other locations for breeding. When overcrowding forces individuals to range outside the area in which they were born to find a mate or food, new populations occasionally arise. Insects often display distinctive abilities in this regard. East African locusts have been found in two forms, a bright green variety, which is sluggish and solitary, and a highly mobile, group-oriented, dark-coloured form that swarms in enormous numbers, eating all plant material in its path. It has been found that if the young of the green variety are raised in large, constricted groups, they metamorphosize into the dark form at maturity. This is called phase polymorphism. As their numbers increase and the food supply thins, the locusts undergo developmental and behavioral changes to produce the widest dispersion pattern possible.

Occasionally, natural selection acts to limit the dispersal of a species. On high mountaintops and isolated islands, for example, the predominance of flightless birds and insects is notable.

Organisms are also spread by passive means, such as wind, water, and by other creatures. This method is hardly less effective than active dispersal; spiders, mites, and insects have been collected by airplanes over the Pacific as much as 3,100 km (about 1,900 miles) from land. Plants regularly spread their seeds and spores by the action of the wind and water, often with morphological adaptations to increase their potential range, as in the case of milkweed seeds.

Seeds are also spread by animals, often as undigested matter in the excrement of birds or mammals, or by attaching to animals via an assortment of hooks, barbs, and sticky substances. Parasites regularly use either their hosts or other creatures as distribution mechanisms. The myxoma virus, a parasite in rabbits, is carried by mosquitoes, which may travel as far as 64 km (40 miles) before infecting another rabbit.

Mountains and oceans can be effective barriers to the dispersal of organisms, as can stretches of desert or other climatological extremes. Some organisms can cross these barriers; birds can cross the English Channel, while bears cannot. In such cases, the paths of the more mobile animals are called filter routes.

Over geologic ages there have been many dramatic changes in climate that have affected distribution and even the survival of many life forms. Furthermore, the continents appear to have undergone large-scale displacements, separating many species and encouraging their independent development. But the greatest factor in the dispersal of organisms, at least during the past 10,000 years, has been human influence.

EFFECTIVE POPULATION SIZE

In genetics, the size of a breeding population, a factor that is determined by the number of parents, the average number of children per family, and the extent to which family size varies from the average is called its effective population size. The determination of the effective population size of a breeding population is necessary for studies of population growth rates and of gene flow.

EMERGENCE

Emergence, in evolutionary theory, is the rise of a system that cannot be predicted or explained from antecedent conditions. George Henry Lewes, the 19th-century English philosopher of science, distinguished between resultants and emergents—phenomena that are predictable from their constituent parts and those that are not (e.g., a physical mixture of sand and talcum powder as contrasted with a chemical compound such as salt, which looks nothing like sodium or chlorine). The evolutionary account of life is a continuous history marked by stages at which fundamentally new forms have appeared: (1) the origin of life; (2) the origin of nucleus-bearing protozoa; (3) the origin of sexually reproducing forms, with an individual destiny lacking in cells that reproduce by fission; (4) the rise of sentient animals, with nervous systems and protobrains; and (5) the appearance of cogitative animals, namely humans. Each of these new modes of life, though grounded in the physico-chemical and biochemical conditions of the previous and simpler stage, is intelligible only in terms of its own ordering principle. These are thus cases of emergence.

Early in the 20th century, the British zoologist C. Lloyd Morgan, one of the founders of animal psychology, emphasized the antipode of the principle: nothing should be called an emergent unless it can be shown not to be a resultant. Like Lewes, he treated the distinction as inductive and empirical, not as metempirical or metaphysical—i.e., not beyond the observable realm. Morgan condemned the 20th-century French intuitionist Henri Bergson's creative evolution as speculative, while proclaiming emergent evolution as a scientific theory. Even so, the theory has not been accepted universally by biologists. With genetics illuminating the mechanism of heredity (and hence the very conditions of evolution) and biochemistry elucidating the workings of the cell nucleus, some biologists are confirmed in their belief that scientific treatment admits only of analysis into parts and not into new kinds of wholes. Thus, they tend to concentrate on the mechanisms of mutation and of natural selection, effective in microevolution—the change from variety to variety and species to species—and to extrapolate these findings to macroevolution, to the origin of the great groups of living things.

Nevertheless, the concept of emergence still figures in some evolutionary thinking. In the 1920s and '30s, Samuel Alexander, a British realist metaphysician, and Jan Smuts, the South African statesman, espoused emergence theories; and later, others, such as the Jesuit paleontologist Pierre Teilhard de Chardin and the French zoologist Albert Vandel, emphasized the series of levels of organization, moving toward higher forms of consciousness. The philosophy of organism of Alfred North Whitehead, the leading process metaphysician, with its doctrine of creative advance, is a philosophy of emergence; so also is the theory of personal knowledge of Michael Polanyi, a Hungarian scientist and philosopher, with its levels of being and of knowing, none of which are wholly intelligible to those they describe.

The golden toad (Incilius periglenes, *formerly* Bufo periglenes) *is believed to be extinct. It was last sighted in 1989.* Charles H. Smith/U.S. Fish and Wildlife Service.

EXTINCTION

In biology, extinction is the dying out or termination of a species. Extinction occurs when species are diminished because of environmental forces (habitat fragmentation, global change, overexploitation of species for human use) or because of evolutionary changes in their members (genetic inbreeding, poor reproduction, decline in population numbers).

Rates of extinction are selective. For example, during the last 100,000 years of the Pleistocene Epoch (about 2.6 million to 11,700 years ago), some 40 percent of the existing genera of large mammals in Africa and more than 70 percent in North America, South America, and Australia were extinguished.

Some species made extinct by humans. Encyclopædia Britannica, Inc.

MASS EXTINCTION EVENTS

Although extinction is an ongoing feature of the Earth's flora and fauna (the vast majority of species ever to have lived are extinct), the fossil record reveals the occurrence of a number of unusually large extinctions, each involving the demise of vast numbers of species. These conspicuous declines in diversity are referred to as mass extinctions; they are distinguished from the majority of extinctions, which occur continually and are referred to as background extinction. Five mass extinctions can be distinguished from the fossil record. Ranked in descending order of severity, they are:

- Permian extinction (about 266 million to 251 million years ago), the most dramatic die-off, eliminating about half of all families, some 95 percent of marine species (nearly wiping out brachiopods and corals), and about 70 percent

The impact of a near-Earth object 65 million years ago in what is today the Caribbean region, as depicted in an artist's conception. Many scientists believe that the collision of a large asteroid or comet nucleus with Earth triggered the mass extinction of the dinosaurs and many other species near the end of the Cretaceous Period. NASA; illustration by Don Davis.

of land species (including plants, insects, and vertebrates).

- Ordovician-Silurian extinction (about 444 million years ago), which included about 25 percent of marine families and 85 percent of marine species, with brachiopods, conodonts, bryozoans, and trilobites suffering greatly.

- Cretaceous-Tertiary (K-T), or Cretaceous-Paleogene (K-Pg), extinction (about 65.5 million years ago), involving about 80 percent of all animal species, including the dinosaurs and many species of plants. Although many scientists contend that this event was caused by a large comet or asteroid striking Earth, others maintain that it was caused by climatic changes associated with the substantial volcanic activity of the time.

- End-Triassic extinction (about 200 million years ago), possibly caused by rapid climate change or by an asteroid striking the Earth. This mass extinction event caused about 20 percent of marine families and some 76 percent of all extant species to die out, possibly within a span of about 10,000 years, thus opening up numerous ecological niches into which the dinosaurs evolved.
- Devonian extinctions (407 million to 359 million years ago), which included 15–20 percent of marine families and 70–80 percent of all animal species. Roughly 86 percent of marine brachiopod species perished, along with many corals, conodonts, and trilobites.

In essence, mass extinctions are unusual because of the large numbers of taxa that die out, the concentrated time frame, the widespread geographic area affected, and the many different kinds of animals and plants eliminated. In addition, the mechanisms of mass extinction are different from those of background extinctions.

HUMAN-INDUCED EXTINCTIONS

Many species have become extinct because of human destruction of their natural environments. Indeed, current rates of human-induced extinctions are estimated to be about 1,000 times greater than past natural (background) rates of extinction, leading some scientists to call modern times the sixth mass extinction. This high extinction rate is largely due to the exponential growth in human numbers: from about 1 billion in 1850, the world's population reached 2 billion in 1930 and more than 6 billion in 2000, and it is expected to reach about 10 billion by 2050. As a result of increasing human populations, habitat loss is the greatest factor in current levels of extinction. For example, less than one-sixth of the land area of Europe has remained unmodified by human activity, and more than half of all wildlife habitat has been eliminated in more than four-fifths of countries in the paleotropics. In addition, increased levels of greenhouse gases have begun to alter the world's climate, with slowly increasing temperatures expected by the middle of the 21st century to force species to migrate 200–300 km (about 125–185 miles) farther north in the northern temperate zone in order to remain in habitats with the same climate conditions. Overexploitation from hunting and harvesting also has adversely affected many species. For example, about 20 million tropical fish and 12 million corals are harvested annually for the aquarium trade, depleting natural populations in some parts of the world.

All these factors have increased the numbers of threatened species: almost one in four mammal species and one in eight bird species were considered at significant risk of extinction at the start of the 21st century.

KIN SELECTION

Kin selection is a type of natural selection that considers the role relatives play when evaluating the genetic fitness of a given individual. It is based on the concept of inclusive fitness, which is made up of individual survival and reproduction (direct fitness) and any impact that an individual has on the survival and reproduction of relatives (indirect fitness). Kin selection occurs when an animal engages in self-sacrificial behaviour that benefits the genetic fitness

Lioness (Panthera leo) with cubs.
Erwin and Peggy Bauer/Bruce Coleman Ltd.

of its relatives. The theory of kin selection is one of the foundations of the modern study of social behaviour. British evolutionary biologist W.D. Hamilton first proposed the theory in 1963 and noted that it plays a role in the evolution of altruism, cooperation, and sociality; however, the term *kin selection* was coined in 1964 by British evolutionary biologist Maynard Smith.

According to the theory of sexual selection, even though some individuals possess certain conspicuous physical traits (such as prominent coloration) that places them at greater risk of predation, the trait is thought to remain in the population because the possessors of such traits have greater success in obtaining mates.

The elements of kin selection (that is, direct fitness and indirect fitness) lead directly to the concept now known as Hamilton's rule, which states that aid-giving behaviour can evolve when the indirect fitness benefits of helping relatives compensate the aid giver for any losses in personal reproduction it incurs by helping.

MOSAIC EVOLUTION

Mosaic evolution is the occurrence, within a given population of organisms, of different rates of evolutionary change in various body structures and functions. An example can be seen in the patterns of development of the different elephant species. The Indian elephant underwent rapid early molar modification with little foreshortening of the forehead. The African elephant underwent parallel changes but at different rates: the foreshortening of the forehead took place in an early stage of development, molar modification occurring later.

Similarly, in man there was early evolution of structures for bipedal locomotion, but during the same time there was little change in skull form or brain size; later, both skull and brain evolved rapidly into the state of development associated with modern human species.

The phenomenon of mosaic evolution would seem to indicate that the process of natural selection acts differently upon the various structures and functions of evolving species. Thus, in the case of human development, the evolutionary pressures for upright posture took precedence over the need for a complex brain. Furthermore, the elaboration of the brain was probably linked to the freeing of the forelimbs made possible by bipedal locomotion. Analysis of incidences of mosaic evolution adds greatly to the body of general evolutionary theory.

NATURAL SELECTION

The process that results in the adaptation of an organism to its environment by means of selectively reproducing changes in its genotype, or genetic constitution, is called natural selection.

In natural selection, those variations in the genotype that increase an organism's chances of survival and procreation are preserved and multiplied from generation to generation at the expense of less advantageous ones. Evolution often occurs as a consequence of this process. Natural selection may arise from differences in survival, in fertility, in rate of development, in mating success, or in any other aspect of the life cycle. All such differences result in natural selection to the extent that they affect the number of progeny an organism leaves.

Gene frequencies tend to remain constant from generation to generation when disturbing factors are not present. Factors that disturb the natural equilibrium of gene frequencies include mutation, migration (or gene flow), random genetic drift, and natural selection. A mutation is a spontaneous change in the gene frequency that takes place in a population and occurs at a low rate. Migration is a local change in gene frequency when an individual moves from one population to another and then interbreeds. Random genetic drift is a change that takes place from one generation to another by a process of pure chance. Mutation, migration, and genetic drift alter gene frequencies without regard to whether such changes increase or decrease the likelihood of an organism surviving and reproducing in its environment. They are all random processes.

Natural selection moderates the disorganizing effects of these processes because it multiplies the incidence of beneficial mutations over the generations and eliminates harmful ones, since their carriers leave few or no descendants. Natural selection enhances the preservation of a group of organisms that are best adjusted to the physical and biological conditions of their environment and may also result in their improvement in some cases. Some characteristics, such as the male peacock's tail, actually decrease the individual organism's chance of survival. To explain such anomalies, Darwin posed a theory of "sexual selection." In contrast to features that result from natural selection, a structure produced by sexual selection results in an advantage in the competition for mates.

ORTHOGENESIS

Orthogenesis, or straight-line evolution, is the theory that successive members of an evolutionary series become increasingly modified in a single undeviating direction. That evolution frequently proceeds in orthogenetic fashion is undeniable, though many striking features developed in an orthogenetic group appear to have little if any adaptive value and may even be markedly disadvantageous. A variety of theories have attempted to explain orthogenesis, but with only partial success. One underlying view in orthogenesis, as espoused by some paleontologists, is that variation in nature is directed toward fixed goals and that species evolve in a predetermined direction irrespective of selection.

PARALLEL EVOLUTION

Parallel evolution is the evolution of geographically separated groups in such a way that they show morphological resemblances. A notable example is the similarity shown by the marsupial mammals of Australia to the placental mammals elsewhere. Through the courses of their evolution they have come to remarkably similar forms, so much so that the marsupials are often named for their placental counterparts (e.g., the marsupial "wolf," "mole," "mice," or "cats").

POLYMORPHISM

In biology, the discontinuous genetic variation resulting in the occurrence of several different forms or types of individuals among the members of a single species is called polymorphism. A discontinuous genetic variation divides the individuals of a population into two or more sharply distinct forms. The most obvious example of this is the separation of most higher organisms into male and female sexes. Another example is the different blood types in humans. In continuous variation, by contrast, the individuals do not fall into sharp classes but instead are almost imperceptibly graded between wide extremes. Examples include the smooth graduation of height among individuals of human populations and the graduations possible between the different geographic races. If the frequency of two or more discontinuous forms within a species is too high to be explained by mutation, the variation—as well as the population displaying it—is said to be polymorphic.

A polymorphism that persists over many generations is usually maintained because no one form possesses an overall advantage or disadvantage over the others in terms of natural selection. Some polymorphisms have no visible manifestations and require biochemical techniques to identify the differences that occur between the chromosomes, proteins, or DNA of different forms. The castes that occur in social insects are a special form of polymorphism that is attributable to differences in nutrition rather than to genetic variations.

SELECTION

In biology, the preferential survival and reproduction or preferential elimination of individuals with certain genotypes (genetic compositions), by means of natural or artificial controlling factors, is called selection.

The theory of evolution by natural selection was proposed by Charles Darwin and Alfred Russel Wallace in 1858. They argued that species with useful adaptations to the environment are more likely to survive and produce progeny than are those with less useful adaptations, thereby increasing the frequency with which useful adaptations occur over the generations. The limited resources available in an environment promotes competition in which organisms of the same or different species struggle to survive. In the competition for food, space, and mates that occurs, the less well-adapted individuals must die or fail to reproduce, and those who are better adapted do survive and reproduce. In the absence of competition between organisms, natural selection may be due to purely environmental factors, such as inclement weather or seasonal variations.

Artificial selection (or selective breeding) differs from natural selection in that heritable variations in a species are manipulated by humans through controlled breeding. The breeder attempts to isolate and propagate those genotypes that are responsible for a plant or animal's desired qualities in a suitable environment. These qualities are economically or aesthetically desirable to humans, rather than useful to the organism in its natural environment.

In mass selection, a number of individuals chosen on the basis of appearance are mated; their progeny are further selected for the preferred characteristics, and the process is continued for as many generations as is desired. The choosing of breeding stock on the basis of ancestral reproductive ability and quality is known as pedigree selection. Progeny selection indicates choice of breeding stock on the basis of the performance or testing of their offspring or descendants. Family selection refers to mating of organisms from the same ancestral stock that are not directly related to each other. Pure-line selection involves selecting and breeding progeny from superior organisms for a number of generations until a pure line of organisms with only the desired characteristics has been established.

Darwin also proposed a theory of sexual selection, in which females chose as mates the most attractive males; outstanding males thus helped generate more young than mediocre males.

SPECIATION

Speciation is the formation of new and distinct species in the course of evolution. It involves the splitting of a single evolutionary lineage into two or more genetically independent ones.

In eukaryotic species there are two important processes that occur during speciation: the splitting up of one gene pool into two or more separated gene pools (genetic separation) and the diversification of one phenotypic form into many (phenotypic differentiation). Many hypotheses are given for the start of speciation, mainly differing in the role of geographic isolation and the origin of reproductive isolation. Geographic isolation may occur with different populations completely separated in space (allopatry); for example, Darwin's finches on the Galapagos Islands may have speciated allopatrically because of volcanic eruptions that divided populations.

A controversial alternative to allopatric speciation is sympatric speciation, in which reproductive isolation occurs within a single population without geographic isolation; an example of sympatric speciation is when a parasitic insect changes hosts. In general, when physical separation occurs among populations, some reproductive isolation arises. The difficulty with this theory is how to explain genetic divergence occurring within a population of individuals that are continually interacting. Most evolutionary biologists maintain that speciation usually occurs by genetic divergence of geographically separated populations.

SPECIES

In biology, a species is a classification comprising related organisms that share common characteristics and are capable of interbreeding.

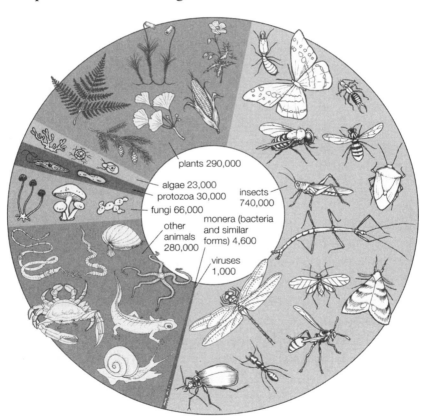

plants 290,000

algae 23,000
protozoa 30,000   insects
fungi 66,000   740,000

other   monera (bacteria
animals   and similar
280,000   forms) 4,600

viruses
1,000

Approximate numbers of described, or named, species, divided into major groupings. Scientists have described about 1.5 million species of living things on Earth, but the majority of species are still unknown.
Encyclopædia Britannica, Inc.

TAXONOMY

The designation of species originates in taxonomy, where the species is the fundamental unit of classification recognized by the International Commission of Zoological Nomenclature. Every species is assigned a standard two-part name of genus and species. The genus is the generic name that includes closely related species; the gray wolf, for example, is classified as *Canis lupus* and is a close relative of the coyote found in North America and designated as *Canis latrans*, their systematic relation indicated by their sharing the same genus name, *Canis*. Similarly, genera that have shared traits are classified in the same taxonomic family; related families are placed in the same order; related orders are placed in the same class; and related classes are placed in the same phylum. This classification system is a hierarchy applied to all animals and plants, as originally set forth by the Swedish naturalist Carolus Linnaeus in the 18th century.

Organisms are grouped into species partly according to their morphological, or external, similarities, but more important in classifying sexually reproducing organisms is the organisms' ability to successfully interbreed. Individuals of a single species can mate and produce viable offspring with one another but almost never with members of other species. Separate species have been known to produce hybrid offspring (for example, the horse and the donkey producing the mule), but, because the offspring are almost always inviable or sterile, the interbreeding is not considered successful.

Interbreeding only within the species is of great importance for evolution in that individuals of one species share a common gene pool that members of other species do not. Within a single pool there is always a certain amount of variation among individuals, and those whose genetic variations leave them at a disadvantage in a particular environment tend to be eliminated in favour of those with advantageous variations. This process of natural selection results in the gene pool's evolving in such a way that the advantageous variations become the norm. Because genetic variations originate in individuals of a species and because those individuals pass on their variations only within the species, then it is at the species level that evolution takes place. The evolution of one species into others is called speciation.

SPECIATION

Subspecies are groups at the first stage of speciation; individuals of different subspecies sometimes interbreed, but they produce many sterile male offspring. At the second stage are incipient species, or semispecies; individuals of these groups rarely interbreed, and all their male offspring are sterile. Natural selection separates incipient species into sibling species, which do not mate at all but which in morphology, or structure and form, are nearly indistinguishable. Sibling species then evolve into morphologically (and taxonomically) different species. Because it is often difficult to distinguish between subspecies and stable species, another criterion has been developed that involves a historical, or phylogenetic, dimension. In this form, a species is separated from another when there is a parental pattern of ancestry and descent.

Speciation may occur in many ways. A population may become geographically separated from the rest of its species and never be rejoined. Through the process of adaptive radiation, this population might evolve independently into a new species, changing to fit particular ecological niches in the new environment and never requiring natural selection to complete its reproductive isolation from the parent species. Within the new environment, populations of the new species might then radiate into species themselves. A famous example of adaptive radiation is that of the Galapagos finches.

The evidence for speciation formerly was found in the fossil record by tracing successive changes in the morphology of organisms. Genetic studies now show that morphological change does not always accompany speciation, as many apparently identical groups are, in fact, reproductively isolated.

IDENTIFYING AND CATALOGING SPECIES

The identification of lineages in species developed tremendously following the advent of molecular biology. Certain kinds of molecular information, especially DNA sequences, can provide clearer support than morphological data ever could for species identification, particularly when species clusters are similar in appearance. Molecular characters can often be identified less ambiguously than morphological characters. Species identification is extremely important for the conservation of biodiversity. About 1.5 million species have been named, yet it is estimated that the total number of species may be anywhere from 3 to 100 million. Large numbers of animals and plants have not been studied. For example, nearly 300,000 species of flowering plants are known, but their true number may be closer to 400,000, with about 2,000 species discovered each year. Even mammals continue to be discovered— including 4,000 to 5,000 in the last 20 years of the 20th century. Occasionally, even relatively large mammals are found still, such as the saola (*Pseudoryx nghetinhensis*), an oryx-like animal discovered in Southeast Asia in the 1990s and placed in its own genus.

Darwin's theory of evolution by natural selection was one of the most significant advancements in science. Not only did it provide an explanation of the appearance of new species, it provided the mechanism by which existing species could adapt to their environment. Despite the challenges to the theory since the 19th century, it has endured—supported and strengthened by new evidence. The synthetic theory, paleontological discoveries, and embryology all served to shore up the legitimacy of evolutionary theory in the human experience.

During the 20th century, additional scientific innovations bolstered the human understanding of evolution. The discovery of DNA and the development of scientific techniques that examined the inner workings and behaviour of DNA molecules allowed for deeper explorations into genetic relationships among species and the development of evolutionary trees of species descent. Such biological systematics continues, enabling humans to better understand their own origins as well as the origins of life on Earth.

GLOSSARY

adaptation The process of species evolving the traits necessary for survival in their environment.

cephalization The evolutionary process by which the sensory organs migrate toward one end of the body.

DNA Short for deoxyribonucleic acid, this acid in the chromosomes of living cells contains the hereditary material that determines the characteristics of all living things.

ethology In zoology, the branch of science that studies animal behaviour.

evolution The process by which a species becomes better adapted to the environmental conditions that surround it.

gene mutation A change to the DNA structure of a gene.

genes Segments of DNA in a chromosome that determines a particular characteristic.

genome The sum total of all the genetic material in the chromosomes, mitochondria, and chloroplasts of an organism.

genotype The genetic constitution of an organism made up of the entire complex of genes inherited from its parent or parents.

genus A taxonomic group made up of closely related species that display very similar characteristics.

heterogeneous Describes a group of dissimilar species or environments.

heterozygous In genetics, describes a trait whose genes from each parent are different.

homology The similarity of the structure, physiology, or development of different species of organisms based upon their descent from a common evolutionary ancestor.

homozygous In genetics, describes a trait whose genes from each parent are the same.

invertebrate A living organism that lacks a spine. These include various insects.

lineage The pedigree of a species.

morphology The form and structure of an organism.

natural selection The process by which species with traits that are best suited for their environment survive and reproduce while those species that are less suited for their environment perish.

nucleotide A string of joined organic molecules composed of a nitrogen base linked to a sugar and phosphate group that make up the structure of DNA and RNA.

phylogeny The history of the evolution of a species or group.

physiology The study of how the bodies of living organisms function.

polymorphism Genetic variation within a species that results in the occurrence of several different forms or types of individuals.

radiometric dating A process used by scientists to determine the age of a material by measuring the rate of decay of the radioactive isotopes. Also called radioactive dating.

species A group of plants or animals having similar characteristics that are able to interbreed.

vertebrate A living organism possessing a spine. These include mammals, reptiles, and fish.

zygote A newly fertilized egg possessing the potential to develop into an embryo.

FOR FURTHER READING

Carroll, Sean B. *The Making of the Fittest: DNA and the Ultimate Forensic Record of Evolution*. New York: W. W. Norton & Company, 2007.

Coyne, Jerry A. *Why Evolution Is True*. New York: Penguin, 2010.

Darwin, Charles. *The Origin Of Species: 150th Anniversary Edition*. New York: Signet Classics, 2003.

Dawkins, Richard. *The Greatest Show on Earth: The Evidence for Evolution*. New York: Free Press, 2009.

————. *The Selfish Gene: 30th Anniversary Edition*. New York: Oxford University Press, 2006.

Dowd, Michael. *Thank God for Evolution: How the Marriage of Science and Religion Will Transform Your Life and Our World*. New York: Plume, 2009.

Fairbanks, Daniel J. *Relics of Eden: The Powerful Evidence of Evolution in Human DNA*. Amherst, NY: Prometheus Books, 2007.

Gould, Stephen Jay. *The Structure of Evolutionary Theory*. Cambridge, MA: Harvard University Press, 2002.

Lane, Nick. *Life Ascending: The Ten Great Inventions of Evolution*. New York: W. W. Norton & Company, 2009.

Mayr, Ernst. *What Evolution Is*. New York: Basic Books, 2002.

McCalman, Iain. *Darwin's Armada: Four Voyages and the Battle for the Theory of Evolution*. New York: W. W. Norton & Company, 2009.

Miller, Kenneth R. *Finding Darwin's God: A Scientist's Search for Common Ground Between God and Evolution*. New York: Harper Perennial, 2007.

Milner, Richard. *Darwin's Universe: Evolution from A to Z*. Berkeley, CA: University of California Press, 2009.

Moore, John A. *From Genesis to Genetics: The Case of Evolution and Creationism*. Berkeley, CA: University of California Press, 2003.

National Academy of Sciences. *Science, Evolution, and Creationism*. Washington, D.C.: National Academies Press, 2008.

Quammen, David. *The Reluctant Mr. Darwin: An Intimate Portrait of Charles Darwin and the Making of His Theory of Evolution*. New York: Atlas, 2007.

Rose, Michael R. *Darwin's Spectre: Evolutionary Biology in the Modern World*. Princeton, NJ: Princeton University Press, 2001.

Scott, Eugenie C. *Evolution vs. Creationism: An Introduction*. Berkeley, CA: University of California Press, 2009.

Shubin, Neil. *Your Inner Fish: A Journey into the 3.5-Billion-Year History of the Human Body*. New York: Vintage, 2009.

Wilson, David Sloan. *Evolution for Everyone: How Darwin's Theory Can Change the Way We Think About Our Lives*. New York: Delta, 2007.

INDEX